S0-EIF-084

EUCLID BEACH PARK

is closed for the season

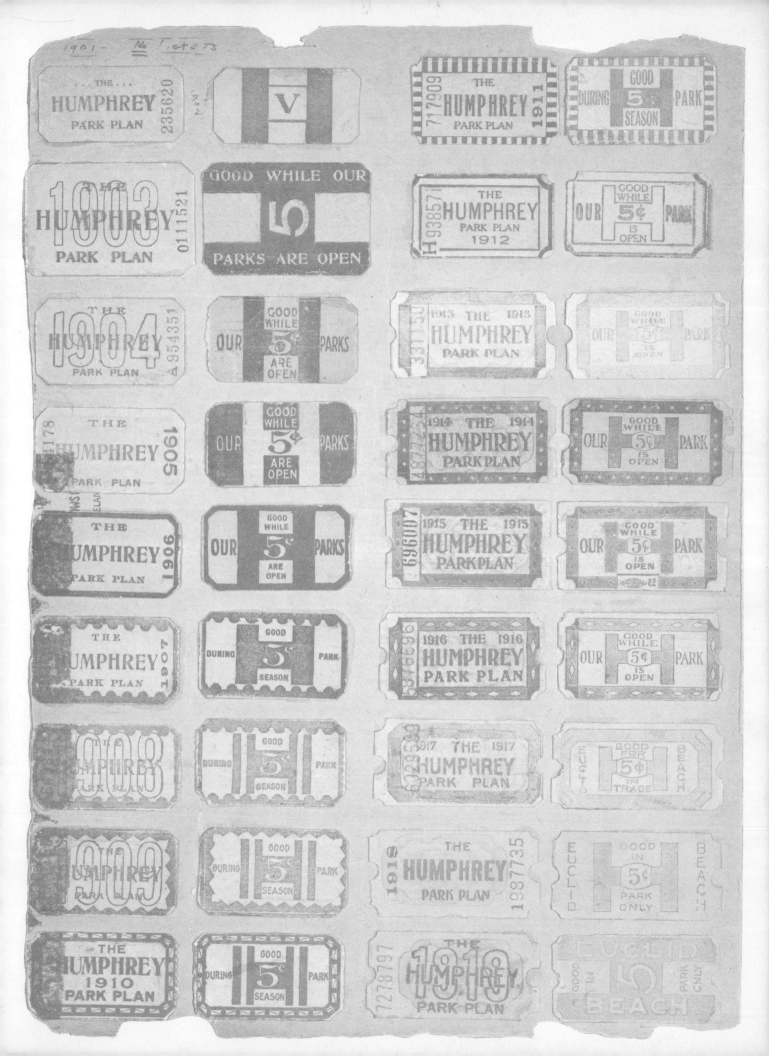

EUCLID BEACH PARK

is closed for the season

by

AMUSEMENT PARK BOOKS, INC.
which is . . .
Lee O. Bush
Edward C. Chukayne
Russell Allon Hehr
Richard F. Hershey

BOOKS, INC.
MENTOR, OHIO

COPYRIGHT © 1977 AMUSEMENT PARK BOOKS, INC.
ALL RIGHTS RESERVED

PRINTED IN THE UNITED STATES OF AMERICA

ISBN 0-913228-22-2
LIBRARY OF CONGRESS CATALOG NUMBER 77-80928

First Printing, 7,000 copies, June, 1977
Second Printing, 10,000 copies, November, 1977
ORIGINALLY PUBLISHED BY DILLON/LIEDERBACH, INC.

Third Printing, 2,500 copies, November, 1978
Fourth Printing, 5,000 copies, March, 1979
PUBLISHED BY AMUSEMENT PARK BOOKS, INC.
Mentor, Ohio 44060

NO PART MAY BE COPIED WITHOUT PERMISSION OF AMUSEMENT PARK BOOKS, INC.

LIBRARY OF CONGRESS CATALOGING IN PUBLICATION DATA

Amusement Park Books.
    Euclid Beach Park is closed for the season / by Amusement
Park Books, inc., which is Lee O. Bush, Edward C. Chukayne,
Russell Allon Hehr, Richard F. Hershey. — Cleveland:Dillon/-
Liederbach, © 1977.

    viii, 331 p. ; ill. ; 29 cm.

    Bibliography: p. 301-305.
    Includes index.
    ISBN 0-913228-22-2

    1. Euclid Beach Park, Ohio—History.   1. Title.
GV1853.E9A48   1977   790'.068'0977132   77-80928
                                                MARC

DEDICATIONS

The spirit of this book is dedicated to my wife, Stephanie; my family; and the memory of my father, Theodore G. Bush, who introduced me to the spirit of Euclid Beach Park.

Lee O. Bush

With this book I honor my mother, Frances, who encouraged me these many years; my loving wife, Carolyn, who gave support and understanding; and Vic Svete, who's guidance encouraged me in the graphic arts.

Edward C. Chukayne

My mother, Mamie Louise, initiated me to the joys of the rides at Euclid Beach; my father, John Frank, sacrificed much during the Depression to get us there; my grandmother, Frances A., shared wonderful tales about the place again and again. It is they I memorialize with this book.

Russell Allon Hehr

To Linda, with love, my patient and devoted wife. And to Jennifer and Barbara, who will always be my little girls. Daddy loves you.

Richard F. Hershey

PARADISE LOST — A VISION REGAINED

I used to sit at my desk and from my twelfth floor window look across the Hudson River watching the lights outline the silhouette of the roller coaster curving high up on the Palisades. Although it was really too far away, I always imagined that I heard shrieks of laughter and the crash of descending coaster cars. Today, instead, there is a forbidding fortress of a housing complex.

And so it is with Euclid Beach Park that was in Cleveland, Riverview Park once in Chicago, Ocean Park in San Francisco and the great old fun parks all over these United States. They have been bulldozed to make room for housing complexes built to perish in much less time. The great amusement parks have given way to the supermarkets of American entertainment.

I grew up across the street from a merry-go-round factory in Brooklyn, and saw the sanded horses piled on a wagon to be drawn by a live horse to some great wonderland. Once a summer, my father piled seven kids on the Lorimer Street car that terminated at the entrance of Prospect Park, which to me was the most enchanted fairyland in the world. These were the family parks where we all had fun together, stuck together and grew up with a respect for each other. But that was then.

Then, American had acres of enchantment everywhere. These developed from earlier picnic groves which, until the beginning of this century, were to be found just a few miles from urban centers at the end of the trolley line, usually installed by the traction companies to increase their revenues. A carousel was one of the first of the amusements to be installed, followed by a shooting gallery, a ferris-type wheel and usually a boat ride on an artificial lake.

The Centennial Exposition of 1876 in Philadelphia, and its architecture; the Columbian Exposition in Chicago in 1893 which featured the great Ferris Wheel; the monumental sculpture of America's native sons, which gave Chicago the appellation of the "Great White City," all were influences on our early amusement parks.

With the advent of the electric light, "Electric Parks" and "White Cities" sprang up across the nation, featuring the incandescent lamps by the thousands, and ferris wheels of various sizes were added. The architecture of these parks followed the patterns set by the States Buildings of the 1876 Centennial, and most of the carousel buildings in modified sizes, testified to that design. The charm of the nineteenth century carried well into the twentieth. After the 1904 St. Louis Fair with its midway, its influence, and especially that of the world's greatest amusement area, Coney Island in Brooklyn, roller coasters and other innovative amusement devices and rides were added to the variety of the American and European amusement parks.

The era of great amusement parks erupted with a brilliance illuminated by thousands of incandescent lamps, and architectural embellishments borrowed from the eighteenth and nineteenth centuries, sometimes called "seashore rococo" and "fairground baroque." For nearly half a century the parks continued to generate the excitement and romantic inspiration of our nation, even through periods of wars, privation and the ravages of time.

To us and our children these parks were historic landmarks, our regret now is that we did not cherish them as such. The pieces are scattered throughout the nation; the sycamores of Euclid Beach Park are no more; the giants of the past have been felled, the sights of its towers piercing the horizon no longer welcome the summer. And as for all the Euclid Beach Parks of the nation, paradise has been lost.

But for the group of dedicated young conservationists who have published this book, the park at the end of the trolley line has not ceased to exist. The fight to keep what is left of our heritage is still going on, and this book should serve as a warning, a guide and a hope. It will be an inspiration to cherish the few remaining old parks and rides. We must fight for their preservation, and unless we do, we shall have our paradise lost.

Frederick Fried
November 6, 1976

(The Plain Dealer)   A Familiar sign that appeared at the MAIN GATE each fall; it had a new
                                      significance in the Autumn of 1969.

PREFACE

For seventy-four years a plot of land, comprised of seventy-five and ninety-three one hundredths acres facing on Lake Erie at the extreme north east corner of Cleveland, Ohio, exerted a magnetic pull on the local citizens. The force behind the magnet was the pursuit of pleasures concentrated within the confines of that acreage; pleasures contemplated in winters, realized in summers. Year after year, citizens built up stores of remembered pleasures associated with the place. In time, their children, and then their children's children, added to the legacy. In such a manner, the area became hallowed.

The official name of the acreage was Euclid Beach Park, but any native could have told you that it was also called Euclid Beach, or just "The Beach."

Regardless of which appelation was used, it always conjured up a kaleidoscope of anticipated or realized pleasures, depending upon the season of the year and the season of one's life. For some it might have been the very simple pleasure of being near Lake Erie or the beach. For some, perhaps, it was the visual pleasure of the lawns, the trees, or the flowers. For others it might have been the pleasure of just sitting and watching other folks go by. Some might have found pleasure in tasting such Euclid Beach specialties as the POPCORN, CANDY "KISSES", the FROZEN CUSTARD, or the LOGANBERRY JUICE. Others might have found pleasure in summering at the CAMP AREA with its tents and cabins. Still others could have delighted in the "sweet cacaphony" that surrounded the ears with a mixture of laughter, fun-screams, and merry-go-round music. For some it could have been the pleasures found at the DANCE HALL — like dancing the "MOONLIGHT WALTZES" or listening to the bands. Or perhps it was the pleasure of skating to the rhythm set by the magnificent old GAVIOLI ORGAN. For many it could have been the pleasures of the rides with their attendant smell of hot grease and electricity — like anticipating the seventy-one feet, five inch plunge that followed the ticking ascent up the first hill of the THRILLER, or like free-wheeling around the curves of the FLYING TURNS. Or it could have been . . . Yes, it *could* have been. But one fateful Sunday in September of 1969, the hallowed park every Clevelander *knew* would be there for future generations was closed forever! The sign at the FRONT GATE had always read "Euclid Beach Park closed for the season," but — closed *FOREVER?*

In time the bulldozers insulted themselves into the buildings and rides, scattering their footings and "broken bones" naked to the elements. Following this wave of destruction came citizens seeking mementos, much in the manner of churchmen seeking relics of a saint. Was this not hallowed ground? And did not each relic from it symbolize a "touch of the garment?"

In like manner the four authors of this book, at first, came seeking only relics. We were all Greater Clevelanders - still are - and each had sought the repertoire of pleasures at the park, changing the selection with the seasons of our lives. Many years before the park was closed, each of us had hoarded articles, slides, postcards, mementos, and films about it. After it closed we pooled our treasures. The resulting corporate collection, as well as the enthusiasm engendered by kindred minds, soon caused us to seek for the "whole garment". Eventually we found so many pieces, as well as so many others who wanted to share their remembrances and relics with us, that we felt it our bounden duty to write this book. It is for those who do not have the time to search, those who have no relics, and also for those generations to come. Past, present, and future will share in the memory of those hallowed acres called Euclid Beach Park.

For two years we pursued the materials for our book, all the while adhering to strict guidelines. First and foremost, we were interested in delineating the pleasure aspect of the park. Quite naturally, in seventy-four years somebody would stub his toe; some machinery would break down occasionally; some accidents would happen; and some forces generated at city or world levels would, from time to time, come nigh the hallowed acres. But, in spite of such collisions, the park stood for the pursuit of wholesome pleasures to millions, year after year, after year. If ghosts there be about the acreage, they are of the essence of pleasures past.

A second guideline was also established from the start. It came out of our having read, reread, and read again, every book we could find on amusement parks. Most of them told a good story, many had pictures, but very few indicated the sources of their information! Could it be that authors and publishers felt such information lacked *eye* appeal? How, we questioned, could books involving such masses of material *not* show their underpinnings? Wanting to reverse such a condition, we decided to include appendices, charts, maps, bibliography, notes, and an index with cross references and citings of all sources, either primary or secondary. Our underpinnings *would* show for more inquisitive readers, scholars, and historians. It is our hope that this pattern may serve as a model for other writers chafing at the bit to tell the story of "their" park.

All of this, however, would not be at the expense of perusing readers wanting merely to reminisce over the park, look through the pictures, or read the book like a story. All these facets would be there. In addition, we would relate the park's chronicle to local, national, and international events. And, as a graphic serendipity, we would show costumes and advertisements of each era in its long history. We wanted something for everyone to share.

But there never could have been something for everyone had it not been for the multitude of people who assisted us — lent us their relics, patiently listened to our pleas, "spanked us" when we gained too much momentum, or tolerated our probing interviews. The enthusiasm of these people was a tonic to us. Some even volunteered their memories or mementos without having been asked. All of this proves that people who knew the hallowed acres so venerated them that they wanted to share their portion of the park's story; surely they wanted to "touch the hem of the garment". In the paragraphs that follow, we would like to make these people known.

The direct descendants of the Humphrey family, Doris Humphrey Mackley and Dudley Sherman Humphrey, III, head our list. The Humphrey family owned, operated, and rigidly maintained their high standards for the park from 1901 until its closing in 1969. Their lineage (which we have traced in one of the appendices) goes back to the Norsemen, then England, then New England, and finally Cleveland. Their staunch New England determination, know-how, and ingenuity are woven into every thread of the garment. The story of Euclid Beach Park is equally the story of the Humphrey family. Doris Humphrey Mackley and Dudley Sherman Humphrey, III, allowed us the honor of copying their huge year-by-year scrapbooks of plans, clippings, plats and reminiscences of the park.

Donald D. Smith of Euclid, Ohio, had faith in our project and shared in most of the peaks and valleys of our journey. To his astute eyes, we must have seemed like four trembling Davids as he helped us plan the strategy to slay the ways-and-means giant. He gave unstintingly of his time and expertise. He has a way about him that can turn stumbling blocks along the path into puddings.

Joel Cedric Warren added his professional skills and time. His was the immense task of copying, not once, but four times, the huge Humphrey scrapbooks and translating them into thousands of slides. His time and effort are equalled only by his love of the park.

The Cleveland Public Library, with its vast research collection and enthusiastic staff, was of great help to us. Most particularly, we wish to thank Marcella M. Matejka, head of the General Reference Department, who went far beyond the call of duty to help us with matters of procedure and legality. Also, her staff was called upon to help us with maps and huge plats again and again. Our thanks to them. Howard A. Novak and his assistants in the Newspaper room and Peggy Wardin and her staff in the History Department lent a hand many times. Janet Coe Sanborn, also of that department, helped us with the Cleveland Picture Collection of primary source photographs. Mr. Jay Beswick and his staff of the Literature Department and Mr. Herbert Mansfield of the Drama section furnished us with advice and primary source materials. We thank them all.

The Western Reserve Historical Society in the persons of Dr. Dennis Harrison and Kermit Pike were of help to us.

Dr. Frederick Fried, eminent authority on carousels and amusement parks, gave freely of his vast storehouse of knowledge, pictures, and powers of identification.

The large Marjorie H. Kekic collection of original photos of the park proved invaluable again and again. Besides, both she and her husband delighted us with personal stories about the park. Both had worked there.

The Frank Jeran collection of photos, memorabilia, and tickets (the tickets are shown in the end papers) were of inestimable value. Because he was the mailman for the park for many years, his effervescent accounts and stories of the "Beach" delighted us many a wintry night.

Professor Robert Cartmel of the State University of New York at Albany, authority on the roller coaster in America, shared his vast knowledge with us. His advice about publishers and details was of much help also.

Mr. John L. Cobb, descendant of the owners of the property on which the park was built, shared his well-captioned original photos, as well as deeds and papers. Indirectly, Mrs. Robert (Betsey Cobb Stewart) Eastwood shared in these materials. Marion Christie Scott Cobb, whose father was Dudley Humphrey Scott, put at our disposal some photos of construction at the park.

Mr. Walter Williams, long time employee, and his wife shared their vast knowledge and experiences about Euclid Beach Park. They still live on the premises.

John W. Stoneback furnished us with most useful verbal accounts of the park and its engineering aspects.

Mr. William Parker furnished us with not only first hand accounts of maintenance at the park, but also photos.

The patient wives, Mrs. Stephanie Bush and Mrs. Linda Hershey, put up with the problems of a book a-borning, absent husbands and a million-and-one annoyances, for the love of the park. And a little later Carolyn Chukayne became a member of this group.

Odelia Hlavka helped us in handling the early stages of correspondence, orders and records.

Joe Erdelac had much faith in our project, demonstrating his keen interest in local history and especially Euclid Beach Park.

Sam F. Chiancone of Keener Printing preferred his skills time and again in our behalf and in his love for the Beach.

Ronald P. Deitz offered his enthusiasm, support and encouragement for our project.

Deborah Hart patiently typed the manuscript again and again, and put up with four divergent tempraments in cloud and sunshine, and occasional, but rare, calm.

David Humphrey Scott, whose father made many contributions to the Park, and who had the rare privilege of living at the place, shared with us his collection of movies made by his father, and his lively tales of behind the scenes maintenance and life at the Beach.

Harry Christiansen, famed Cleveland author, was most enthusiastic and helpful in assisting us.

Doctor Phillip J. Kaplow, who worked at the Park in its later days, lent us many pictures taken from the operator's viewpoint.

Rex L. Zirbes patiently proofread the text and offered valuable suggestions.

Mrs. Frank Kapel and William F. Kapel shared their memorabilia and first hand accounts of the whereabouts of many of the devices from the Park.

Bob Legan, collector extraordinaire, with his storehouse of facts, clarified many technical details for us in regards to the Penny Arcade.

Directly or indirectly, the following persons had a hand in the making of this book: Edward Andres, Alden M. Armstrong, Charles J. Avellone, Kaye Ballard, DeArv G. Barton, John Battle, III, Eric Beheim, Mr. and Mrs. Rudy Beheim, James G. Billson, Jr., Wayne Boggs, Jerry J. Borden, F. Robert Boyce, Art Broze, William Burkhardt, Frank A. Emde, Art Farrar, Zani Garbincus, Rudolph H. Garfield, Cecil Golly, James C. Hackley, Viola Hennie, Harry H. Hershey, Sr., Dave Hyman, Peter Iversen, Everett Jones, Emma (Gollon) Karnatz, David Kirbish, Olive Kozlik, Frank Kustra, Gary Lamb, Charles Lehman, Martin Linsey, James P. Marcus, Russell Milan, C. Aubrey Moore, Carl L. Mower, J.O. Murray, John Murray, Robert Pettay, Kitty Phelan, Kermit J. Pike, Henry M. Prekel, Eddie Robinson, Ronald Salter, Henry "Hank" Schneider, Alan R. Schuessler, Emil Sholle, John Wallace Skinner, Frank Strasek, Eugene Stuart, Vic Stuart, John Tierney, Lewis J. Trebar, John Urbancic, Erwin R. Wahl, Robert J. Ward, Edward I. White, Frank Yankovic, Mrs. Jennie Zaman.

And now, if the reader will indulge the authors by letting them address the park directly:

EUCLID BEACH PARK, here is *your* story; the story of the great family that guided you; the story of the thousands who created your parts, worked on you and kept you running; the story of the millions who came to your acreage; the story of the trillions of pleasant memories carried away from you in the minds of all who loved you. The four of us had the honor of finding and putting together all the memories of you we could find; we never could have found them all, earthbound as we were. But somewhere out there in the timeless scheme of things, the remainder of the memories still linger with those souls on some sunnier shore. With that host afar, and with those here below who still remember you, the authors now join in a thunderous thank you for all the pleasures you gave us. You see, to us you are *not* closed forever. Euclid Beach Park, you are only closed for the season.

Cleveland, Ohio
1977
AMUSEMENT PARK BOOKS, INC.
Lee O. Bush
Edward C. Chukayne
Russell Allon Hehr
Richard F. Hershey

The Authors: (left to right) Ed Chukayne, Richard Hershey, Russell Hehr, and Lee Bush, and a restored RACING COASTER CAR at the Hershey residence.

CONTENTS

FROM ENDPAPER TO ENDPAPER

Chapter 1
THE FIRST SEASONS, 1895-1900

The cover of the promotional booklet published by the Euclid Beach Park Company for the season of 1899.

LEE HOLTZMAN
GENERAL MANAGER.

Euclid Beach Park.
CLEVELAND, O.
SEASON 1899
WARD & SHAW.
PRINTERS.
CLEVD, O.

TELEPHONES :   General Manager's Office : Park-Glen 10.   Office, 225 Superior St.: M. 2222.   Boat Office, foot of Superior St.: M. 2487.

(Amusement Park Books, Inc.)

1

The thought that there could be a Cleveland, Ohio, without a Euclid Beach Park seems to be a contradiction in the minds of many who knew the park over the years. A drive by its former site on Lake Shore Boulevard presents a scene that today seems unreal, as high-rise apartments are revealed instead of the towering coasters with their pennants flying, or the tip of the ROCKET SHIP ride, or the LOG CABIN at the end of the main parking lot. The new buildings appear as illusions to the eyes of those who passed the "Beach" so many times for so many years.

Located on the southern shore of Lake Erie, eight miles east of Cleveland's Public Square, Euclid Beach Park flourished for seventy-four seasons. On a brisk September day in 1969, the letters placed on the sign by the main gate announced for the last time that Euclid Beach Park was "Closed For The Season." Many an anxious eye had watched that sign through the successive springs, waiting for the words to change to a date that would hold the promise of another season. But what of the first seasons and the beginnings of Euclid Beach Park?

The 1880's saw the initial development of the elements that formed the "traditional American amusement park." New York's Coney Island became the parent of most major rides, concessions, and attractions and was influential in their early development. Also, with the spread of the interurban lines and the street railway systems, the so-called "trolley park" emerged as the transit companies built these parks at the termination points of their lines to stimulate traffic on weekends, when few people had need of street car transportation. Amusement parks, or "summer resorts" as they were called, sprang from many a picnic grove or just a pasture, and certainly the presence of a body of water helped attract the crowds who had just realized the wonder of "sand bathing" or even real bathing amid the waves. The meeting of the land and the water offered a great number of diverse recreational pleasures and the hope to beat the heat of the city.

It seemed only reasonable to the original founders, the Euclid Beach Company, that in the 1890's there was the potential for a major summer resort to thrive in the city of Cleveland. There were numerous parks in business in the greater Cleveland area, but not a single pleasure resort of any stature had been developed which fronted on Lake Erie. The words of the original prospectus for the Euclid Beach Park Company read like an incredible prophecy. (Illus. 1.)

Prospectus of the Euclid Beach Park Company.

'The Euclid Beach Park Co. was incorporated under the laws of the state of Ohio, October 23, 1894, by Albert E. Thompson, John Flynn, John Irwin, Jerome B. Burrows, and Hylas B. Gladwish.

'The Capital Stock is Three Hundred Thousand Dollars, composed of 3000 Shares of One Hundred Dollars each. The Incorporators are convinced that a Summer Resort within easy reach of Cleveland, properly appointed and conducted, will be both popular and profitable.

'The Incorporators have secured an option on 63-6/100 acres of land at Twenty-Three Hundred Dollars per acre, payable as follows: Thirty-Six Thousand Dollars January 1, 1895, balance in five equal annual payments with interest at 6% per annum, the property lying directly north of Collinwood which has a Lake frontage of 1700 feet.

'This site is especially adapted for a place of resort having a broad beach 75 to 100 feet wide backed by a bluff, and extends 1500 feet south to The Lake Shore Boulevard with a frontage thereon of 2080 feet.

'The design is to enclose the property, lay out drives and walks, plant and transplant trees, put in an Electrical Fountain, build a Casino, Bath and Boat Houses, Toboggan Slides and such other attractions as may be deemed advisable.

'A Dance Pavilion, Eating House, Green House, Ice House, Water tank and Engine House with engine capable of furnishing water for all Buildings, Fountains sprinkling lawns and flower beds, also capable of lighting entire grounds with electric light, — in fact, make Euclid Beach to Cleveland what Coney Island is to New York.

'The Company also holds an option on two passenger Steamers especially adapted for this service, with capacity for 800 people each, which will land passengers at our own docks at The Park.

'After having made a conservative estimate of the number of people who have paid admission the past year for a day's outing from Cleveland and Vicinity, we find the following:

June 15th to Sept. 15th

Put-in-Bay, by Boat,	40,000
Beach Park,	15,000
Forest City Park,	100,000

Minor Resorts; such as, Adams Avenue, (Lake Front,) Silver Lake, Corrage Grove Lake, Meyers' Lake, Cuyahoga Falls, Geauga Lake, Rocky River, Dover Bay Park, The Mulberrys', West Dover, Randall's Grove, Lake Breeze, Oak Point, Vermilion, Linwood Park, Shaddock's Grove, Ruggles' Beach, Sages' Grove, Cedar Point, etc., ... 300,000

TOTAL 455,000

'Would it not naturally imply with a resort like this, with all its natural and other advantages, two street car lines and two steamers, that Euclid Beach Park should receive the greater part of this patronage annually?

The Aggregate Cost the First Year will be:

First Year's Payment on Land,	$36,320.83
First Year's Payment on Boats,	10,000.00
Dock for Large Boats,	5,000.00
Dock for Small Boats,	500.00
Dancing Pavillion,	11,000.00
Casino,	3,000.00
Bath House,	2,000.00
Toboggans,	500.00
Twenty Boats,	500.00
Electric Fountain,	5,000.00
Ice House,	1,000.00
Electric Light and Water Plant,	10,000.00
Estimated Operating Expenses,	15,000.00

TOTAL $100,820.83

Estimated Receipts the First Year:

Two Boats in service from June 15 to Sept. 15, 16 trips per day, 150 Passengers each trip @ 50¢ per person (90 days), ... 108,000.00

Passengers from street cars, 500 per day @ 25¢ (90 days), ... 11,000.00

Receipts from Bath House, Boat House, Dining Hall, Refreshments, Privileges, etc. $50.00 per day (90 days), ... 4,000.00

TOTAL $123,750.00

Less First Year's Disbursements,	$100,820.83
Amount on hand at close of Season 1895,	$ 22,929.17

Second Year's Disbursements:

Payment on Property, (2d Installment)	$21,792.50
Interest 6% on same ($108,962.50),	6,537.75
Interest on Investment 33-1/3% Capital Stock, # 6%	6,000.00
Steamers, (2d Installment)	6,000.00
Interest on same,	1,800.00
Improvements,	10,000.00

$52,130.25

Second Year's Receipts:

Boats, Street Cars, Perquisites,	$123,750.00
Increase over 1895, (10%),	12,375.00
Amount Brought Forward 1895, Cash on Hand,	22,929.17

TOTAL $159,054.17

Less Disbursements,	52,130.25

Balance on hand at close of Season 1896, ... **$106,923.25**

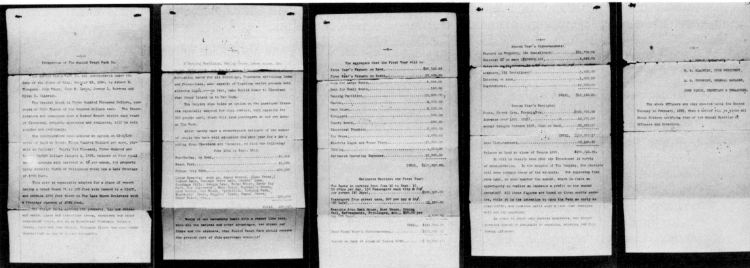

(Russ Milan)

(Illus. 1) The Prospectus (of the original Euclid Beach Park Company) was offered to solicit funds for the new venture.

'It will be readily seen that the Investment is worthy of consideration. In the opinion of The Company, the receipts will even surpass those of the estimate. But supposing they were half, or even quarter the amount; where is there an opportunity to realize so handsome a profit on the amount invested? All these figures are based on three months service, while it is the intention to open the Park as early as practicable, and continue until such a time that receipts will not pay expenses.

'In order to enter into certain contracts, the Incorporators deemed it advisable to organize, electing the following officers:
J.R. IRWIN, *PRESIDENT,*
H.B. GLADWISH, *VICE PRESIDENT,*
A.E. THOMPSON, *GENERAL MANAGER,*
JOHN FLYNN, *SECRETARY & TREASURER.*

The above Officers are only elected until the Second Tuesday in February, 1895, when a notice will be given all Stock Holders notifying them of the Annual Election of Officers and Directors.'

(Amusement Park Books, Inc.)

(Illus. 2.) William R. Ryan, Sr., the first acting manager of Euclid Beach Park, was later owner and operator of the nearby competitor, Manhattan Beach, later known as White City.

So, with this remarkable document the prospect of Euclid Beach Park was predicted. However, not even those enterprising men could see just what the future of the proposed resort might be.

For the directing head of the new park, William R. Ryan, Sr., was chosen as Euclid Beach's first acting president and manager after the park's opening. *(Illus. 2.)* Ryan was an active figure in Cleveland's business and political circles. With modest but enterprising beginnings, he developed a business dealing in candy, cigars, and tobacco and also operated a drug store. From these interests he became associated with the development of amusement and resort places. Through his involvement in the establishment and development of amusement centers, he became known as "the father of Cleveland's summer resorts."[1] William Ryan was to remain as president of the Euclid Beach Company through the 1897 season. Later he was to own and operate Manhattan Beach, which became White City Park.

So it was that early in 1895 the property was enclosed and walks and drives laid out along with the planting and transplanting of trees. *(Illus. 3.)* This land, having been sold at twenty-three hundred dollars an acre a year before, was becoming Euclid Beach Park. Forty years earlier, twenty-three acres of it had been sold by Manners West to Alexander Ross for the sum consideration of one hundred dollars. It was to yield a great deal more, not only in monies but pleasures and memories.

As the feeling of spring came to Cleveland in 1895, and as the breezes that came off the lake got warmer, the people of the city and the surrounding areas began to think of outings, the beaches, and the joys of summer. The newspapers began to advertise excursions to Put-In-Bay via the D & C Lines' steamers; boat trips to Niagara Falls were touted, and familiar local names, such as Forest City Park, Edgewater Park, and Glenwood on the Lake Front, made their bid for the summer crowds. Amid these ads, beckoning the throngs to come and play, was a simple and seemingly first appearance of a significant name. It said: "EUCLID BEACH PARK, Saturday, June 22. Steamers leave foot of St. Clair St., 8 A.M., 1 P.M., and returning 9 A.M., 4 P.M., and 7 P.M. Music in attendance, boating, etc. each Round Trip, including admission to grounds."[2] Thus it was announced that Euclid Beach Park was in its initial season. Throughout the following week, the papers carried ads announcing the times for boat departures and informed the public that the visitors to the park

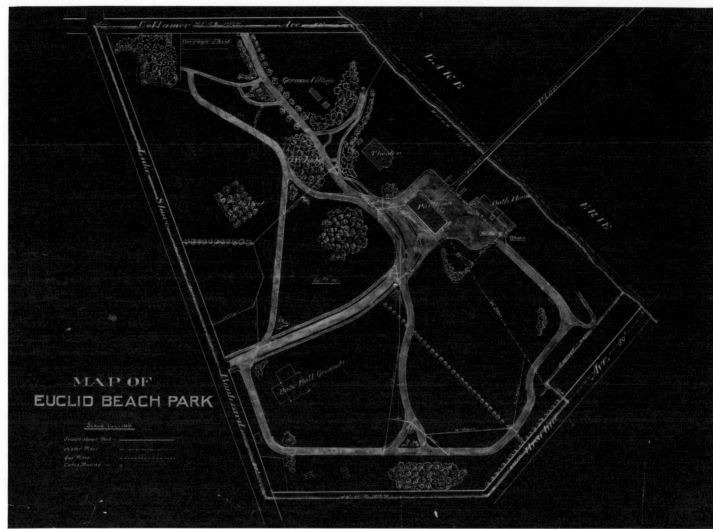

(The Humphrey Company)

(Illus. 3.) Plan of the park as it was developed for the season of 1895. The original structures, the DANCE PAVILION, THEATRE, PIER, and BATH HOUSE are shown as is the line of Poplar trees running east to west in the camping area. These trees are also visible in Illus. 68a., Chapter IV., p. 64.

(Amusement Park Books, Inc.)

(Illus. 4.) View of the PIER from the 1899 booklet taken from the area of the DANCE PAVILION. One of the "TUBS" is moored at the PIER'S end. Down the center of the deck of the PIER, a dividing rail is evident.

could hear the Iowa State Band in concert, for free, on June 26, 28, and 30th. Even though the public was invited to the park as early as the 22nd, not until June the 30th did the park claim: "EUCLID BEACH PARK, Today - Open for Business, Docks Completed. *(Illus. 4.)* Open Daily All Summer."[3] A late completion of the docks may have delayed an earlier opening than the end of June, a date considered well into the season. It was also stated at this time that the Iowa State Band under Bandmaster Frederick Phinney would be making numerous appearances at Euclid Beach during early July. *(Illus. 5.)* Indeed, the Iowa State Band was popular in Cleveland that summer, making many concert appearances at Pain's Amphitheatre, Wade Park, and Euclid Beach. Band concerts were a staple in the diet of attractions at summer resorts and would continue to be for many years to come.

Then came the 1895 Fourth of July, the paramount summer holiday and the ultimate American self-celebration. Where more fitting than at an amusement park could it be celebrated? Though every park claimed the grandest fireworks display on this holiday, Euclid Beach would initiate a tradition that would live throughout its many seasons. A fireworks display, reported to have cost $1,000, was offered in the afternoon and evening. Certainly it was a success, and it was announced in the papers that, "This is where they went! Everybody [was] there the Fourth!"[4] The management declared that 50,000 patrons attended the park on the Fourth of July, 1895.

(The Cleveland Plain Dealer)

(Illus. 5.) Newspaper ad announcing the performance of the Iowa State Band as it appeared in the Cleveland Plain Dealer, Monday, June 24, 1895.

Certainly many of those 50,000 visitors to the park — and others who attended the park that season and the next five seasons — came to the park on one of the two steamers owned by the Euclid Beach Park Company. The "DULUTH" and the "SUPERIOR" were ferry steamers 98 feet in length, built in Cleveland in 1890. After five years of service on Lake Superior, they were brought back to Cleveland in May, 1895, by the park owners to make daily trips from downtown Cleveland to the "Beach." Painted white with bright red lettering, these two boats were affectionately called the "EUCLID BEACH TUBS." *(Illus. 6.)* This service continued until 1901.

(The Cleveland Plain Dealer)

(Illus. 6.) One of the Euclid Beach "TUBS" is shown at its downtown Cleveland dock.

(Illus. 7.) View of the DANCE PAVILION as seen from the PIER, familiar to visitors as they arrived via the "TUBS".

(Amusement Park Books, Inc.)

(Illus. 8.) Two views of the DANCE PAVILION showing the exterior cupola and a second floor outside balcony while the interior view exhibits the open beam work and stage for musical ensembles.

(Amusement Park Books, Inc.)

Those who traveled to the park were greeted by a scene familiar to visitors throughout the park's history: the long PIER, with the DANCE PAVILION at its land end. (Illus. 7.) This building stood as a land mark until it burned after the park's closing in 1969. Dancing, too, was a main ingredient in the fare of entertainments offered to the summer fun seekers. (Illus. 8.)

Mid-July brought another delight to the ears of Clevelanders. The Cleveland Plain Dealer gave a glowing account of the success of Innes' Band which had musically triumphed at Savin Rock in Connecticut and were to concertize in Cleveland and at Euclid Beach Park. Innes' Band, a large aggregation, performed some of the newest marches and had an assemblage of vocalists who finalied their appearances with works called "War and Peace" and "A Day at the World's Fair." (Illus. 9.) The article summarized that Innes' Band "will appear at Euclid Beach Park every afternoon of the present week. Besides the band, there will be numerous attractions, such as boating, dancing, bathing etc. Thousands visit the park daily. It is one of the finest resorts in America."[5]

The "TUBS" and the street car lines continued to bring patrons to the park as it offered a diversity of entertainment for the summer of '95. (Illus. 10.) There was Professor Loisettes Stork Circus; the awakening of Santelli's Sleeping Boy [sic], a side show; Diadumune, the first woman to sleep for seven days; and Professor Kirk's Military Band. (It was Kirk's ensemble which played at the opening of Euclid Beach Park.) Throughout August, a varying fare of vaudeville and band concerts was also presented. The Retail Butchers held their annual outing at the park on August 22nd, and the event was highlighted by an ox killing, a "Novel Event" as the headline read. From September 9th on, the park remained open on weekends and closed for the summer on the 28th of the same month. The first of seventy-four seasons had terminated.

The 1896 season was proclaimed and commenced on May the 29th. To entice customers to come to the Park, a new list of attractions was presented: The CRYSTAL MAZE, "the mystic wonder of the century"; "Bonner, the wonderful talking and trick horse"; The SWITCHBACK RAILWAY, (similar to the invention of LaMarcus A. Thompson which is now considered the beginning of the modern roller coaster); a "FERRIS" WHEEL; SWINGS; and a MERRY-GO-ROUND. There were also concerts featuring the Centennial Band. Transportational service was increased as the street railway offered departures from downtown Cleveland every ten minutes, and a schedule of nine round trips daily was made by the "Tubs."

(The Cleveland Plain Dealer)

(Illus. 9.) Ad in the Cleveland Plain Dealer, Wednesday, July 10, 1895 marking the appearance of Innes' Band at the Amphitheatre and the Iowa State Band at Euclid Beach.

(The Humphrey Company)

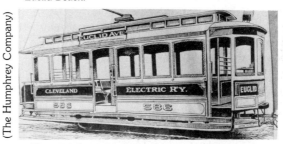

(Illus. 10.) Streetcar similar to those that brought the first visitors to the park.

(Cleveland Public Library)

EUCLID BEACH PARK.

IS NOW OPEN FOR THE SEASON.

BONNER

The Wonderful Talking and Trick Horse.

Crystal Maze

AND OTHER ATTRACTIONS.

Music, Boating, Dancing and everything to amuse.

Boat leaves foot of St. Clair Street every hour after 8 A. M. Cars leave the Square every 10 minutes, through without change

(Illus. 10a.) Ad for Euclid Beach in TOWN TOPICS magazine, Saturday, May 23, 1896.

Also, the C & B steamer "OHIO" would supplement the "TUBS" on Sundays and holidays. The Fourth of July, 1896, would offer a $5,000 fireworks display. Among the attractions for this season were a balloon ascension and parachute jump, an operatic presentation of "la Somanbula" [La Sonnambula by Bellini], and Sevengala [Svengali] the Hypnotist. Pawnee Bill's Wild West Show appeared along with selected vaudeville acts.

Fads were as evident then, as ever, and the year 1897 must have been the year of the bicycle, at least in Cleveland and Euclid Beach. The fifteenth of a mile BICYCLE TRACK, located west of the Lake Shore Boulevard MAIN GATE, was to be busy all season with lady bicycle riders. (Illus. 11.) Championship riders would appear at many sites in and around Cleveland and finish the season at the park. Two ladies, May Allen and Helen Baldwin, were among the finalists competing as the end of the summer neared. The management of the park recognized the public interest in the bicycle and even offered prizes in a contest to design a bike pavillion. The structure was to be erected at the cost of five hundred dollars.[6]

William Ryan made every effort to bring the spirit of Coney Island to Euclid Beach. He brought a personality from Coney Island to present a water show in Cleveland. This man was Captain Paul Boyton, who is now credited with forming the first outdoor amusement park, as such, in America. His Seal Lion Park was at Coney Island, Brooklyn, New York. Although there had been numerous concessions on the "Island" for more than fifteen years, Boyton was the first to collect a number of diverse attractions in a park, fence it in, and charge admission at the gate.

Sea Lion Park had a number of shows, trained water animals, a chute-the-chutes, a loop-the-loop (360°) coaster, and other attractions. Sea Lion Park opened for the Fourth of July, 1895. Euclid Beach was not far behind. As of the 1895 season, Euclid Beach had no major rides, but Ryan certainly saw the Coney Island pattern and brought it to the "Beach." By the season of 1896, Euclid Beach boasted a Thompson coaster called the SWITCHBACK RAILWAY. (Illus. 12.) Also offered to the public for their approval was a Herschel track MERRY-GO-ROUND, (Illus. 13.) and a ["Ferris"] PLEASURE WHEEL. (Illus. 14.) A CHUTE was built down which bathers could slide into the lake. (Illus. 11.) Also, the DANCE PAVILION, BATH HOUSE, and THEATRE which had been there since the first season, helped fill out an impressive roster for the young park. (Illus. 11.)

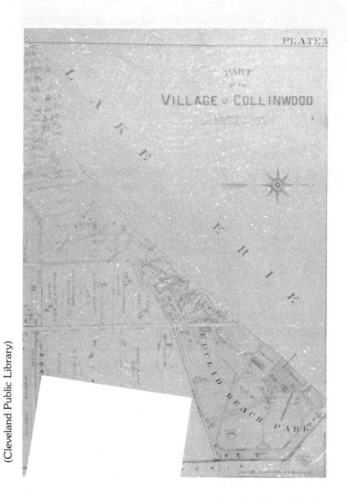

(Cleveland Public Library)

(Illus. 11.) Plan of Euclid Beach Park for the season of 1897, showing the location of the SWITCHBACK RAILWAY, CRYSTAL MAZE, THE EDISON, and FERRIS WHEEL.

(The Cleveland Press)

(Illus. 11a.) Cleveland Press ad proclaiming the popularity of the bicycle as a park attraction, Saturday, May 31, 1897.

9

(Amusement Park Books, Inc.)

(Illus. 12.) The SWITCHBACK RAILWAY claimed a course 1000 feet in length. It was the ancestor of the ever popular modern roller coaster.

(Amusement Park Books, Inc.)

(Amusement Park Books, Inc.)

(Illus. 13.) Track MERRY-GO-ROUND, possible a product of Armitage-Herschell or Herschell-Spillman, with unusual conical roof, an early landmark.

(Illus. 14.) One of the two "FERRIS WHEELS" to appear at Euclid Beach Park was this machine built by the Buckeye Observation Wheel Company.

10

(Illus. 15.) Various ads for Euclid Beach Park (1895-1900) as they appeared in many of Cleveland's publications.

(Cleveland Plain Dealer, Cleveland Press, Cleveland Leader, and Town Topics.)

The format of attractions also continued with acts that were in the style of those found at Coney Island: Minerva the World's strongest woman; Boyton's Water show; a diving horse; plus a number of minstrel acts. D.D. Fulton's Mamoth Imperial Minstrels and Billy Williams' Minstrels joined the parade of acts to be offered to the public. By 1897, Euclid Beach had also become the spot for a number of annual outings: the retail grocers, the butchers, the Press newsboys, and the Knights of Pythias, to name a few (Illus. 15.)

The United States approached a military showdown with Spain in the spring of 1898. Euclid Beach announced Clara Morris would open the "new" THEATRE with her refined vaudeville company since "high class" vaudeville was touted as the usual fare at the park.

As the country began to contract war fever, signs of current events began to show at the local parks. Forest City Park presented "The Battle of Manilla" and the "Blowing Up of the Maine" that May. Big vaudeville acts such as Hilda Thomas and Frank Barry with a large troop were appearing regularly at Euclid Beach. Also, further enticement was offered as the boat fare was reduced to a nickel for a round trip, five cents cheaper than a trolley ride. The car lines offered direct routes to Collinwood and a special 5-cent bus line that then conveyed the riders directly to the PAVILION.

The first week in June brought the attack of American forces on Puerto Rico and Manila, and that same week brought Arthur Deming and more "high class" vaudeville to Euclid Beach

11

(Amusement Parks Books, Inc.)

(Illus. 16.) Pictures of the AVENUE THEATRE, showing its exterior before the facade was installed, and the interior with the stage set for a production as part of the 1899 promotional booklet's enticement to prospective patrons.

Park. (Illus. 16.) The naval forces of the United States gave their Fourth of July present to the country by destroying the Spanish Fleet outside Santiago Harbor. Euclid Beach presented fireworks by Arbuckle and Katz, a baseball game, a double attraction at the THEATRE, a balloon ascension, and a band concert. The first still picture presentation to be made at the park was a patriotic piece called "The Biograph."[7]

Throughout the summers of 1898 and 1899, Euclid Beach continued to offer vaudeville, band concerts, plays such as "Lady Macbeth," and a variety of side show attractions. A "Ladies Week" was featured, and all the ladies who attended the park were admitted to the theatre without charge. (Illus. 16.) The retail grocers had their outings at the "Beach" and in 1899 offered a $500 carriage as a raffle prize. A number of other oganizations held their picnics at the park, including the telephone company. Euclid Beach advertised itself as the "Coney Island of the West" and "The Seashore of Ohio."[8]

(Illus. 16A.) 1899 Ad "Coney Island of the West"

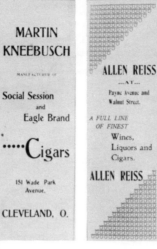

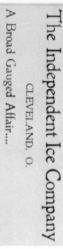

(Illus. 17.) Pictures appearing in the 1899 booklet produced to promote Euclid Beach Park under new management. Lee Holtzman replaced William Ryan as manager while the latter developed his own park a few miles to the west - Manhattan Beach (later known as White City).

(Amusement Park Books, Inc.)

13

A new manager, in the person of Lee Holtzman, took over the direction of Euclid Beach Park for the 1899 season. A lengthy and extravagant booklet was put out by the new management announcing the coming attractions for the summer of 1899. The very atmosphere of the times, the romantic '90's, and the approaching turn of the century are reflected by the advertisements and lilting verse that accompanies pictorial scenes of the park. A welcome is offered, and a verse above a picture of the original MAIN GATE READS:

"Those who enter here, leave care behind,
Find rest for the body and peace to the mind."[9]

In every way, the park reflected a midwest view of the Coney Island image. *(Illus. 17.)*

The summer of 1900 brought a new resort to Cleveland, "Manhattan Beach," named after a section of Coney Island, New York. This park was a mere four minutes from Euclid Beach and was on Lake Erie across from East 140th Street. Its owner was William Ryan, formerly Euclid Beach's manager. He now beckoned the summer crowds to see "high class" vaudeville at Manhattan Beach. Although Euclid Beach would be presenting the usual fare of acts, plays, band concerts and special attractions, such as Totzke, the "Dental Marvel" (he slid down a 40-foot rope suspended by his teeth), in 1900, there were a number of new attractions offered. These included free transportation via the "TUBS" and free dancing in the afternoons. The Coney Island look was being marketed just down the shore, and the Euclid Beach Park Company looked for a way out. There was evidence that the directors of the park were so unsure of their course that they even failed to advertise until after the Fourth of July, 1900.

There were others, too, who had been at the park during its early years, doing business, observing, and forming distinct and substantial ideas of their own, all the while peering out from behind the popcorn stand counter. *(Illus. 18.)*

(The Humphrey Company)

(Illus. 18.) Early popcorn stand at Euclid Beach Park operated by an unusual family as pictured in Amusement Park Management Magazine - International Association of Amusement Parks.

(Illus. 18a.) Buying a bag of popcorn and catching the last streetcar from Public Square sometimes caused a number of problems. c. 1901/1902

Chapter 2
The Humphreys and
Euclid Beach/

A family affair

Occasionally in the process of history, there are elements of seemingly remote origin that come together as if their convergence was chiseled in the granite of destiny. This seemed to be the case when the family of Dudley Sherman Humphrey II and a plot of land situated in the Western Reserve came together, first in the year 1896, and finally in a lasting marriage that began in 1901. Humphrey ancestry can be traced back to their arrival in England with William the Conqueror in 1066 and subsequently to America as early as 1640. But who were these people, the first elements of this marriage, what were their ideals and ideas, and how did they happen to be at Euclid Beach Park in the era that just preceded the turn of the century?

THE FAMILY

The Humphreys had settled in New England in the mid 1600's and lived in Massachusetts and Connecticut. Dudley Humphrey was born in Goshen, Connecticut, in 1770 and came to Ohio in 1837 to be patriarch of the Ohio branch of the family. His son, Dudley Sherman Humphrey I, was also born in Goshen, Connecticut, and the date of his birth was 1814. D.S. Humphrey I moved to Parma, Ohio, along with his brother William in 1834. He married Mable F. Fay, the first white woman born in Parma, in 1847. He and his family then settled in Townsend, Ohio, in Huron County in 1849, due to lack of lumber in Parma. From this man and his notable sons and daughters came the beginning of the trek to Cleveland and Euclid Beach.

The Humphreys had come from New England to Ohio to explore the forests and the possibilities of the saw mill business. D.S. Humphrey Senior was successfully involved in the lumber business, but after the loss of a hand in a saw mill accident, he had decided to devote all his attention to his farm. *(Illus. 19.)* This twelve hundred acre farm straddled the Wakeman-Townsend townships line. The farm was well equipped with the proper machinery of the day. Son Dudley S. Humphrey II became skilled with machines and was at home with the principles of mechanics and, in addition, showed a great deal of aptitude in contriving new machines and modifying others. His early aspiration was to be a civil engineer. The Humphreys had been successful lumbermen in New England but had decided to speculate on the rich forests in Ohio. Their speculations were rewarded with further success in the woodlands of the Buckeye State. So, as a member of a very prosperous family, Dudley Sherman Humphrey II set out to realize his goal of becoming an engineer. Off to Buchtel College (later to be Akron University) he went while his older brother Harlow and his younger brother David decided to pursue the duties of the farm.

The Humphreys were an extremely close-knit family of rugged and tenacious stock, seasoned by many a fierce New England winter and accustomed to persisting until any appointed deed was accomplished. They were also people of high moral character dedicated to that which they saw as clean, open, and charitable. The latter was a quality which lead to the exodus from the Wakeman-Townsend farm.

Dudley S. I was a man who indeed lived by his beliefs. He was approached by neighbors who owned and operated a saw mill and barrel factory with the request for financial backing. He responded in an expected fashion, in the spirit of generosity and neighborliness, even though he obligated a considerable portion of his assets. This investment was promptly followed by a series of disasters that were to turn a financially solvent house into a place of monetary tragedy. An explosion occurred at the factory which resulted in great cost and numerous damage suits. This was followed shortly by the Jay Cooke panic of 1873. (Jay Cooke and Company, a prominent banking firm, went bankrupt and brought an end to a period of inflation and expansion. The resulting depression was marked by many business failures and widespread economic distress.)

(The Humphrey Company)

(Illus. 19.) The Humphrey farm house at Wakeman, Ohio.

As for the Humphreys, a situation developed in which they found themselves operating a saw mill and barrel factory formerly owned by the neighbors they had helped. This development marked the end of Dudley S. Humphrey II's formal education; he returned home to aid his father and take over management of their involuntarily acquired businesses. Despite the acquisition of a large barrel contract, the economic climate proved insurmountable. The orders for barrels resulted in a loss, and the Humphreys were unable to meet their current $25,000 deficit. Even with young Dudley Sherman's energy and experience in the sawmill business and a work force of seventy workmen, the mill and factory faltered.[10] This indebtedness forced the family to mortgage the farm and sell a four-hundred acre parcel. In 1876, Dudley S. Humphrey I died and left sons David and Harlow to run the farm while D.S. II managed the faltering mill. Despite the great effort of the members of the family, they could not successfully challenge the times and continued to slip deeper into debt. The year 1879 marked a high point in disaster. The mill burned and left the Humphreys with an additional $45,000 deficit. It was also the year that Dudley S. Humphrey II chose to get married. Together, he and his lifetime partner assessed the future. It would seem that it was not an ideal time to start a marriage; and it would be a rough road in the days ahead before the course of events would be smooth.

With great determination, Dudley Sherman Humphrey II, his wife Effie, his brothers David and Harlow, and his sister Linnie set to the task of making the farm productive as a means of erasing their debts. By 1889, $15,000 of their debt had been liquidated. The fall brought a bumper crop of 20,000 bushels of potatoes. In addition, to increase revenue and productivity the Humphreys had invented a device to plant potatoes called the "concave potato knife", indicative of their ability to use initiative. This tool enabled a planter to cut more potatoes for planting in a shorter time and was marketed by the "Humphrey Bros. Seed Grain and Seed Potato Growers".[11] It indeed now appeared as if they were on their way to recovery. However, more frustration beset them. The farm market of 1889 was extremely poor, and as a result the family decided to hold over the potatoes by storing them under ground to sell the following spring. They were disappointed the next season, for the potato market fell to a record low. This along with the farm crops was the final blow.

With everything they owned now mortgaged — including their personal property — the Humphreys went to their banker and declared that they were "through", and suggested a sheriff's sale. It was hoped that there would be a sufficient return from this sale to meet their debts with perhaps a little left over. However, the sale turned into quite a different story. The banker was the high bidder on almost every article of value. It soon became apparent to the many friends and neighbors of the Humphreys that the banker (mortgage holder) intended to "bid in everything". In view of this, the competitive bidding stopped, and, as the sale continued, it became a mere formality. When everything was totaled, all their belongings were sold, and the Humphreys found themselves still $20,000 in debt. The sale was in the fall of 1890, and the family remained on until March of 1891 to look after the property.

With $100 they had borrowed, the Humphreys (with Dudley's two children and mother Humphrey) moved to Glenville, near Cleveland.

In Glenville the atmosphere was one of hope. The suburb was a horse center and the location of the popular race track operated by the Cleveland Driving Park Co. — first amateur harness racing club in America.[11a] David and Harlow, both experienced horsemen, obtained a contract to train all the colts owned by a large stable operator. They were contracted to break and train horses for $30 a head, per month. In addition, Dudley was writing articles with some success for farm journals while the women contributed a substantial income from paying boarders with their home-cooked meals.

At this time a significant development took place which would later prove basic to the Humphreys' arrival at Euclid Beach. While traveling about Cleveland, Dudley frequently bought popcorn from the many vendors along the streets of the city. Dudley Humphrey noted that this corn did not taste as good as that which the family made in an iron kettle back at the farm. The common procedure used by these sidewalk vendors was to pop their corn exposed to the air and then add seasoning. The Humphreys had a different way of making popcorn. Dudley related that, ". . . we used to put our corn into the hot kettle, mix the lard and salt right with it, cover the lid, and stir it up with a big spoon. That kept all the sweetness of the corn in the popped kernel and seasoned it at the same time".[12] Harlow had devised a wooden top with a hole in it for the popper so the corn could be stirred without opening the kettle. Dudley refined this idea by fitting a skillet to a Russian drum that could be turned by a hand crank.[13] The invention was patented, and Dudley Humphrey set out to sell his new corn popper.

It was a success initially. Carting his child of resourcefulness from vendor, to vendor and store, to store, he vanquished all differing methods of popping as he masterfully displayed the proper way to pop corn. However, the victory was temporary. In a short time, every possible buyer within reach was sold the new machine at the price of $5.00 apiece, with the totals showing twenty-five sold with no prospective customers within sight.

Sometimes the tests that are given out by the circumstances of life are harsh enough to cause a complete withdrawal from any sort of self determination. Dudley's eyes had been giving him continued pain as he went about his writing, and upon examination he was told that his eyes would be fine if he discontinued his writing. Harlow and David met with additional misfortune as their fee was reduced to $20.00 a head per month. To add to this trend, the women's boarding business began to decline. It was indeed a time of desperation. The boys decided to seek work, and Dudley answered an ad that inquired for: ". . . A man experienced in the sorting of hardwood lumber; apply in person. Steady work".[14] Certainly this was a job that Dudley was well qualified to handle. However, he was refused the position, and the advertiser advised Dudley to "make his own job".[15] He was, in essence, overqualified to work for someone else.

A summary of the situation presented a picture most people would evade. They would flee in panic to some refuge of despair. However, these folks looked ahead with determination rather than back in dejection. The failures at the farm and mill, the bad fortune at the race track and stables, Dudley's eyes, and the diminishing boarding house business were interpreted as sign posts pointing a way from a series of endeavors and to a new enterprise. At age forty, Dudley Humphrey II could have resigned himself to failure and subsistence at best *(Illus. 20.)* He was, though, at this juncture, reminded of the many lessons in perserverance and ingenuity that his father had taught him. The tenacity of belief and principle and the employment of "Yankee resourcefulness" would spur the Humphreys to a new achievement.

(The Humphrey Company)

(Illus. 20.) Dudley S. Humphrey II at age 40.

It was common — almost ceremonial — in the Humphrey household to hold regular and frequent family councils. Dudley brought home with him from his aborted job interview a new idea that seemed so apparent he must have felt it incredible no one else had thought of it. He gathered the family and made his proposal. The fact had been established that there were no new buyers for their popper, but that many vendors were making a living selling popcorn in the city of Cleveland. Not only that, it had been clearly demonstrated that the Humphreys' way of popping corn in its own seasoning was superior to any other method then being used. They would fit their old wagon with a popper and go into business. The perfect opportunity was at hand. Dudley had seen in the newspaper, along with the lumber job ad, an announcement that a big carnival was coming to town. "Nobody laughed," said Humphrey, "though my wife admitted later the notion sounded crazy."[16] They were ready for this move, this incredible move, that brought the Humphrey family ever closer to their rendezvous with Euclid Beach. They packed all their possessions into the old delivery wagon, borrowed fifteen dollars for corn, gasoline to run the popper, some food, and set out for the site of the coming carnival.

1893 was a year for action. President Grover Cleveland called a special session of Congress to repeal the Sherman Silver Purchase Act in hopes to stem the panic that was crippling the economy. In the spring, the World's Columbian Exposition opened in Chicago, and on the evening of June 23rd, the Humphreys opened a popcorn stand outside the carnival grounds. The carnival was being held at Cable Park, which was located on grounds west of where Hough Avenue met East 105th Street (400 feet north of Mount Sinai Hospital). The Humphreys were fortunate enough to locate a house to rent on Edmonds Street near the scene of the carnival. The rent would not be due until the end of the first month of occupancy. The carnival itself featured an extravagant production of Pain's "Last Days of Pompeii." The high point of this work was a colossal fireworks display. During that hot evening, made even more uncomfortable inside the wagon by the heat of the gasoline-fed popper, the family sold popcorn as fast as it could be popped. The night's tally showed receipts of $8.50 with the corn going at a nickel a bag. A competitor, with a much more elaborate rig and a better location, registered only $.50 for his evening's efforts. Dudley S. II bought him out for $15.00, which was to be paid at the end of the week. With two locations now in operation the result of the next day's business was $30.00. A pattern began to take shape. The Humphreys bought out other vendors who could not make a go of their businesses. By July Fourth, they owned four rigs and on that holiday did $125.00 in business. *(Illus. 21.)* It was announced by Dudley Humphrey II, after assessing the fruits of their labors, that, "We'll stay in this business."[17] After their success at the carnival he and his family set their rig at East 107th and Euclid Avenue on Cleveland's East Side. David, Harlow, and Linnie chose locations in other areas of the city. Dealing strictly in cash, the Humphreys prospered at all their locations. Through the next few years they continued to buy out competitors and erase their debts. In 1895, Dudley secured a site on Public Square at the southwest corner of Ontario and the Public Square, the center of the city. (This locale is today the Higbee Company's main display window of their downtown store.) It was literally a hole in the wall, a four foot by eight foot store front, rented at $45.00 a month. *(Illus. 22.)* The landlord scoffed at the idea of selling popcorn from this location, but by two years time, the Humphreys were leasing the entire building.

(The Cleveland News)

1905   **1939**

(Illus. 22.) Public Square Stand of The Humphrey Company, 1905, and its later 1939 occupant.

(The Humphrey Company)

(Illus. 21.) A typical Humphrey Popcorn Cart from about 1900. The setting appears to be near the RAVINE at the park.

(Illus. 23.) The Articles of Incorporation for the Humphrey Company, 1893.

(The Humphrey Company)

The year that the "hole-in-the-wall" was rented, Euclid Beach Park opened. The next year, 1896, Dudley Sherman Humphrey II, his brother David, and their families operated a popcorn concession at the Park. (Illus. 18.) This unusual family affair had a thriving business amid the diving horses, side shows, parachute jumps, and vaudeville acts that were so prominent at Euclid Beach in the late 1890's. However, they did not like the place. This family, the Humphreys, whose name eventually became synonymous with Euclid Beach Park, disliked the resort to the extent that they left it in 1899. ". . . we didn't like Euclid Beach Park,"[18] said Dudley S. Humphrey II. "It didn't help us to be there. The biggest attraction was a BEER GARDEN. Gamblers, fakers, and questionable side shows littered up the place."[19] It was obvious that the way in which the park was run was in no way subject to the approval of the Humphreys. D.S. Humphrey suggested to the management that the BEER GARDEN and the undesirable shows be discontinued and a decent trade stimulated. His suggestion was met with a laugh and countered with the argument that these were the things that were the money makers. The side shows stayed and the Humphreys left.

THE LAND

In two years the Humphreys would return to claim the second element of the marriage — the land which was the site of Euclid Beach Park. But many years before the advent of the Humphrey popcorn business, as the grandparents of Dudley Sherman Humphrey I were working in the forests of Connecticut, there were interests in that very same state looking westward. In 1796, the Connecticut Land Company sent a group of surveyors to map and divide the Western Reserve. (Illus. 24.) This party was led by Moses Cleaveland, whose name, with slight adjustment, was adopted by the City of Cleveland. It is also due to this man and his party of surveyors that the township of Euclid got its name and made possible the first part of the park's name. To somewhat appease the surveyors, General Cleaveland drew up a contract with his men to form a township east of Cleveland, with each man having a share. They called it Euclid in honor of the geometrician and surveyor. Although all the

(Illus. 24.) The Western Reserve.

proposed plans for the town did not mature, the town was established and named. It would seem that as early as the 1790's, there would be some chance that would bring the New England Humphreys and the land of the Western Reserve together. A full blown migration from the east to the Western Reserve was evident by 1817, and as we have seen, the Humphreys came to Ohio in 1837.

The land that was to be the site of Euclid Beach Park was in two tracts established in the Western Reserve. The basic and larger portion where the amusement area would be developed was in Tract #16. The southeast corner, later to be the larger area of the Euclid Beach trailer camp, was in Tract #15. The acreage that was positioned in Tract #16 when purchased by the original Euclid Beach Park Company was in the village of Collinwood. The City of Cleveland annexed the village of Collinwood on January 21, 1910. The smaller Tract #15 section of the park property was originally in Euclid Township, then later, in the village of Nottingham, which, in turn, was annexed by the City of Cleveland on January 14, 1913. The property north of Lake Shore Boulevard, as well as the area south of the street, eventually known as "Humphrey's Field," was, prior to the opening of the park, a farm owned by Caius Cassius and Brutus Junius Cobb. *(Illus. 25.)*

 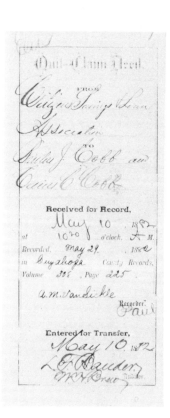

(Illus. 25.)

(Illus. 25.) Some of the maps and deeds to the property that was to become Euclid Beach Park which was owned by the Cobb family during the period before the park was opened.

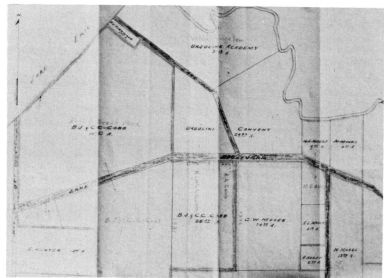

22

(John L. Cobb Collection)

(John L. Cobb Collection)

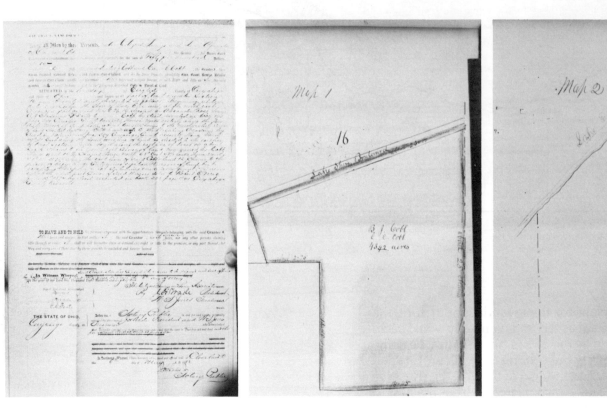

(Illus. 25.)

(John L. Cobb Collection)

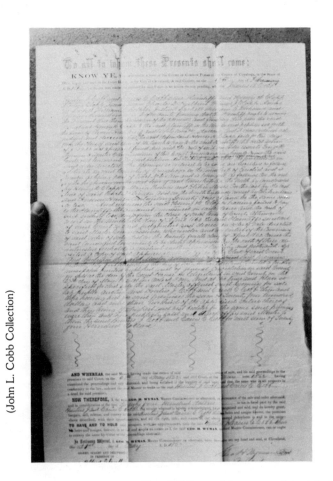

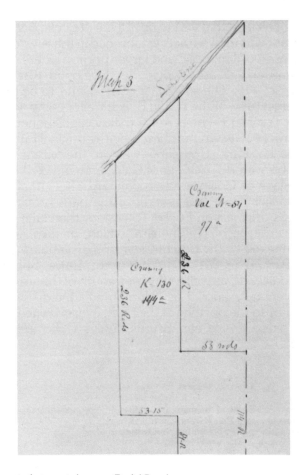

(Illus. 25.) Some of the maps and deeds to the property that was to become Euclid Beach Park which was owned by the Cobb family during the period before the park was opened.

The Cobb brothers, including a third brother, Junius Brutus, were in the book business, a business they had learned while working for Moses C. Younglove & Company. In 1852, the Cobbs took over the firm and it became J.B. Cobb & Company. The business grew and later became known as Cobb, Andrews & Company. This firm was finally bought out by its chief competitor, The Burrows Brothers Company, in 1888. During this period, the Cobb family had been acquiring property that would eventually be the site of Euclid Beach Park. They had bought this land as early as 1854. More acreage was purchased in 1866 and 1870. The final parcel bought by the Cobbs was acquired the 6th of May, 1882. It is speculated that the wife of Caius Cobb, Helen Margaret Andrews Cobb, named the farm that faced the lake "Euclid Beach." This land was all within Tract #16. *(Illus. 25, 26a-b.)*

The property immediately east of Cobb's Euclid Beach Farm, which was partially in Tract #15 and partially in Tract #16, was sold to The Ursuline Academy by George and L.A. Gilbert in 1874. (Lakeshore Boulevard had been originally named Gilbert Avenue after this family.) The Humphreys would not finally acquire all the property that is commonly attributed to them and Euclid Beach Park until 1914. The Cobbs, from whom the basic section of land was obtained, would remain associated with the Humphreys and the park for many years after the Humphreys took control of Euclid Beach Park. How did the two elements, the Humphrey family and this land, come together?

(John L. Cobb Collection)

(Illus. 26a.) The Cobb farm house was utilized as the park's office building in the early years. The farm was originally named "Euclid Beach."

(Illus. 26b.) East 156th Street was originally called Collamer, and before the building of the park, the road was a dirt lane.

(John L. Cobb Collection)

As has been noted, there were those (the Humphreys) who had watched the early seasons of Euclid Beach Park proceed. They had not been quiet concerning the conduct of the park, but the management declined to accept any such advice. It might have been that the fame, the notoriety, and popularity of Coney Island in Brooklyn, New York, had set the principle trend of what was to be featured by this new business, the business of Amusement Parks. Coney Island was indeed referred to both in the prospectus of the Euclid Beach Park Company and in the advertising for the early Euclid Beach. A number of other new parks across the country would claim that to be the "Coney Island of the West, or South or . . ." was certainly desirable. In a few short years there would be the appearance of Luna Park in the city of Cleveland, and it would be unashamedly influenced by its namesake at Coney Island. In Cincinnati, the slogan "Coney Island of the West," supplanted the official name of a new park, "Ohio Grove." This famous park was to be known as "Coney Island" until its closing in the 1970's. No one could deny that the East Coast Coney Island was one, if not the most significant, influence in the amusement park business in the '90's. However, this strip of land on the Atlantic Ocean, just north of New York harbor, was not known as a center of moderation. Certainly the use of spirits was present at the many concessions that dotted the "Island." However, it was not the only activity that might be objected to by conservative people. Every and any type of activity could be found there.

To recognize real alternatives is indeed a gift, and certainly the Humphreys saw that there was another way to run an amusement park. After the Humphreys closed their popcorn stand at Euclid Beach Park in 1899, Dudley S. Humphrey II, his brothers and sister moved to expand their already flourishing vending business. Plans were made to open a chain of popcorn stands in Chicago similar to those that had proven so successful in Cleveland. While in the "Windy City" Dudley S., by chance, picked up a Cleveland newspaper. That paper informed him that Euclid Beach Park had failed, and the land was to be sold off and developed as an allotment. The plans for the Chicago popcorn stands were cancelled, and Dudley S. moved as swiftly as possible to get home. Once again the family was gathered. It was time to make a new and momentous commitment. To take over Euclid Beach Park would be the perfect opportunity for the Humphreys to prove that their views on park management were not only feasible, but could be very profitable.

The former management was faced with the loss of more than half their investment if they sold the land for building development, and it was established that the original Euclid Beach Park Company was losing twenty thousand dollars a season. They jumped at the Humphrey offer and consequently leased the park to the Humphreys for five years at twelve thousand dollars a year.[20]

THE MARRIAGE

The decision to commit to this project had to be made quickly, but, in essence, it had been prepared for many years and was viewed by Dudley S. Humphrey II and his family as the chance of a lifetime. It was not only to be the chance of a lifetime for the Humphreys, but it made the possibility real for many of us to experience a great number of pleasures over the years to come. So it was that in the spring of 1901 the Humphreys went about renovating the park and prepared to put every bit of experience and judgment they had to work. The marriage had been accomplished. The Humphreys and Euclid Beach park were now a family affair.

To conduct an open and clean business meant every one could see what was going on. The high board fence that surrounded the property was torn down. This was something Dudley S. had asked the previous management to do so that decent people could see what was happening on the grounds of the park. Obviously, the old management didn't want this kind of observation; the Humphreys did. Next, all the questionable concessions and the GERMAN GARDEN (the beer concession) were eliminated. No more freak shows and questionable games of change would be found at the park. Significantly, there would be no more gate charge, which D.S. felt would be like charging admission to a drug store. Dudley S. conferred with the street car people who agreed to charge only one fare to those passengers coming to Euclid Beach. In return, he retired the two steamers from service that had brought passengers to the park's dock. With the institution of these features, Euclid Beach Park, under the management of the Humphreys, assumed a slogan that was to become well known: "One Fare, Free Gate, No Beer." There were those who had been associated with the park business who thought this procedure was "business suicide." Not only that, but what would be the policy toward those who would not be considered welcome by the management? Dudley S. stated they would find a way to keep them out — which he did — even though it took a Supreme Court ruling. Euclid Beach Park would be a place for decent people to bring their families and enjoy a beautiful landscape and amusements that were clean and wholesome.

Did the Humphreys estimate correctly, or was the Coney Island syndrome the basic and only premise on which to run an outdoor amusement park? Could such an operation survive without the beer trade and the profit made by games of "not such a good" chance? "The old park," said Dudley S. "collected 90,000 gate admissions during the previous season. We had that many people visit the park in a single day."[21] Yes, Cleveland approved, and would continuously approve for many seasons to come. The Humphreys had informed the churches and the newspapers of the policies on which the family would run the park. Cleveland responded.

The season of 1901, which opened for the first time under the Humphreys on May 27th, gave the family all the encouragement they needed to keep and develop their ideas and ideals. As a gauge of the increase in patronage, a look at the popcorn stand gave clear indication. Its best season before Humphrey management was 2,000 dollars. The 1901 season showed an increase to 10,000 dollars. During the summer of 1926, that same popcorn stand did 60,000 dollars worth of business. The direction was established during the early days of the 1900's. Indeed, the elements of experience that had tried the Humphrey family since the 1870's, the failing procedures of the original Euclid Beach Park Company, and the handy work that nature provided on those acres in Tracts #15 and #16 in the Western Reserve had come together in the Spring of 1901 — a fitting way to start the century. The new plan was an almost instantaneous success; in fact, in 1902, the Humphreys were to boast that almost one and a half million people visited Euclid Beach in 1901. (Illus. 27.) With a free gate, income was made by charges at the individual attractions, a practice maintained until the park closed in 1969.

(Illus. 27.) A dramatic increase in annual attendance as announced in a 1902 full page ad, clearly stating the Humphrey's position concerning the management policies of Euclid Beach Park.

ATTENDANCE NEARLY 1,500,000 LAST SEASON.

Our EUCLID BEACH PARK

DANCE PAVILION

A BIG SUCCESS

WE made the most remarkable demonstration at Euclid Beach last season ever known in the history of summer resorts. Under our management we have cut out the entrance charge, the beer garden and all freaks, fakes and gambling devices. *Everything* is of a highly moral and elevating character. From previous attendance of less than 200,000, with the beer attractions and disorderly crowds and loosing deal, doing away with these injurious features we boomed this resort to 1,500,000 happy visitors and very satisfactory financial results. ✪ ✪ ✪ ✪ ✪

ONE FARE   FREE GATE
NO BEER
✛

Everyone walks RIGHT in on the ground floor— None HIRED to come.
✛

SCORES of amusement and entertainment features. ✪ *Many of them new and novel.* Besides dancing, bathing, boating, bowling, roller skating, etc. ✪ ✪ ✪ ✪

GRAND CAMPING SCHEME.

Pure water, pure air, lovely shade, thousands of good people to associate with, and more attractions than any other resort in the world. Have a few weeks of it. *Look for details later.*

(The Humphrey Company)

INTERIOR OF AVENUE THEATER AT EUCLID BEACH

(The Humphrey Company)

(Illus. 28a, b.) Letterhead of the Humphrey Company reflected the style of the early part of the 20th century.

With the popularity that seemed apparent in 1901, the Humphreys, at David's suggestion, moved to become owners of the park. This move was initiated before a third of the 1901 season had passed, and in two weeks the Humphreys had purchased eighty per cent of the company stock. Some stock holders, who saw the trend the Humphreys were setting, were reluctant to sell. Ultimately, the family acquired all the stock. Because of the popularity of the new park policy, the price of individual shares went from twenty-five cents on a dollar to seventy cents on a dollar.[22] Values of every kind were rising at Euclid Beach Park. (Illus. 28.) Much of the success that the park enjoyed was due to the elimination of rowdies and trouble makers. Dudley S. was outspoken on the subject of undesirables. It had to be firmly demonstrated that those who did not

conform to the policies the family had set down would be ejected from the grounds — forcibly, if need be. Sometimes it was necessary. The Supreme Court supported the Humphrey view and stated that the park manager need give no reason for barring undesirables from the park. Numerous damage suits were leveled at the Humphreys; they were all fought and won by the family. Over the course of this first season of new management, it was established what type of clientele was welcome at the "Beach." One instance is related that a man of some political influence came to the park that year (1901) and purposefully misbehaved. This was simply a challenge, and he dared the Humphreys to put him out. Dudley S. did not put him out; however, he had the huskiest park policeman on the force follow this man everywhere he went. (Illus. 29.)

(The Cleveland Plain Dealer)

(Illus. 28c.) Pennants flying from the CIRCLE SWING, women in long dresses and men in hats, coats and tie. This was how the BEACH at the "Beach" looked in 1904. The CIRCLE SWING had its original GONDOLAS and was decorated gaily. A worker can be seen on the CIRCLE SWING tower and a young boy looks toward the PIER from the BOAT LIVERY. Families were present everywhere.

On the occasions of this man's visits to the park, he always had this uninvited companion. Finally, the man apologized to D.S., agreeing that the way the Humphreys were running the park was indeed correct and would they please call off the big policeman. The basic ideal that was to be the guideline for Euclid Beach Park under the Humphreys was stated by Dudley S. Humphrey II: "We have a clean park because we've not been afraid to fight for it. Anybody can throw out a friendless bum in rags — but that gives only superficial cleaness. If you want REAL cleaness, you must stand ready to throw out the man in immaculate dress — if he isn't clean inside. We've done that. There has been no compromise with influence, position, or money. The success of Euclid Beach has proved that the great majority of people are decent and will patronize a decently conducted thing."[23]

(Illus. 29.) Park police of Euclid Beach were under the direction of captain John MacDonald for most of the park's operation under The Humphrey Company.

(The Humphrey Company)

28

(Illus. 30.) 1908 panoramic view of Euclid Beach Park showing the east portion of the grounds from the DANCE PAVILION to the SCENIC RAILWAY.

(Kekic Collection)

A number of the attractions inherited by the Humphreys when they acquired direction of the park were older structures. the DANCE PAVILION, the BATH HOUSE, the THEATRE, and OFFICE (originally the Cobb farmhouse) were buildings that were on the property from 1895. The SWITCHBACK RAILWAY, the old track MERRY-GO-ROUND, a "FERRIS" WHEEL (a pleasure wheel), a CHUTE slide into the lake, and a set of SWINGS dated from 1896. As might be expected, the Humphreys went about making changes. Some rides and buildings were altered, replaced, or just plain eliminated. (Illus. 30.)

Before the SWITCHBACK RAILWAY was replaced, an ESCALATOR was installed to help riders get to the cars. In 1904 this earliest of coasters was replaced by a later design called the FIGURE EIGHT. The location of these two coasters was in the area next to the ROLLER RINK.

The ROLLER RINK was built in 1904 and lasted for many decades as a center for enjoyment at Euclid Beach Park. Renovations and enlargments were made to it in 1909.

By the season of 1903, a new and unique carousel was added to the roster of attractions at the park as the Humphreys proudly advertised the appearance of the new "JAPANESE FLYING PONIES." In 1910 another significant machine was placed in the park. That year brought the beautiful CARROUSEL to Euclid Beach that was to be the classic ride of its type in the park until the time of the Beach's closing.

The Humphreys set about bringing new rides to the park frequently. Euclid Beach increased its list of roller coasters when the SCENIC RAILWAY was constructed in 1907. In addition, the area just to the lake side of the roller rink, that had already seen two roller coasters, and now saw a third in 1909. Originally called the NEW VELVET COASTER, this roller coaster was later to be known to many as the AERO DIPS.

A ride of great popularity, and a landmark to visitors to the park and those passing by in their boats as they traveled Lake Erie, was the CIRCLE SWING, later to be known as the ROCKET SHIPS. This ride was a favorite until the last days.

Another distinguished and famous citizen of Euclid Beach's ride population was the RACING COASTER. Originally, it was called the DERBY RACER and remained to delight riders from 1913 until the end of the final season.

(Illus. 31.) The policy of the Humphrey Company regarding dress at the DANCE PAVILION was characterized by this 1907 cartoon of D.S. Humphrey II and an improperly attired unfortunate.

If you went to a company or community picnic at Euclid Beach Park, you were familiar with the "LOG CABIN." This building, one of the first to be viewed when leaving the MAIN PARKING LOT and entering the amusement area, was to serve as an organization headquarters for annual outings and as a dance hall. The original structure was built for the Pan American Exposition of the Work of the People of North and South America and was called the Forestry Building. The Exposition was held at Buffalo, New York, in 1901. The building was disassembled then reconstructed at Euclid Beach in 1902 and called the LOG CABIN. (Illus. 196, 197, 198.) The new management began to reshape their park, as new structures were introduced.

In the years preceding World War I, the physical look of the park was not the only change basic to the Humphrey direction of Euclid Beach Park. The rules of conduct were strict, very strict, and were exemplified by a cartoon that appeared in a by-line entitled "Who's Zoo in Cleveland."[24] (Illus. 31.) Anyone who did not wear a collar in public was not a gentleman, and anyone who was not a gentleman would not be allowed on the dance floor. Thus, those who appeared collarless would be removed from the dance hall. Also, the subject of bathing attire was clearly regulated. Even though the management had to bear the criticism of the *Cleveland Leader* for being overly conservative, the Humphreys stated plainly that a bathing garment would be long enough to cover the limbs, high enough to conceal the chest, and definitely not be gaudy in color.[25] The management of Euclid Beach Park was never afraid to

(The Humphrey Company)

GENTLEMAN—A well-bred and honorable man; a man of education, high principles, courtesy and kindness; a man who never appears in public without a white collar, the badge of his gentility.—Humphrey's Revised Dictionary.

Beau Brummel, the greatest dude of any age, set the sartorial standard for gentlemen. Since then, in intervening generations, have appeared men who won fame by spreading Beau Brummel's doctrines and keeping his memory green.

Such a man is Dudley S. Humphrey.

Dudley S. goes farther than Beau Brummel ever thought of going. He says every man who wears a white collar is a gentleman.

Presumably he believes that a man who does not wear a white collar is not a gentleman, for he rules all such from the dance floor of Euclid Beach.

Now don't be confused. When he talks about gentlemen, Dudley S. means gentlemen. He does not refer to gents who wear vici kid shoes tied with white strings, yachting caps and automobile goggles.

Dudley S. is one of three brothers who have made lots of money in a few years. They used to sell popcorn from a wagon, but now they scoot around in bang-bang chaises and hire men to count their money. Their principal field of endeavor now is Euclid Beach, and Dudley S. is the main squeeze out there. What he says goes. That's the reason why when he says no collarless humans of the male persuasion shall squeeze supple waists in the mazes of the dance, they bounce them off, that's what they do.

Signed, Dudley S., Detector of Gentlemen.

take their case to the public. In an article by A.L. Allen in the "Echo," the question of how a public place should be run is addressed to the people: "Euclid Beach — Ask Anyone!" It is subtitled, "The Best Advertisement that the Humphrey Company Has Is the Manner in Which Euclid Beach is Conducted."[26] (Illus. 32.)

The public had become aware of what was going on at Euclid Beach Park, and in a relatively short time. Not only was the population of Cleveland, Ohio, aware of the growing reputation of this rejuvenated park, but the beginnings of a national image were in the making. In the New York Herald of Sunday, August 10, 1902, a full page article on the front page of the amusement section, with numerous pictures, appeared, extolling the Humphreys and Euclid Beach Park. "Pop-Corn Brought a Fortune — The unique Road that led from a Push Cart to Wealth in a few short Years."[27] (Illus. 33.)

In addition, an interesting bit of verse was composed by Herb C. Palin, a renowned writer, reported to be the highest paid writer in the world. After a visit to the park, he wrote: (Illus. 34.)

Euclid Beach Ask Anyone

The Best Advertisement that The Humphrey Company Has Is the Manner
In Which Euclid Beach Is Conducted

By A. L. Allen

(The Humphrey Company)

(Illus. 32.) A statement concerning the popularity of the Humphrey Company park policy.

"How the Humphreys Humped"

Thirty-seven years ago this story did begin,
    That tells of troubles bravely fought and how the right did win,
It tells of how—from not a thing a splendid project grew,
    And teaches some great moral truths that may appeal to you.

The Humphrey boys, the story runs, lived out upon a farm,
    With parents' care surrounding them and shielding them from harm,
Where healthy in the open air they rugged grew and strong,
    And learned to till the fertile soil and tell the right from wrong.

Their father passed away one day and left the farm in debt,
    The farm was large—a fortune due—which they must some way get,
But brightly did they set to work though weighted down with claims,
    For fourteen years they battled on determined in their aims.

But when the fight was nearly won a slump in values came,
    That threw the boys clear off their feet although they still were game,
The Sheriff sold them out one day—to Cleveland did they come,
    With not a cent to call their own but much more grit than some.

They wrote a while 'bout farms and things, but that did never pay,
    They worked and worked and worked again with not a chance to play,
Hard luck turned worse and then grew bad until in Ninety-three,
    A new invention of their own began the light to see.

The "thing" popped corn and popped it well, but not a soul would buy it,
    Although the Humphreys saw its worth the minute they did try it,
They started in to pop good corn and pop the hard luck question,
    To give the people something good but not give indigestion.

The tide had turned, good money came, they got a corn concession,
    Then got the pop-corn trade, you know, right in their own possession,
At Euclid Beach they toiled away just popping corn and popping,
    The nickels in their pockets, too, continually were dropping.

The place ran down, for want of care, the owners cash were losing,
    Though Euclid Beach was beautiful and of the public's choosing,
The Humphrey boys did get control—control with pop-corn money,
    Which fact is true as true can be although it may seem funny.

They made the Beach a beauty spot, and that in fullest measure,
    A well protected Picnic Ground for public, ease and pleasure,
Their ladies helped with chaste advice and strong co-operation,
    'Till Euclid Beach stands out to-day an object to the Nation.

And Euclid Beach is up-to-date in atmosphere and tone,
    Throughout the land 'tis spoken of and morally is known,
The moral of this rhyming truth is handed in a lump—
    The thing that made the Humphreys' win was just the Humphrey "hump".

(The Humphrey Company)

(Illus. 34.) Even the poets praised the energy and policies of the Humphreys. The poet was Herb C. Palin.

(Illus. 30.) 1908 panoramic view of Euclid Beach Park showing the east portion of the grounds from the DANCE PAVILION to the SCENIC RAILWAY.

(Kekic Collection)

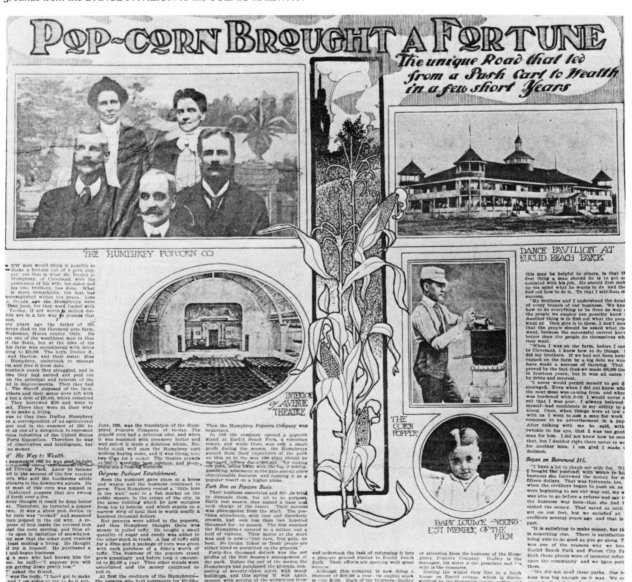

(The Humphrey Company)

(Illus. 33.) The success of Euclid Beach Park and the Humphreys spread quickly and widely as attested to by this article in the New York Herald, August 10, 1902.

The basic principles on which the park was run were high morality, temperance, and wholesome fun; indeed, Dudley S. Humphrey was building a highly successful amusement park on these premises — as he and his family interpreted them. There was no compromise even where the Armed Forces were concerned. The *Cleveland Clipper* of November, 1906, reported that members of the crew of the U.S.S. Wolverine were barred from the dance floor because their attire didn't conform to the dress code. *(Illus. 31.)* Once again Humphrey forwarded the consideration that all are equal when it comes to these rules, and no uniform would get special privileges, including police, firemen, or the Salvation Army.[28] The rules of apparel stood.

Perhaps the most outstanding change in the park's policy, and one that was tested from time to time, was the view on intoxicating beverages. When the Humphreys took over the park in 1901, the first concessions to go were those which sold beer, wine, and liquor. The GERMAN VILLAGE was closed, the last load of empty bottles returned. The visitor to the "new" Euclid Beach sipped lemonade. Not only was there no alcohol to be purchased in the park, but those who chose to have a drink or two before entering the park found their admission denied — they were most unwelcome.

Directly across the dirt road which was then Lake Shore Boulevard, stood a tavern run by one Peter Schmitt. Guards at the gate of the park watched the patrons of the tavern carefully, and if they attempted to come to the park, the way was blocked. Not so much as the smell of liquor on the breath of an intended patron was allowed. The park management made it clear as they posted a sign that simply said: "Any Person Going to the Saloon across the Way Cannot come into This Park."[29] *(Illus. 35.)* An underlying feud between the saloon and the park management surfaced in a number of ways. Dudley S., in addition to his sign, had spotlights playing on the entrance to Mr. Schmitt's establishment to keep track of its patrons and discourage their plans to cross the street and come into the park; however, the opposition had its plan too.

It seems that one Gotlieb Lieber, a liquor salesman by profession, intended to show a humanitarian side and went about informing a Bedford justice — a justice who would listen — about a deplorable and downright "nasty" [sic]! practice that was going on out at Euclid Beach Park on Sundays! There were college boys, toiling at their various labors while working at the concessions and rides, tending to the comforts of

(The Humphrey Company)

(Illus. 35.) The protagonists - The Peter Schmitt Tavern and Euclid Beach Park. The sign clearly states the case. D.S. Humphrey had spotlights play on the entrance of the Schmitt establishment to discourage patrons of the bar from crossing the street.

others, but being denied any of their own. Mr. Lieber intended to stop this cruelty! The poor lads were bathed in their own perspiration and, with the whirling of the rides and the accompanying rush of air, were in grave danger of contracting neuralgia. Justice L.D. Cox of Bedford issued eighteen warrants, and a constable delivered them to the park. They were intended to include the Humphreys and Mr. Shannon (then manager of the park) plus sundry other employees. In the meantime, it was discovered that Mr. Lieber was in the employ of one A.J. Lukwinski, who, by some coincidence, was a liquor wholesaler, and did, it was noted, supply one Peter Schmitt. All such parties, Schmitt, Lukwinski, and/or associates, denied any knowledge of the action. The Park management, having been forewarned of the warrant delivery, received the constable with great calmness. He first arrested Dudley S., then D.H., and proceeded to find Shannon. The manager was eating with Justice Murphy of Cleveland Heights, who calmly stated that he, a justice, could accept bonds and ordered the release of the Humphreys and Shannon on their own personal bond.[30] The park remained open on Sundays right to its last day in 1969 — a dry, but "working" Sunday.

(The Humphrey Company)

(Illus. 36c.) The last car home from the Beach, 1907.

(Illus. 36a.) Streetcars originally stopped at a building later known as the popcorn and refreshment stand.

(Harry Christiansen Collection)

(Illus. 36b.) Around 1908, the station was moved south toward Lake Shore Boulevard near the PONY TRACK.

(Russell Allon Hehr Collection)

The first ten years of the new century would continue to see the Humphreys employing constant expansion and adjustment. In 1902, the family bought Forest City Park, located on Cleveland's east side. Forest City Park had been in existence since the latter part of the 1800's and under Humphrey control would assume the same policies that were in effect at Euclid Beach. Forest City Park would be sold in 1906 as way was made for yet another venture, the Elysium.

The street car tracks that brought the trolleys into Euclid Beach Park had run to a location along side the MAIN POPCORN STAND, just south of the DANCE PAVILION. In 1907, the Humphreys and the street car company moved the disembarkment area south nearer Lake Shore Boulevard (near the southern end of the future COLONNADE and KIDDIELAND). *(Illus. 36.)*

The Finest Summer Outing and Camping Resort in the

is our justly famous

EUCLID BEACH PARK

The Pride of Cleveland and Northern Ohio. It is now drawing patrons from far and near, all delighted and satisfied. The Humphrey's have spent over $100,000 on improvements and in beautifying the grounds since last season.

Family Gatherings

And picnickers are safe to come on short notice—as coffee and lunch are in abundance at purely nominal prices.

Good order, genteel deportment and well meaning people only desired.

The Children

Find no end of harmless amusement in the Penny Arcade.

Box Ball Alleys

Another new feature this year—at present under construction—will be finished soon—a very popular exercise and pastime wherever introduced.

THE NEW SCENIC RAILWAY

This Wonderful and Fascinating production is entirely new—artistic and beautiful in construction—is brilliantly lighted— just completed and in perfect running order. It is the Largest and most expensive Scenic Railway in this country — es a safe yet thrilling ride of over a mile in four minutes. Equally entertaining to old and young. Don't miss it.

BOWLING.
BILLIARDS.
POOL.
BOATING.
BATHING.
CAMPING.
CIRCLE
SWING.
CAROUSAL.
MERRY-GO-ROUNDS.
OCEAN WAVE
FIGURE 8.
FLYING
DUTCHMEN.
Etc., Etc., Etc.

THE DANCING PAVILION

Think of it—a handsome structure on the shore of old Lake Erie, and (20,000) twenty thousand square feet of perfect floor surface—always smooth and glossy—making dancing easy—accommodating 800 couples (1,600 people) without crowding. It's the wonder of Ohio in this line.

ONE FARE—FREE GATE—NO BEER.

This was the original announcement to the general public of the start toward the HIGH MORAL TONE in everything that pertains to Euclid Beach Park and its management.

This "High Moral Tone" has continued ever since and will continue as long as the Humphrey's own it.

Well meaning people only desired, in reality means that the other kind are not tolerated—and this applies to all.

When you come here you are in good company.

THE ROLLER SKATING RINK

Provides a deservedly popular amusement and exercise. The floor has been enlarged to a surface equal in size to our famous dancing pavilion—20,000 square feet of skating surface.

We have just adopted a new and easy method whereby one may learn to skate in an hour. The rink is, very popular this year.

From 12 to 3 and from 6 to 7.30 beginners can skate free, including use of skates.

Moving Picture Theatre

This was the first Theatre in the country exclusively devoted to the exhibition of Moving Pictures. It has a large seating capacity and shows bright, clear, entertaining, instructive, funny but clean pictures only. Include it in your trip.

MOVING PICTURE THEATRE

THE CIRCLE WAVE

This new and novel, safe and amusing feature, "The Circle Wave," is being erected and will certainly prove a very popular sport for the children. As it was not completed in time to be photographed for this issue you will have a pleasant surprise awaiting your arrival.

Figure Eight

A long and pleasant ride, entertaining alike to old and young. You will recommend it to your friends after you have enjoyed it yourself.

Circle Swing

A safe and thrilling ride through the air. Many have enjoyed this wonderful sport. If you haven't, get busy your next trip.

THE LOG CABIN

Just the place for private parties, conventions, etc., where the company desires to have a "headquarters" together—part of the time, at least. Speak early for dates for log cabin.

Address: **THE HUMPHREY CO.**

Euclid Beach, Cleveland, Ohio.

America's Greatest Camping Opportunit

TENTS AS THEY LOOK TODAY ON LAKE DRIVE

It is interesting to know just how comfortable and homelike these cosy tent-homes are. Everything is there for you to move in. All you need is bedding, food and clothing. If you select a 4-room home, you have a living room, 2 bedrooms and a combination dining room-kitchen, or you may have 4 bedrooms if desired, with 4 double beds, each with a substantial iron bed with good springs and mattress. But the surprise will greet you in the dining room-kitchen—there you will find everything but linen—you find table, dishes, gas cooking stove, refrigerator, cooking utensils—all complete.

Grocery, huckster and ice wagons visit each avenue daily—in addition thereto, a good grocery is near at hand. If you want a perfect camp, come. Over 40 acres devoted to camping.

Best Possible Accommodations.

Tents already constructed with floor, double roof and one, two, three, four, or five rooms, as desired.

Artificial gas connections for lighting and cooking with each camp.

Popular Prices

Camping Facilities.

Police protection, well lighted ground, A No. 1 sanitary toilet arrangements. Tents are waterproof—1, 2, 3, 4 and 5 rooms each. Screen doors, screen windows, awnings, gas for cooking, gas jet in each room, pure water in abundance, ample shade. Well meaning people only invited. All applicants must furnish satisfactory references. There is nothing in the camping line that cannot be had at this popular resort.

We have expended over $40,000.00 in improvements on our camping grounds this year.

DOUBLE ROW OF SOLID COMFORT

Our entire camp is thoroughly equipped with excellent sanitary conditions. Grounds well policed by our special watchmen. You can rent an outfit furnished or unfurnished, as you prefer. Streets made, graded, sewered, plenty of shade trees. In fact, our camp is certainly "The Finest Ever."

THE GOOD PEOPLE OF OHIO

And adjoining vicinity no longer have to hunt for a desirable camping location—they have the best right at home.

No more long trips to Michigan or other northern states—you have the very best right here on the cool shore of old Lake Erie.

No matter where you live—write, telephone or wire for detailed information.

A handsome illustrated booklet mailed you free on application.

WE HAVE TENTS FURNISHED FOR SLEEPING, INCLUDING BED, LINEN AND COVERINGS CARED FOR EVERY DAY. IN FACT, A HOTEL UNDER CANVAS OF FROM 1 TO 4 ROOMS.

A Portion of the Camp in Process of Construction. Office at the Right.

A PEEP INTO CAMP VIOLA

THE 1907 CAMPING SEASON IS NOW OPEN

Wise People Will Apply for Accommodations Early—In the Past We Have Been Unable to Accommodate all Those Who Have Applied for Tents

CALL ON OR ADDRESS THE WAGNER MANUFACTURING CO. TENTS   H. W. roud.

BOTH PHONES.   CORNER VIOLA AVE. AND MAGNOLIA LANE, EUCLID BEACH GROUNDS, CLEVELAND, OHIO.

(Russell Allon Hehr Collection)

(Illus. 37.) The CAMP GROUNDS had a wide range of attractions which were promoted by the Humphrey Company.

By the 1907 season, Euclid Beach Park would boast of offering "America's Greatest Camping Opportunity."[31] The camping facilities would offer tents, which were already erected, with floor and double roof, and options including one, two, three, four, or five rooms, with natural gas for cooking. The grounds offered the most modern toilet facilities to provide the utmost in comfort for the summer visitor. *(Illus. 37.)*

One of the most enjoyed features of the "Beach" was, indeed, the DANCE PAVILION, which was advertised as having an 18,000 square foot dance floor polished to a surface as smooth as the mirrors that lined the walls of the ballroom. The dance restrictions were as strict as any rule to be found at the park. There was to be not the slightest hint of ungentlemanly or unlady-like conduct or immediate expulsion would result. The dress code has been already mentioned and was adhered to at all times.

Improvement to existing buildings and rides was constant in an effort to keep Euclid Beach Park as new and appealing as possible. The Humphreys even worked with those outside the park to make travel to the Beach better. In 1909, Lake Shore Boulevard was paved and extended east to Wickliffe as a main thoroughfare. This was fostered by the Humphreys and the local citizens.

Another feature of this era was CASTLE INN, which was located at the north-east corner of the park in the camp area. "The view from the spacious veranda is beautiful, the well kept lawn reaching down to the shore is most satisfying and restful to the city dweller." claimed the ECHO of 1909.[32] Mrs. Ida Magner was the proprietress. She also leased the RESTAURANT on the second floor of the BATH HOUSE, which overlooked the lake. All the cooking and baking was done on the premises to assure freshness.

In 1912, a cement terrace or promenade was poured around the DANCE PAVILION. The cement pouring process utilized a machine developed by the Humphreys. It was also used to pour the ramp at the land end of the PIER and to construct a number of SUMMER COTTAGES on the CAMP GROUNDS. *(Illus. 38.)*

(Kekic Collection)

(Illus. 38.) An important Humphrey development, extensively used throughout the park, was the innovative cement pouring machine, here seen pouring the ramp leading to the PIER. c. 1912

The Humphreys were mindful of new events and had an eye for using new developments to encourage a visit to the park. In 1911, Harry Atwood, a pioneer aviator, flew from Cedar Point at Sandusky, Ohio, to Euclid Beach Park. Thousands were to greet the young flyer. Again in 1914, a young woman aviator, Lily Irvine, made a similar trip. Flying was to be an interest of the Humphreys throughout the years.

While aviators buzzed in and out of Euclid Beach and new rides and new features were constantly introduced at the park, another pattern emerged that was basic to making Euclid Beach Park what it was. Workers would come to the park from the early part of the century through the twenties and stay on as employees, as would many of their sons and daughters. Some of these families would work for the next forty and fifty years at the "Beach." It was as though they were absorbed into a larger family, larger than the Humphreys, larger than their own. It was the "Euclid Beach Family." *(Illus. 39.)*

Roy Mizner, a former park employee, recalls his days at the park. He came to the park in 1906 and worked with two brothers, Ed and Cliff Johnson from Pickway, Ohio. Ed was boss of the MAIN LUNCH by the ROLLER RINK. When the STREETCAR STATION was moved to a site nearer Lake Shore Boulevard in 1906, a new lunch area was opened. It was called the CHESTNUT GROVE. Ed Johnson sent his brother, Cliff, later to be called "Kicky," to open the CHESTNUT GROVE. This peaceful refreshment area was amid a grove of trees at the site that would later become the COLONNADE and KIDDIELAND.

Roy went back to visit the park more than fifty years later and found Cliff Johnson still at work at the refreshment stands, as intent as ever at performing his duties at Euclid Beach.

Harry Shannon, the park manager, would be a land mark himself as he remained to manage the park until the fifties. Trained as a lawyer, he was a

(The Humphrey Company)

(Illus. 39.) The park managers during the early teens of this century would become members of the Euclid Beach "Family" with long terms of service.

(Kapel Collection)

(Illus. 39a.) Glenn Curtis seen taking off from the BEACH at the park in 1910; Harry Atwood flew to Euclid Beach the following year.

shrewd businessman and was in no small way responsible for a great deal of the park's early and continued success.

In the first two decades of the twentieth century, there is no doubt that Euclid Beach Park was successful. The crowds on some days were enormous. Roy Mizner, along with his fellow workers, would arrive at the park at 8 A.M. on a Saturday, Sunday, holiday, or special picnic day. They would make a thousand ham sandwiches. Later they would sell lemonade as fast as they could mix it. "It was made in a big glass crock, and we would add syrup instead of sugar," remembers Mr. Mizner. Also, since the location of the CHESTNUT GROVE was right by the relocated STREET CAR STATION, many an overheated street car passenger would stop for refreshment before going on to the fun. The coffee was a big seller, since many patrons brought their own picnic baskets and needed to buy a beverage. That, too, sold as fast as they could make it. The lunch stands sold ham sandwiches, ice cream (vanilla only, "brought in by Tellings"), Vernes pies (there were five flavors, which could be a la mode), lemonade, and coffee. Some days, the busier ones, would be fourteen and fifteen hours in length. Some of the employees had tents at the camp grounds, and many a tired worker would just sleep in a friend's tent and not even bother going home. The wage for a regular full time worker was eleven dollars per week, regardless of the hours worked. An "Extra" or part time employee would work for twenty cents an hour.

Once in the park, visitors could find more than plenty to tempt the taste. The Humphrey Company always took pride in what was sold at the concession stands. The taffy (pull candy) became a legend, and day after day, visitors could watch Russ Ramsey, distinguished by his big black mustache, toss the taffy to the pulling hook some fifteen feet from where he stood. He never missed.

The success of the Beach could also be gauged by the competition. White City (formerly Manhattan Beach) would have a hundred or so people on a given day, while a short distance away Euclid Beach would have thousands. Even the popular Luna Park would not be as favored as Euclid Beach. It seemed that the citizens of the area desired a park managed in the Humphrey manner.

The rules were strict. A gentleman never attempted to hold his lady too tightly while dancing, or he would have to leave the dance hall.

Employees were not permitted to smoke, and Linnie Humphrey took it upon herself to make sure the workers didn't. She would hide behind telephone poles or go as far as to sneak into the men's lavatory, under the DANCE PAVILION, to make sure no park employee was indulging in tobacco.

Most of all, it seemed that a man knew he could take his family to Euclid Beach Park and be assured that there would be no violence or rowdyism. He could feel assured that there would be no ill mannered drunks to spoil a day's outing. In every way, it was a family place. It was a place for the families of the public, for the Humphrey family, and, in its own way, for its own family. More than one set of brothers, like the Johnsons, or sisters, like the four Robinson girls (all cashiers), or fathers and sons would work, eat, sleep, and live at Euclid Beach.

The pattern was set in the spring of 1901; the result was a unique amusement park. With no gate charge, no alcohol, and no shabby games of chance, Euclid Beach presented a distinct image like no other park anywhere.

By the time the echoes of World War One died down and the world tried too hard to hide from the realities of total war, Americans embarked on having fun. . . in a grand style. The three decades to follow the end of World War I would be dramatic as basic changes in every area of life would take place. Within the confines of Euclid Beach Park there would be many changes too, but there would always be present the core of principle that gave this place its unique and popular tone. There was the idea of a well kept, safe, and wholesome recreation facility with hundreds of trees and cool walkways. A conservative atmosphere, coupled with the latest developments in rides, attractions, and conveniences, would be the mode of operation for this park. The Humphreys had proven beyond a doubt that there were very many people who desired this kind of place, and it would be shown that this popularity would increase.

From the beginning of the 1901 season until after World War I, the pattern emerged that made Euclid Beach an institution. The park was directed by a strict but aggressive family that made the Beach a well supervised facility. They employed constant additions and modifications in order to offer the patron a better way to enjoy himself. Also, during this period, it can be noted that many employees and their families came to Euclid Beach Park and stayed for tens of years. They became members of the Euclid Beach "Family." In every way the Beach had become a "family affair."

(The Humphrey Company)

(Illus. 39b.) An impressive list of facilities for the Euclid Beach of 1904.

39

(The Humphrey Company)

The Greatest Week in Cleveland's History

BEGINS TOMORROW (SUNDAY) AT

EUCLID BEACH

Everybody in Cleveland and All Northern Ohio Will Be There to See

THE DOLL SHOW

ALL WEEK IN THE LOG CABIN

The wonderful popularity of the doll show last year—the large increase in entries—the additional cash prizes, aggregating more than $300, which The Cleveland Press offers, insure your approval of this all-week exhibit, beginning tomorrow, Sunday, the 24th.

BULLETIN:

Wednesday, "Suburban Day" in Cleveland, was selected to provide opportunity for not only city residents but all Northern Ohio to see

The Children's Parade

On Wednesday, August 27th

STARTING at 4 P. M. on the newly erected board walk, 1000 feet in length, built especially for this purpose.

For 22 years a like carnival has been an annual event at Asbury Park, N. J., where the entire city is given over to the celebration. The efforts of The Cleveland Press, The Humphrey Co., the 10 merchants offering 30 silver trophy cups, the care, thought and enthusiasm of the numberless exhibitors assure unequaled pleasure at the cost of carfare only.

Children's Parade Prize Trophy Cups on Exhibition in the Log Cabin
Grand Prize $50 in Gold Given by The Cleveland Press

DIVISION I: Baby coaches and go-carts in any decoration.
Trophies donated by The Higbee Co.
DIVISION II: Doll coaches, including costume of child.
Trophies donated by the boys' clothing department of The Wm. Taylor Son & Co.
DIVISION III: Express wagons, pedalmobile, marathon racer, o-cycles, driven or drawn by one or more children.
Trophies donated by The May Co.
DIVISION IV: Costumes in fancy dress.
Trophies donated by The Burrows Bros. Co.
DIVISION V: Floats. Attendants in costume.
Trophies donated by The Bailey Co.

DIVISION VI: Costumes in college and school colors.
Trophies donated by The B. R. Baker Co.
DIVISION VII: National costumes of any country.
Trophies donated by The Webb C. Ball Co.
DIVISION VIII: Costumes in burlesque.
Trophies donated by B. F. Keith's Hippodrome.
DIVISION IX: Pony, dog and goat turnouts.
Trophies donated by The Belle Vernon-Mapes Co.
DIVISION X: Flowers. Dressed to represent any flower.
Trophies donated by The Fairchild's Flour

The Humphrey Company

(Illus. 39c.) Full page newspaper ad of August 26, 1911, announcing a week of children's attractions at the park.

Chapter 3
Three Sides of a golden era

20's

30's

40's

Euclid Beach Park endured a tenuous infancy from its opening in 1895 until it was rescued by the Humphrey family in 1901. The first two decades of the twentieth century saw the pattern that was to be the Beach's mode of operation take /shape. The Humphreys, established as champions in sobriety and conservatism, suitably injected aggressive action in providing new and exciting entertainment to the park. They added attractions that gave Euclid Beach the stature of a major amusement park and introduced policies found few other places in the country. Rides like the CIRCLE SWING, the SCENIC RAILWAY, the big CARROUSEL, and the RACING COAS-TER ranked the ride attractions along with the larger parks of the day. These, teamed with the DANCE PAVILION, the ROLLER RINK, and the AVENUE THEATRE, established the park's stature without question. *(Illus. 40.)* This period from 1901 to 1919 could be seen as the childhood and adolescence of Euclid Beach Park.

(Illus. 40.) Musicians played from the balcony of the AVENUE THEATRE to announce show performances. (The musicians, probably Lou Currier, Trumpet, and Eddie Purcell, Piano.) The inset also shows the design of the facade as it looked during the early part of the twentieth century. The larger picture depicts alterations that were made to the front of the building later.

(The Humphrey Company / Tom Oldham)

But if the park's first nineteen years of operation were its infancy, childhood, and adolescence, then the twenties brought Euclid Beach to full maturity. The roaring, clattering, and banging twenties were an era golden in the annals of the amusement park business and in the history of Euclid Beach.

"The '20's"

As skirts went up and prices followed suit, the appetite for greater thrills and more exhilarating rides was met. The design and construction of the roller coaster built in the twenties reached a degree of execution such that those coasters still activate that special sense in the pit of the stomach with as much intensity as most other rides now in use. It was during this decade that John A. Miller ran about the country putting up roller coasters as fast as they could be built. His handy work will be remembered by many who rode the fearful Cyclone at Puritas Springs Park (closed 1958) on the west side of Cleveland. It was in this same period that the National Amusement Device Company of Dayton put up the coaster still in operation at Geauga Lake Park, southwest of the city, in Aurora, Ohio. As for Euclid Beach, one of the favorites of park patrons, also built in the twenties, was the THRILLER.

The art of the carved Carousel horse had been perfected for some time, and Euclid Beach had already known four glorious carousels. But in 1921 a new and novel ride was installed, the GREAT AMERICAN RACING DERBY. The

1905 Philadelphia Tobaggan machine had been retired as was the original Herschell track MERRY-GO-ROUND. In 1921 the park now featured three noteworthy carousels.

To utilize space and heighten the visual effect of ride design, ride structures would frequently be interwoven until the individual rides were nearly indistinguishable. (Illus. 41.) The MILL CHUTE, constructed in 1921, was the Beach's first water ride. Its loading platform was located just west of and next to the SCENIC RAILWAY station, making that platform almost one with the familiar four-towered loading area of the 1907 roller coaster. The tunnel, through which the boats moved in darkness, weaved in and out about the wooden framework of the "old SCENIC."

It is important to note that as major structures were installed, Euclid Beach Park assumed the look it would have until its close in 1969. (Illus. 42.) The memory of this look, the atmosphere, the very tone of the park, is something that is not easy to forget or easy to find anywhere else. The rides that were installed were of a permanent nature, not fold-up carnival attractions that gave the feel of here-today-gone-tomorrow. The buildings and rides were integrated into the surroundings and cushioned by the many trees. The ever-present Sycamore with its shedding bark provided a flavor unto itself. (Illus. 43.) From the time of the Humphrey take-over in 1901, there was an effort to introduce more trees and heighten the look of a peaceful grove. In addition, the colors used to paint the buildings were muted in a general variety of greens to blend with the trees. The park generated feelings that it had always been there and that it was as substantial as the trees on the property. Yet, against this backdrop was posed, in bold relief, the most adventuresome of rides which exemplified the park's thorough dedication to having fun. The essence of the park captured the rarest of properties in human endeavor — balance. There was an aura of tranquility mixed with the excitement of anticipation upon entering the Beach. There was also the absence of the usual midway and the serene lack of barkers yelling at their "marks." The only screams heard were those of delight from children and riders as they were rushed about on their various courses.

(Illus. 42.) Aerial view showing the abundance of trees throughout the park. The circular pool is evident before the fountain was installed and after the SEA SWING was removed. The THRILLER'S first hill is shown and the wooded area next to the THRILLER platform was the future site of the FLYING TURNS.

(The Humphrey Company)

(Illus. 41.) The tangle of structures shows the great array of coasters present at the Beach in the '20's. From left to right: the THRILLER, the double tracked RACING COASTER, SCENIC RAILWAY, and MILL CHUTE.

(Kekic Collection)

(Illus. 43.) Many strolled amid the Sycamores on the BLUFF-WALK overlooking the BEACH and were dressed for the occasion, no matter what the temperature. The SEA SWING is visible behind the line of trees.

(Kekic Collection)

The feeling again was evident when leaving the main parking area and entering the park itself. A sort of transformation in status took place as sounds crept to the visitors from different quarters, but nothing overpowered the ear or eye. There was an intense softness about the texture that met the senses. The entering of a different world was even more apparent when leaving the STREETCAR gate and moving into the amusement area by walking under the COVERED WALK. It was a different place. The sounds, sights, and smells were suspended amid the trees and never obliterated the sounds of the birds or the lake. It was a romantic place too. The wooded areas gave the park the illusion of being larger than it was as groupings of trees seemed to give the feeling of many different places within one park.

The area just east of the LAKE LUNCH, which was formerly the BOWLING ALLEY, was a grove of well aged trees with numerous picnic tables. (Illus. 44.) There had been a RAVINE that ran west of the THEATRE down to the BEACH, and with its elimination, a handsome PICNIC GROVE was established. Many a picnic basket and checkered table cloth traveled there on family and company outings.

The sandy BEACH itself was a bustle of activity with the BOAT LIVERY as popular as ever. The sands were lined with frolicking bathers, all seeking to elude the heat of July and August. (Illus. 45.) To add to the pleasures of the water, in the Teens a new device was placed in the circular pool at the foot of the PIER next to the BATH HOUSE. This water merry-go-round or SEA SWING, as it was called, was publicized in the *Popular Science Monthly*, and the magazine opinioned that, "This merry-go-round furnishes great enjoyment for bathers who must have [a] more or less reckless variety."[33] The power source was an electric motor that revolved the upper steel framework. (Illus. 46.) Visitors to the park in later years will remember the circular pool with a WATER FOUNTAIN in it showing many different colored lights at night.

The PIER itself was reported to be 800 feet in length. Any visit to the park was incomplete without a stroll to the end of the PIER. (Illus. 47.) Even though regular boat service to the park landing at the PIER had long since ceased, this long finger pointing out into the lake was a busy location. It was from the end of the PIER that many a Fourth of July fireworks extravaganza was launched. The crowds would line the banks

(Kekic Collection)

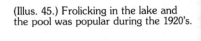
(Illus. 44.) It was a fine outing as a picnic lunch was enjoyed by the whole family.

(Illus. 45.) Frolicking in the lake and the pool was popular during the 1920's.

(Kekic Collection)

and witness a hallmark of Euclid Beach Park as America's birthday party was "finalied." And certainly many a perch was extracted from Erie's waters by ardent fisherman, young and old, even when the park was closed. *(Illus. 48.)*

A visit to the end of the PIER often occurred during an evening of dancing. The DANCE PAVILION and its glass-like floor had achieved national prominence and dedicated patronage. The BALLROOM featured the finest local and traveling orchestras, and many a visitor's main reason for coming to the park was to "trip the light fantastic."

The Humphreys not only made it a policy to bring new rides to the park, but they were mindful of the need to constantly improve existing attractions. The list of taste tempters that were offered at the Beach's concession stands could be considered an amusement park gourmet menu. One of the favorites for many years was the GINGER ALE and LOGANBERRY drink stand. The unique carbonation, mixing, and cooling process, which was the predecessor of the modern method used at many soft drink fountains, was developed by David Humphrey, Dudley S. II's brother. The tanks for the ingredients and carbonation were stored below

(Kekic Collection)

(Illus. 48.) Fishermen frequented the PIER during much of the park's history.

(The Humphrey Company)

(Illus. 46.) Popular Science Monthly published an aritcle in 1920 about the SEA SWING at Euclid Beach Park. This ride and variants of it were popular at many parks during the '20's.

(Kekic Collection)

(Illus. 47.) The PIER was always a popular location for those who visited Euclid Beach. The concrete ramp is clearly visible.

(The Humphrey Company)

(Illus. 49.) Harris C. Shannon, general manager of Euclid Beach from the early part of the century until the 1950's.

(The Cleveland Press)

(Illus. 50) Howard Stoneback was characterized in this drawing.

the serving counters in a basement, and the ingredients were mixed and traveled up to the customer area through a series of hoses. The ability and desire to constantly improve, expand, and innovate gave Euclid Beach Park a unique signature signed indelibly on the memories of many a visitor.

The twenties could amost be thought of as a season unto itself when it comes to the Beach. It not only represented a time when the park and the Humphreys further fortified themselves as a Cleveland institution and an amusement park with a world-wide reputation, but it was a time when another quality began to emerge. Working at Euclid Beach was addictive. There were those, like Harry Shannon, who worked for and managed Euclid Beach for more than fifty years. *(Illus. 49.)* The twenties was a period during which many families came to the park and, in time, would make their own indelible mark on her.

An amusement park is like a theatre, and like a stage production, much of that which makes a play successful is done behind the scenes, back stage, and in preparation long before the curtain opens. Consider that with all the mechanical devices, special structures, unique effects, and potential crowd capacity, there must be at least a thousand and one details requiring attention during, before, and after each season. We could see the producer as the Humphrey family, the playwright as many of the employees, the stage hands many of those same employees, and the stars as the attractions. The joy of the performance was, of course, that each visitor could put the acts in any order he or she liked, and the cast of characters could be any facet of the park on any given occasion.

Park people share a kinship with others in the business of entertainment but have a unique position. Their arena is a stationary group of structures that have to be ever exciting. It's not

feasible to make many changes at short intervals, so that which is offered has to be very special. Likewise, there is the ever present consideration of safety. Park people are different, in their own special way, and Euclid Beach Park had many very special park people, far too many to speak of completely.

Special people are not always easy to understand. In the spring of 1923, a very serious but talented man came to Euclid Beach. *(Illus. 50.)* Howard Stoneback and his family of seven lived in a tent just east of the RACING COASTER during the first season of employment. Stoneback had been hired to train under the retiring head carpenter, Mr. Maclevie known as "Mac." Howard Stoneback came to Cleveland with high qualifications; in fact, he had been a foreman for the Philadelphia Toboggan Company since he was thirteen and had traveled the country erecting carousels and building roller coasters. He also was a talented wood carver and would design, carve, and build a patented kiddie ride. During the winter of 1923-4, he supervised the construction of the THRILLER in conjunction with that same Philadelphia Toboggan Company. *(Illus. 51.)* His signature also appeared on many a drawing that had altered, improved, and made unique the rides and buildings of Euclid Beach Park. "He was an engineer without a diploma," said Bill Parker, another of the park's very special people. It will be noted that Mr. Stoneback only had an eighth grade education. Stoneback remained at the park as head carpenter and then head of maintenance until his unfortunate death in 1959. He was known as a perfectionist, a moody person, and one whose chief obsession was working at Euclid Beach. In fact, Howard's two sons became part of the park family when they became Beach employees.

(The Scoop Newspapers)

(Illus. 54.) A later picture of Walter Williams.

(The Humphrey Company)

(Illus. 53.) Dudley Humphrey Scott was chief engineer at Euclid Beach for many years.

Bill Parker was one of the most liked and respected members of the Euclid Beach family. In the mid twenties, he came to the park as a welder when he proved that he could handle a special job at the Elysium. His was the task of welding the pipes of the Elysium's ice-making device to keep the brine liquid from leaking and melting the ice skating surface. From there he went to the park and remained until the '60's. "Wild Bill," as he was called by some, was famous for his walk on the radial arms of the CIRCLE SWING (ROCKET SHIPS) 80 feet above the ground while the ride was in motion. Bill was merely checking the cables that supported the passenger space. His only request was that the operator not stop the ride while he made one of these frequent surveys. (Illus. 52.)

A special feature of Euclid Beach Park which was provided by workers like Stoneback and Parker was its capability to repair, renovate, and produce almost anything that happened to be needed and, furthermore, do it in the park's own shops. Many an improvement, modification, or complete ride was designed, engineered, and manufactured on the park grounds.

There were many behind-the-scenes people scurrying about the attractions, basically unnoticed by the patrons, making sure everything was as it should be. Dave Scott recalls riding his father's shoulders when he was too small to walk the entire park himself. His dad, Dudley Humphrey Scott, would take him from powerhouse to powerhouse checking the temperature of the motors and examining the oil levels to see that the bearings were getting their proper lubrication. Scott, the chief engineer, was dedicated to safety, and all the park men were urged to constantly watch and listen to the rides. (Illus. 53.) Many times a possible malfunction could be detected by a sound.

(Bill Parker)

(Illus. 52.) "Wild" Bill Parker living up to his nickname high above the park on one of the radial arms of the ROCKET SHIP ride.

(Kekic Collection)

(Illus. 51.) The THRILLER under final stages of construction with the original second hill pictured. Later this hill was decreased in height.

There was intense interest in every aspect of the business of amusing people. Employees of Euclid Beach took many a busman's holiday, visiting other parks. Dudley Scott made many trips to parks in different parts of the country investigating new developments in the field. A remarkable photographer, he carried his trusty Bell and Howell wind-up movie camera on these trips and photographed possible attractions for Euclid Beach Park. He also took many pictures of existing rides at Euclid Beach in slow motion to analyze the workings of the various mechanisms. There was dedication to the cause of bringing new and exciting attractions to the park and the the cause of safety on every operating ride.

The year 1921 brought Walter Williams to Euclid Beach. (Illus. 54.) He worked at the park for as long as almost anyone; he was there the day the last season ended. He was also there helping to build the MILL CHUTE and DODGEM, and helped install the GREAT AMERICAN RACING DERBY in that same year.

(Illus. 57.) They poured in for a day of fun. Remember the old "Flivvers"? The parking lot is almost full as the cars pass through the MAIN GATE. (Kekic Collection)

Euclid Beach ①

I think Euclid Beach is a regular fairyland for the kids of Cleveland. We live in an apartment on the third floor. We have no yard we can not run and jump. Once a week we go out to Euclid Beach here we can run and jump and stretch our selves so we can grow and we can ride on the different rides and have all kinds of fun. So we feel fine when we go home so if it is that way with us children it must be good for the tired mothers and the worried fathers. They can not go out here and see all the fun and ride on the rides and still come away feeling the same. No they come away feeling great their minds are clean swept by going flying

(Illus. 58.) A prize winner's letter appeared in the Cleveland Press/Euclid Beach Essay Contest. (The Humphrey Company)

(Kekic Collection)

(Illus. 55.) The COLONNADE was an excellent example of the Humphrey concrete pouring process. The complete construction took two years. This building provided a large area for visitors if the weather turned a bit damp. KIDDIELAND, numerous refreshment stands and eating areas were housed within this structure.

In 1925, Euclid Beach management, along with the Cleveland Press, sponsored an essay contest for children. The object was to have the entering essayists state why they liked the park. A winner in the contest answered the Humphrey Company in the following manner after he received his prize:

My dear Mr. Humphrey,

I kindly thank you for the five dollars ($5.00) you sent me for my prize in the Euclid Beach Cleveland Press Kiddies Day Contest. I also thank very much for the little surprize you sent me. I really did not expect the tickets for the Press said nothing about them.

I love Euclid Beach Park better than any essay can express . . . (Illus. 58.)

It perhaps summed up the general feeling of those who visited the park.

The Humphreys were indeed innovators. Their own process of pouring cement was well ahead of its time, already having been utilized in constructing the DANCE PAVILION, the PIER, the OFFICE, and the CAMP GROUNDS. In 1924 a new structure was poured by this process, and the large concrete housing to be known as the COLONNADE was built. (Illus. 55.) As it was located just south of the DRINK CONCESSION and the DANCE PAVILION, it necessitated the moving of the former street car terminus to its final Lake Shore location. The COLONNADE was to shelter KIDDIELAND and various stands of refreshment. The BOULEVARD STAND was established at the new STREETCAR gate. Open year round, it was staffed by "Es" Judd, his brothers, and Otto Price, all Euclid Beach perennials.

(Illus. 56.) The Humphrey Company stated its own case in this special full page ad.

(The Humphrey Company)

Indeed, the twenties was an era that saw Euclid Beach thrive on the premise stated by its slogan: "Nothing to Depress or Demoralize." (Illus. 56.) The policy of prohibiting alcoholic beverages was now a national policy (since 1920), but it had been established by the Humphreys at the park since 1901 and certainly had been accepted to the satisfaction of the patrons. The park itself as a recreational and entertainment facility was now in its full bloom, and Cleveland and any area within reach was patronizing Euclid Beach avidly. (Illus. 57.) The roster of entertaining features numbered four roller coasters, three carousels, the CIRCLE SWING (AEROPLANES), the BUG, the DODGEM, a new KIDDIELAND, the DANCE PAVILION, ROLLER RINK, THEATRE, and all the BEACH facilities. It was a golden era.

Beyond the great success of the park, Dudley S. Humphrey received more recognition as the twenties approached a perilous end. Mr. Humphrey was president of the National Association of Amusement Parks and presided over the eleventh annual convention in December of 1929, held at the Stevens Hotel in Chicago. D.S. was also elected president of the Citizen's League (Cleveland). This golden season was crowned with great honor for the dean of the amusement park industry, but as he addressed the membership of the park convention, he spoke of the challenge ahead: the crash had come.

The twenties saw much of the world looking for new leadership, while in America the primary object of search was fun. The country turned inward, and the quest for amusement brought a heyday to the park business. The United States declined League of Nations membership, and roller coasters got higher and faster. Gershwin became famous, and names like John McCormick, noted vocalist; Fritz Kreisler, violinist; and W.C. Fields came to Cleveland. October, 1929, marked the stock market catastrophy with Black Thursday and Black Tuesday; the first signs of a depression were visible. September 3, 1929, marked the golden wedding anniversary of D.S. Humphrey II and his wife Effie. *(Illus. 59.)* Just as the Humphreys had experienced fifty years prior to the 1929 occasion, there would be trying times ahead.

"The '30's"

There is a saying that is well worn even for a cliche. It simply asserts that, that which goes up must come down. With the coming of the depression, the priorities of endeavor switched from a quest for fun and frolic to the hope of survival. As many a fortune was obliterated in almost an instant, and the changes that swept the country were far reaching and penetrating, the Humphreys and Euclid Beach found themselves better prepared than most for the coming trials.

It was common practice in the amusement park industry to borrow money from a financial institution in the fall and pay it back in the spring, usually by June 15th. Since parks in the northern part of the country had a very limited season in which to make their way, this procedure for acquiring capital for the winter months was common. In 1930, the capital was not available, and the Humphreys and the Beach were faced with a dilemma that had in one way or another confronted many at this time in history. The

(The Humphrey Company)

(Illus. 59.) Mrs. M.M. Humphrey, (D.S.'s "Effie").

management went to their employees and asked if they would forego most of their winter pay and accept due bills in lieu of payment until June 15th. By then, business would have resumed. The "Euclid Beach Family" agreed and contributed greatly to the park's ability to remain open. Cleveland Trust had offered to lend the park the money, but a controller would have had to be placed in the park. D.S. remembered the losses of earlier days and wished for no repeat of those calamities. In essence, the employees became the Park's bank and were indeed paid back by June 15th.

The thirties had one distinct positive function in that this period brought people closer together. In many cases it was the only way to survive. In relation to Euclid Beach Park, it encouraged and helped solidify the core of the park's existence. The principle put forth and successfully practiced since 1901 allowed Euclid Beach to be patronized even if there was only the price of a trolley ride available. The free gate was a gift to many a depressed soul who could enjoy the scenes, the trees, and the lake at the Park. Sometimes, just sitting and watching other people was entertainment enough. *(Illus. 60.)* And, if there was a quarter or a dollar that could be lavished on luxury, there was a strong chance it would be spent at the Beach.

Those who found themselves absorbed by the park felt that working there was more than a job and became more dedicated to its preservation, each in his own way. Many a member of that working family could relate that it was impossible to get rich running a roller coaster or repairing a carousel, but they would hasten to say that the Humphreys were good, decent people who showed no pretense of wealth or even seemed interested in being rich.

(Illus. 60.) The shade of the many trees and the familiar green park benches formed an essential element of Euclid Beach. A visitor could spend endless hours watching others. The above scene is south of the BALLROOM looking east toward the DODGEM.

(Kekic Collection)

(Illus. 61.) The cover of the "Euclid Beach Special" edition of Amusement Park Management Magazine - August 1930. The periodical was published by the National Association of Amusement Parks and in 1930, this organization held their summer convention at Euclid Beach Park. The cover shows Dudley S. Humphrey II, president of the Humphrey Company.

Perhaps it was a signal of encouragement from some quarter that the summer convention of the National Association of Amusement Parks was held at Euclid Beach Park in August of 1930. *(Illus. 61.)* The Humphreys hosted the guest members in a not extravagant, but friendly manner which was their way. There was, however, one very large treat in store for the visitors - a new and exciting ride to titilate the senses called the FLYING TURNS, which opened for the 1930 season and was an example of the epitome of the art of "scream-extraction." *(Illus. 62.)*

Amusement Park Management

EUCLID BEACH SPECIAL

D. S. HUMPHREY
PRESIDENT
EUCLID BEACH PARK

AUGUST 1930

(International Association of Amusement Parks.)

52

Euclid Beach's New Sensation

"Flying Turns," built by the Humphreys and J. N. Bartlett during the winter, is operating to capacity and will be an interesting sight for visiting park men.

(International Association of Amusement Parks.)

UPPER: The entrance to "Flying Turns." A crowd is usually waiting there for the ride to open each day. It is getting 25 cents per trip.

LEFT: A three car train approaching one of the turns.

RIGHT: This picture gives a fair idea of the structure.

BOTTOM: These little cars were built in the Humphrey machine shop. They are constructed of as good material as an automobile.

(Illus. 62.) A full page ad that appeared in the August, 1930 issue of Amusement Park Management announcing the opening of the FLYING TURNS - "Euclid Beach's New Sensation."

(The Humphrey Company)

(Illus. 63.) This cartoon depicts the "event of the century" as Humphrey and McLaughlin duel over the merits and demerits of popcorn and beer.

While 1930 brought the convening park men to Euclid Beach and the brunt of the depression to the country, the subject of alcoholic beverages was assessed with the same perennial condemnation by the Humphreys. D.S. Humphrey went so far as to make a radio broadcast that year extolling the virtues of popcorn and reaffirming his attitudes toward the spirits. This broadcast was taken as a challenge by certain persons, namely one Robert McLaughlin, who was a champion of barley corn, a chief ingredient of beer. Mr. McLaughlin felt D.S. had gone too far and forwarded for the public's consideration, via the newspapers, the thought that any doctor would only confirm that beer was not the harmful commodity of the two. McLaughlin proposed a duel in which he and Humphrey would consume matching quantities of beer and popcorn balls respectively and see who came out the worse for wear. *(Illus. 63.)* The newspapers printed a series of answering articles which were then followed by answers to the answers and so on. The volleying of rebuttals was like a tennis match with the views going from side to side. But alas, the proposed event was never realized as D.S. announced that he and Mr. McLaughlin were old friends and surely Bob was not serious. Woefully it was announced that the "competitive event of the century" would not take place. The park remained dry.

Yes, Euclid Beach was a respectable place, *(Illus. 64.)* and the president of the Humphrey Company who directed the Park was indeed a respectable man. D.S. Humphrey did not seclude himself in the comfort of a successful business but was well known in many a Cleveland civic organization. The following list gives some indication of his involvement:

Cleveland Municipal Research Bureau
National Research Council
Cleveland Engineering Society
Ohio Good Roads Federation
Cleveland Citizens League
American Concrete Institution
American Road Builders Association
National Association Of Park Men
National Chamber of Commerce
Cleveland City Club
Cleveland Automobile Club
Cleveland Athletic Club
Cleveland Mid Day Club 34

(The Cleveland Press)

(Illus. 64.) Respectability was all present at the Beach. The matter of wearing apparel was always carefully prescribed; only children were allowed to wear shorts.

(The Humphrey Company)

(Illus. 65.) Condolences and tributes proffered at the time of the death of Dudley S. Humphrey II from many different areas and persons.

The direction of Euclid Beach Park was in the hands of a man interested and active in the community around him. Even though D.S. was active in the city of Cleveland, due to his great interest in concrete road construction, he was also familiar both in Columbus and Washington D.C.

However, he frequently stated that the family kept in touch with their farm heritage. A source of great satisfaction, the recovered Wakeman farm, brought back into the Humphrey family in 1928, was actively worked as corn and other crops were harvested. Mr. Humphrey credited their activity on the farm as helping to keep their feet

on the ground. As for wealth, he said that there was not time to become absorbed in it; the park and its direction furnished him with all the satisfaction he needed. Euclid Beach was his pride and joy. "There isn't anything like it in the world," was Dudley's view.

On September 7, 1933, Dudley Sherman Humphrey II left that world. He was 81. He died at his home on the grounds of Euclid Beach Park. The obituaries reminded Cleveland and the amusement park world of the loss of one of their deans. (Illus. 65.) The rites were held on the following Saturday, and the park was closed until 6 P.M. It was the first time in the park's history that the gates did not open for a full day of Saturday fun during the season. Also in 1933 the German nation found a dubious leader, a man who stood for the antithesis of that leader who was lost forever to the land he loved so well.

The direction fell on the shoulders of Dudley's son, Harvey. He was equal to the task. Harvey Humphrey had two sisters, Mabel and Louise. Mabel was the wife of Perce Killaly; Louise was married to Jack Lambie. The Humphreys, Killalys, Lambies, and Scott families made up the "directing family" of Euclid Beach. *(Illus. 66.)* Then, in 1938, the park and family of the Beach lost another principle member, Dudley Humphrey Scott. Besides being chief engineer, Scott had been instrumental in developing a number of lighting effects for the dark rides and, in particular, the LAFF-IN-THE-DARK. His loss was great.

The '30's saw the disappearance of the "old SCENIC," the redesigning of the MILL CHUTE, the appearance of the WITCHING WAVES and its subsequent replacement, the LAFF-IN-THE-DARK. Of course, there was also the fearful FLYING TURNS. Rides like the BUBBLE BOUNCE and RED BUG BOULEVARD were also attracting riders during this decade. The Beach continued to host many a company or community picnic with attendance figures exceeding ten thousand persons during many of these outings. Great marble shooting tournaments were held during the thirties. Near the end of the decade, a Press reporter attempted to

In Respect for the Memory of
Our President and Founder

D. S. HUMPHREY

EUCLID BEACH PARK

WILL BE CLOSED SATURDAY,
SEPTEMBER 9, UNTIL 6 P. M.

The Humphrey Co.

evaluate the rides with "Ride-O-Graphs," and children who rode on the park's numerous attractions outlasted the devices. Indeed, Euclid Beach Park did not succumb to the depression of the '30's but continued to grow and solidify as a place of recreation and as a substantial institution in Cleveland.

The year 1939 marked the end of the decade, and just as twenty years earlier a boom time was ushered in, a new boom of a different variety was being felt in Europe and Asia.

(Illus. 66.) Members of the family in the 1920's including: "Albert Peters, Tom Harrison, Carol Scott, Mother Humphrey, Kathryn Greenland, Lou Greenland, David Scott, Louise Scott, Louise Humphrey Lambie, Perce Killaly, Mabel Killaly, Marion Scott, Jack Lambie, Kathryn Humphrey, Dud Humphrey, Kathryn Greenland."

56

(The Humphrey Company)

(The Cleveland Plain Dealer)

(Illus. 67.) The platform at the THRILLER station was one of the most popular areas in the park. Eager riders anticipate the 71' 5" plunge. The THRILLER exemplifies its popularity in this 1946 scene.

"The '40's"

The turmoil and agitation that had been fomenting throughout the world erupted in September of 1939. It no longer could be ignored; the world was at war. The fear of the nation's involvement in an international conflict spread across the country. A spokesman for the National Association of Amusement Parks supported the thesis that fear had a paralyzing effect on the population, and the best way to expel that paralysis was healthy diversion - good clean fun. He went on to assert that the function of the amusement park was clear in helping to keep the nation in balance. The amusement park was an ideal place to forget your troubles, fears, and, in general, negative thoughts. Whether it be an economic depression or the threat of world conflict, these sanctuaries served a purpose.

The year 1941 saw the closing of the ELYSIUM after thirty-three years of operation. Built on land owned by Case Institute of Technology, the structure reverted back to the original land owners as rumors were circulated that the premises might be incorporated in the war effort since, during World War One, the ELYSIUM had served as an army barracks.

May 10, 1942, marked the loss of yet another member of the Humphrey family. Louise Humphrey Lambie died as a result of burns sustained when her housecoat caught fire. She had contributed numerous architectural ideas for the Beach's improvement, and her husband, John E. Lambie, Jr., was active in the park's management.

Despite the war and the losses, Euclid Beach persisted in hosting thousands as major companies like White Motor, Richman Brothers, and Goodyear held their annual picnics there. Cities like East Cleveland, Euclid, and Garfield Heights also brought thousands to the Beach.

The spirit of the times and the war effort were reflected in many ways at Euclid Beach Park. (Illus. 68.) The year 1943 saw watermelons and a ton of coal auctioned off for $100 war bond purchases. War time outings were sponsored with reduced rates for a number of attractions. Bathing was only twenty cents, and the forty boats of the BOAT LIVERY were offered for a quarter an hour. Dancing was only six cents or one ticket per dance. Roller skating was six tickets ($.37) from 3 P.M. to 5:30 P.M., and eight tickets ($.50) from 8 P.M. to 10:30 P.M. Of course, the cost of travel was excessive due to the scarcity of petroleum, rubber products, and the country's need of them for war-time purposes. Instead of driving to distant places, the citizens of Cleveland were encouraged to come to the Beach. The idea was, of course, to have fun and save on vital fuels. The park was even visited by a group of former Italian soldiers who, after capture and internment as P.O.W.'s had volunteered to serve in the United States Army. Certainly, people from all walks of life and areas of the world drew on Euclid Beach for entertainment and refreshment during that period of world conflict.

Perhaps a major turning point in our nation's history began to show itself after the signing of the peace treaties in 1945. The operation of Euclid Beach Park had gone on as usual during World War II, but many changes in personal, local, national, and international views were to modify the public's tastes and attitudes. Some of these changes hung like a stormcloud off on the horizon. Many who had sacrificed during the depression and sacrificed again during the war felt that the post war prosperity should be almost religiously pursued. To many, affluence presented the preferred path, and those institutions identified with the past were to be challenged or forgotten.

Although a number of unpleasant incidents occurred at various park attractions during the season of 1946, that year was heralded as a banner year, as was 1948. The Humphrey Company subsequently announced in the spring of 1949 that they expected another fine season. How many more fine seasons would the park offer? Few could predict the effect that the world conflict would have on the country, the city, the park.

The period from 1901 through the '30's was one of growth, innovation, experimentation, and dedicated patronage. The forties demonstrated a plateau with the continued popularity of Euclid Beach Park. But the very fiber of American life had been altered by World War II. Technology directed the attentions of Americans to different forms of entertainment. Passivity came into vogue. Going and doing took a back seat to sitting and witnessing, and, therefore, the public taste was incredibly altered. Euclid Beach began to show the signs of an emptying arena. Future games would be played in living rooms - not in the PENNY ARCADE.

Euclid Beach neared its fiftieth anniversary under Humphrey management. In retrospect, the Humphrey Company could see a colorful and important contribution to the Cleveland community. Most of all, the spirit of the park had been the quest for fun, a fantasy through which individuals could escape their concerns while refreshing their spirits. This ideal was never forgotten as a priority, even to the Beach's last day. Clearly, this ideal embodied an infinite number of details, a thousand stories, and a community of unique attractions and significant events which unmistakably identified Euclid Beach Park.

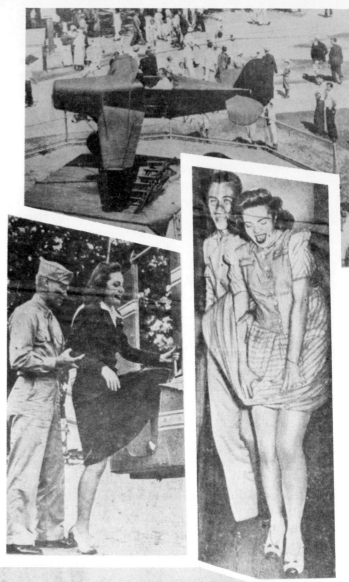

(Illus. 68.) Uniforms of members of the Armed Forces were present frequently during World War II.

(The Cleveland Plain Dealer, The Cleveland Press.)

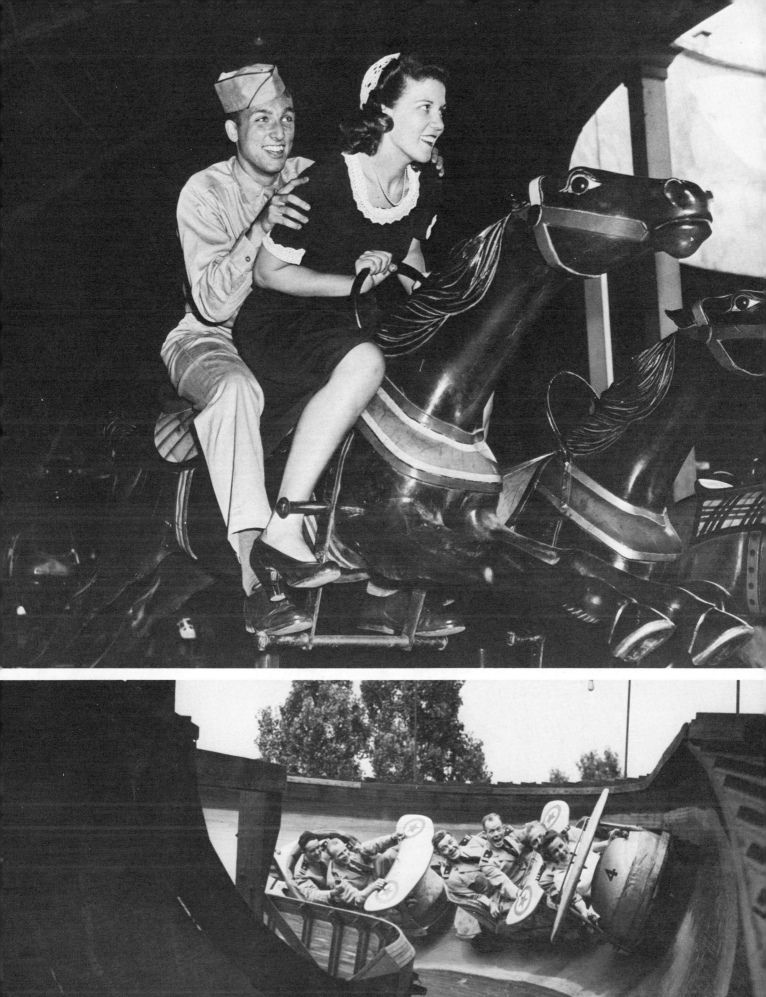

Chapter 4
FUN AND RiDES

(Illus. 68b.) The plunge - the THRILLER'S first hill.

(The Cleveland Plain Dealer)

Fun & Rides

The pleasures provided by the rides in an amusement park are based on the simplest of principles, the simplest of ideas. To think that a simple force like gravity is used to pull a rolling car down a hill or that a power source can turn a group of fun-seeking riders around in a circle to produce pleasure, such "uplifting" joy, is, indeed, worthy of consideration.

The one feature that distinguishes an amusement park from other centers of recreation is the presence of special rides — rides that are of a permanent and grand nature, not just traveling carnival devices. The development of the individual rides, the intermingling of differing buildings and structures produce the most prominent feature of an amusement park. Almost every park is unique in its layout and selection of rides. The organization of twists and turns, the towers and the unusual roofs, the array of flags and pennants, and all the other shapes that are proper to a park define its personality visually. It has been said that all shapes recognizable to the eye are either straight or curved. Upon witnessing the variety of shapes that compose a park, it seems strange that all the details of the composition are such simple elements.

However, it is not only that which confronts the eye that identifies an amusement park. The sounds, the glorious roars, the clatter and bang, the music of the band organs, and the whir of a hundred mechanical devices, and, of course, the giggles, screams, and sounds of the people themselves make a special and holy music to the lover of this institution, the Great American Outdoor Amusement Park.

And there are myriad aromas to delight the sense of smell. There is always the scent of popcorn and candy, the fragrance of a mustard-laden hot dog, and that special odor furnished by the strained rubber driving belts and the grease and oil lubricants. Although it is hardly Chanel No. 5, it is as sweet as any rose to the nose that seeks it out. It is one of the fantastic sensations produced only by an amusement park.

Euclid Beach Park was in no way immune to providing these special assaults on the senses. No petrified young girl, holding on to her hat, her boyfriend, or both, while ascending the first hill of the THRILLER, could ignore the clatter of the ratchet dog under the car, or miss the smell of things electric and petroleum as the vehicle moved up to its downward plunge. There was an ever-present roar as the GREAT AMERICAN RACING DERBY whirled its teams of horses and riders around in determined competition. The ringing of the starting bell that accompanies any self-respecting carousel, the volleys of thuds provided by colliding DODGEM cars, the rush of air near the CIRCLE SWING (ROCKET SHIPS), and the buzz of the chain drive that moved THE BUG in its never ending, tail-chasing course, made up a thousand orchestrations that tossed through the air creating a most beautiful din.

Any true lover of Euclid Beach can tell you that the "Beach" had its own particular symphony, its own theme and variations, its own song. Perhaps it was the situation of the park on the shores of Lake Erie, with the varying breezes that tossed the sounds of the park in a unique manner. Perhaps it was the grouping of the coasters in one area and the carousels in another. Perhaps it was inside the ear of the person, each unto him/herself. Regardless of the origin, regardless of the reason, it was there. And in great part the sights, the sounds, and, indeed, the smells too, were due to the rides, those special structures that in the imaginations of children, grandpas, romantics, and parkmen live.

If you happened to be at the park on that last of all days, Sunday, September 28th, 1969, you would have seen a number of people moving about the park looking from place to place to drink in every last bit of sight, sound, and smell. Some of the younger people would look at some of the rides, like the FLYING TURNS, as if they were witnessing dinosaurs on the brink of extinction. It was the last day for these giants that "roamed" over the park, and those that were not so giant. Although each had had its day; they had provided many people with a thrill, a laugh, or even a fright, and most of all — delight. Throughout its many seasons, Euclid Beach would provide its visitors with a choice of rides to delight the soul. If you remember, as many do, the view from Lake Shore Boulevard, two great coasters stood dominating the vista. The first and highest inclines of the RACING COASTER and the THRILLER were familiar reminders to many of us that yet another spring would come, and we would travel those hills again — but not always. Few could remember *all* the rides because Euclid Beach was different to each generation. Few knew her for all of her seventy-four summers. Even so, there was essentially just one Euclid Beach Park and basically one identity from the Spring of 1901, when the Humphreys assumed management, to its last day in 1969.

UPS AND DOWNS

Although it may be possible to have an amusement park without a roller coaster, it would seem unlikely. In fact, it would seem that the roller coaster could be considered essential to such an establishment. What vista would present the necessary park qualifications without the familiar wooden framework of twists and turns of spaghetti track? No, a "rolly coaster" was, and is, a must.

Few are present to tell of the special qualities possessed by the earliest coasters. Just as few are able to tell of the sounds during the '80's and '90's of the prior century, and still describe the tonality of that era when streets were covered with dust or mud and the only sounds were those of hoofs and occasional street cars. Earliest roller coasters too were quieter devices than their offspring. The original American roller coaster was gravity all the way, except for the help of a modicum of manpower.

The SWITCHBACK RAILWAY made its appearance at Euclid Beach for the summer of 1896. *(Illus. 12.-68a.)* This ride was patterned after the original design erected at Coney Island, New York, in 1884 by LaMarcus Adna Thompson and was heralded as the first successful roller coaster. Thompson was a native of Ohio, having been born at Jersey, Ohio, in Licking County. He moved about the country and, while involved in many different occupations, constantly showed a great deal of creativity in building original wooden articles. His ultimate creation was an instantaneous success at Coney Island. His Switchback Railway at that East Coast resort brought Thompson five to seven hundred dollars a day in fares, numerous contracts to build copies of the patented ride, and a number of competitors. His venture blossomed, and he was considered a major gravity-ride builder until the 1940's. Although the SWITCHBACK RAILWAY was a twelve-year-old design in 1896 when it appeared at the Beach, it was popular until its removal in 1904.

(Illus. 68a.) The SWITCHBACK RAILWAY with a group of frolicking passengers - the safety regulations were a bit different in those days. (c. 1900) The line of Poplar trees and the CAMP-GROUND can be seen in the background.

(Kapel Collection)

The mode of propelling this ride, the SWITCH-BACK, was gravity and a number of strong backs. The cars which conveyed the passengers traversed two sets of parallel tracks in a series of gentle rolling hills. At either end of the course was a tower, ascended by stairs to the top where the cars were boarded. Gravity was to do the rest. However, the momentum always failed to propel the cars to the top of the tower at the opposite end, and a group of workmen had to push it up to the summit after disembarking the riders. This shortcoming seemed in no way to distract from the fun, and the SWITCHBACK'S popularity seemed to forecast the roller coaster as one of the most important elements of the outdoor amusement park industry.

As was their policy, the Humphreys made improvements on almost every item brought into the park. A Remo escalator with leather saddle-like seats was installed on the SWITCHBACK RAILWAY to alleviate all the stair climbing to the top of the tower. The rider sat astride the seat which had a rein affair to hold onto, as on horseback, and was brought to the starting point of the ride. *(Illus. 69.)* The idea of having a chain or cable pull coaster cars to the summit of the highest hill was developed by Thompson's competitors, as was the idea of a closed oval circuit. These developments nullified the need for stairs or escalators.

(Illus. 69.) The Remo Escalator, called the "ESCALADER", that replaced the long climb by the stairway to the top of the SWITCHBACK RAILWAY, Eager riders mount the device to get to the thrills of the early coaster.

(The Cleveland Press)

(Illus. 70.) A model of the early FIGURE EIGHT roller coaster. An example of this ride appeared at Euclid Beach during the early 1900's.

(The Humphrey Company)

With the razing of the SWITCHBACK, room was made for enlarging the ROLLER RINK and building a new coaster. The new gravity ride, built in 1904, was called the FIGURE EIGHT. The ground plan of this ride was indeed a figure "8". (Illus. 70.) The cars carried four riders in two seats and were pulled up the highest hill by chain. The car on the track was stablized by a set of side wheels that ran against a side track. Even though the speed of the ride was very modest, like other coasters of the time, it was popular. The manufacturer of the Beach's FIGURE EIGHT was the famous Philadelphia Toboggan Company. (Illus. 71.)

(Illus. 70a.) The loading platform of the FIGURE EIGHT and the wooden walkway that ran north and south between the DANCE PAVILION and the coaster.

(The Humphrey Company)

(Illus. 71a.) The loading platform of the FIGURE EIGHT with an obviously carefully posed group of riders and crew men. The manufacturers plaque is evident, 1904.

(Illus. 71b.) Three cars of the FIGURE EIGHT ascending the first incline. The Philadelphia Toboggan sign is clearly posted.

(Frederick Fried Collection)

(Frederick Fried Collection)

Scenic Road at Night, Euclid Beach, Cleveland

(Illus. 73b.) The loading building of the SCENIC RAILWAY as it was brilliantly lit after dark.

(Russell Allon Hehr Collection)

(Illus. 72.) Upper - The Thompson SCENIC RAILWAY, as advertised in 1907.

(The Humphrey Company)

(Illus. 73c.) Fully loaded trains of the SCENIC RAILWAY as they traverse the course of the ride.

(Russell Allon Hehr Collection)

In 1907, L.A. Thompson made another contribution to Euclid Beach Park with the building of the SCENIC RAILWAY. (Illus. 72, 73.) This ride, constructed at the cost of $50,000, was a landmark at the park with its detailed four-towered loading station. The SCENIC RAILWAY incorporated the use of cables to draw the three-car trains up the starting hills of its four course circuit. Beneath the cars of the train was a clutch apparatus that was engaged as a wheel and lever device were triggered by a raised rail located between the two main rails. On the three-car trains, the two brakemen, or "brakies" as they were called, controlled the speed of the train and brought it to each of the cable sites at "cable speed." If this wasn't accomplished, as it sometimes wasn't, the ride might have to shut down and a crew reposition the train before operation continued. To reduce the crew size during the twenties, the length of the trains was reduced to two cars and one brakeman. (Illus. 74.)

As with most rides built at Euclid Beach, the "old SCENIC" received its share of alterations. According to the original design of 1907, the last circuit made by the cars went around the outside of the station building at about a second story level. In 1916, this was enclosed so as to make a dark tunnel and increase the thrill. As George Reinhart, Jr., related, it was not as fast as some of the later coasters, but "you could give 'em a pretty good ride."[35] The speed of the ride was somewhat determined by the way in which the "brakie" handled his assignment. George's father, George, Sr., demonstrated the limits one evening during a camp grounds picnic. He negotiated the tunnel section just a little too fast and wound up with a derailed train. (According to some who reminisce about the incident, male riders contributed by pulling their dates toward them as they entered the tunnel and thus shifted the weight to the outside of the turn. This, combined with the speed of the car, was enough to cause the train to jump the track). No damage or injury was sustained, but it demonstrated the limitations of the speed of the SCENIC RAILWAY. Unlike later designs, this coaster ran on railroad-type flanged wheels without the benefit of under-friction wheels found on rides like the THRILLER. (Added under-friction wheels would virtually lock the cars into the track and make derailment impossible). Under the guidance of Howard Stoneback, the "old SCENIC" was lengthened and made faster in the late Twenties. The course, then in its final form, was comprised of four lengthened circuits. But despite its modest pace, the SCENIC RAILWAY pleased thousands of riders as it provided entertainment from 1907 until 1937.

(Russell Allon Hehr Collection)

(Illus. 73a.) The ornate structure that housed the loading areas of the SCENIC RAILWAY.

(Russell Allon Hehr Collection)

(Illus. 74.) There was no doubt that the SCENIC RAILWAY was a popular ride as can be seen on the faces of these riders, 1920's. The carved dragons' heads can be seen on the front of the lead car, the brakeman also can be seen at the rear of the first car.

(Kekic Collection)

(Illus. 74a.) The loading area and building of the SCENIC RAILWAY with the tunnel on the second floor level. The RACING COASTER is on the right.

(Illus. 75a.)

(Kekic Collection)

(The Humphrey Company)

(Illus. 75b.)

(Kekic Collection)

(Illus. 76a.)

(Kekic Collection)

John A. Miller was a significant roller coaster designer and, due to his designs, prolifically left his impressions on millions of stomachs. He was to make two contributions to Euclid Beach. His first was the 1909 roller coaster; it was a small ride (in later times it was ideal for introducing a youngster to the joys of negotiating the drops, rises, and turns of a gravity ride). Its original name was the NEW VELVET COASTER, later to be known as the NEW VELVET RIDE, VELVET COASTER in the Teens, and finally the AERO DIPS (often misprounounced AREEO DIPS). Even though the VELVET COASTER was modest in size, it delivered the maximum for its stature — it was a Miller coaster. *(Illus. 75.)* It stood just north of the ROLLER RINK and the MAIN LUNCH, replacing the FIGURE EIGHT, and thrived until 1965. *(Illus. 76.)*

Thus, by the end of the first ten years of the twentieth century, Euclid Beach boasted two respectable "high" rides or gravity-propelled devices that were constructions of considerable height for the times. People were enthusiastically riding both the SCENIC RAILWAY and the VELVET COASTER. *(Illus. 77.)*

Euclid Beach Park was amazingly free from the terror and destruction of fire. This can only be attributed to the care and safety-mindedness of the employees and management. However, the AERO DIPS was once threatened in 1930 by a fire that started in a storage building located under the ride. Fortunately, the damage was contained, and only 400 dollars' worth of repairs had to be applied to the coaster.

(Illus. 75a.) The first hill of the AERO DIPS may appear modest, but to the youngster riding it for the first time, it was terrifying.

(Illus. 75b.) The course of the AERO DIPS took it over the ROLLER RINK and MAIN LUNCH building. The coaster produced an ever present roar to those inside.

(Illus. 76a.) The AERO DIPS is visible to the east, the BALL ROOM is on the right.

(Illus. 76b.) Looking East, the FIGURE EIGHT is seen on the site where the AERO DIPS would later appear.

(Kekic Collection)

(Illus. 76c.) The view to the west from the AERO DIPS site reveals the DANCE PAVILION and the CIRCLE SWING. Barrels filled with water were stored on the roof as a fire precaution.

(Illus. 77.) This postcard (c. 1909) exhibits the "NEW VELVET RIDE" as the coaster's name (later AERO DIPS). The view is to the Northeast showing part of the BALLROOM promenade.

(Russell Allon Hehr Collection)

In 1913, John Miller brought a second successful, yet different, ride to the Beach. Miller, who contracted for many firms, built this ride for the Ingersoll Engineering and Construction Company of Pittsburgh, Pa. The DERBY RACER, often shortened to the DERBY, or RACING COASTER, a later name, was an innovation for its period and was built at the cost of $45,000. *(Illus. 78.)* It utilized two separate but parallel sets of tracks on which the two trains raced. Actually, there was only one continuous track designed in such a manner that a train starting on the east side of the station would finish on the west side and vice versa. In this way, no switching was needed, and each set of cars got an alternate chance to negotiate each of the courses. *(Illus. 79.)*

(The Cleveland Plain Dealer)

(Illus. 78.) Ad announcing the opening of the NEW DERBY RACER in the Cleveland Plain Dealer, May 30, 1913.

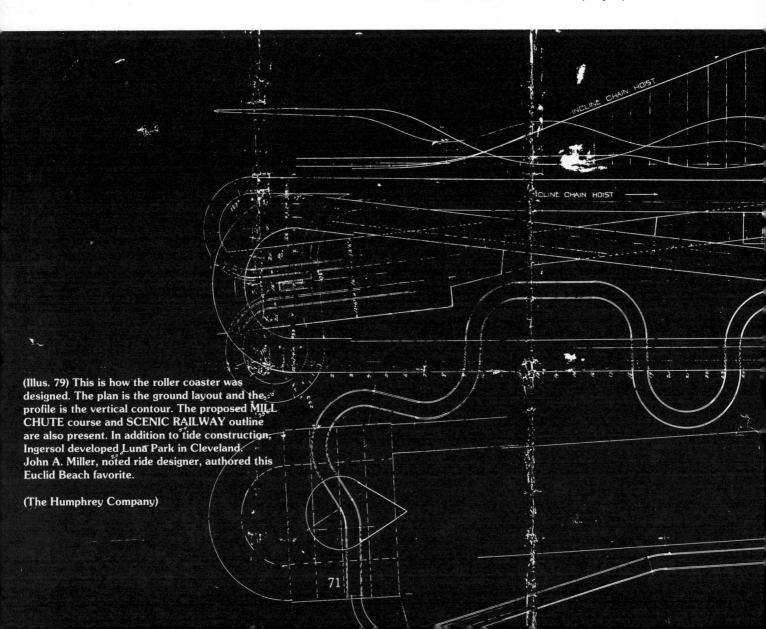

(Illus. 79) This is how the roller coaster was designed. The plan is the ground layout and the profile is the vertical contour. The proposed MILL CHUTE course and SCENIC RAILWAY outline are also present. In addition to ride construction, Ingersol developed Luna Park in Cleveland. John A. Miller, noted ride designer, authored this Euclid Beach favorite.

(The Humphrey Company)

71

(Illus. 80.) The two trains of the RACING COASTER "locked" in competition, much to the delight of the riders.

(The Cleveland Plain Dealer)

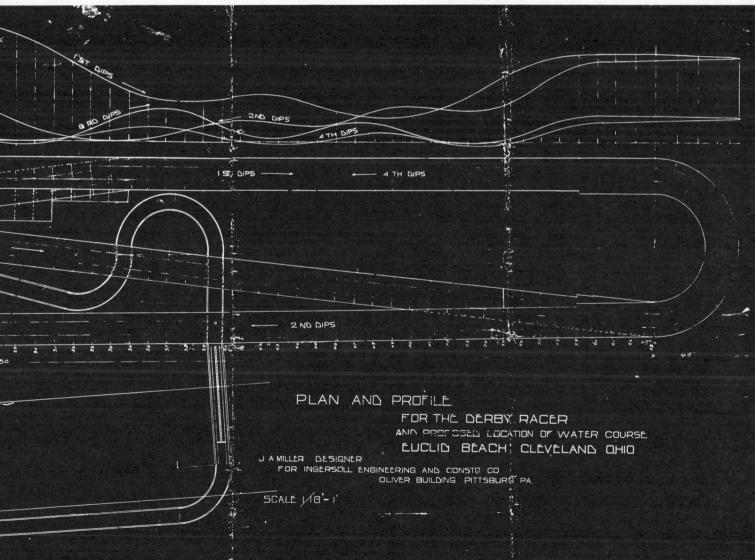

PLAN AND PROFILE
FOR THE DERBY RACER
AND PROPOSED LOCATION OF WATER COURSE
EUCLID BEACH CLEVELAND OHIO

J A MILLER DESIGNER
FOR INGERSOLL ENGINEERING AND CONSTG CO
OLIVER BUILDING PITTSBURG PA.

SCALE 1/16" - 1'

(Illus. 81.) Who will win? Perhaps the man in the tower knew.

(Kekic Collection)

(Illus. 82.) The second turn around of the RACING COASTER went over the loading pavilion. The SCENIC RAILWAY is on the left. The control tower is also visible in the view looking northward.

(Kekic Collection)

At many an outing, groups of frolicking picnickers would choose sides and mount their respective trains. Someone would wager that the red train was faster, or that the yellow one (circa the '20's) was a sure winner; or yet others would simply choose the first available seat on either train. The competitive spirit shone forth from the riders' faces as this popular coaster became an institution at Euclid Beach. Riders would lean, push, shove, or just hope as the cars moved around the course. (Illus. 80.) As the trains entered the final length of track leading to the station, the winners would signal victory, and the losers would chide "next time" or revenge. "What a great ride!" What many a rider did not realize was that fortunes of victory and defeat were not always up to chance, the weather, or their talent as passengers. There was a controller's tower situated near the end of the unloading platform from which the entire course could be viewed. (Illus. 81.) Either the ride manager, Jack Anderson, or the assistant manager, Roger Rheardon (a railroad worker who took off summers to work at the Beach), would scan the progress of the various trains and make significant contributions to the outcome of many of the competitions. One

(The Humphrey Company) (Illus. 83.) This overhead view of the RACING COASTER shows the wooden RED BUG BOULEVARD course, the area where the SCENIC RAILWAY stood (left), the little village for the MINIATURE RAILROAD. (Note the absence of the higher second THRILLER hill.)

of the safety features of the RACING COASTER was a series of brakes located strategically around the ride which could stop the progress of one or both of the trains if any malfunction or damage was detected. These brakes could be used for other purposes too, like slowing one of the trains. So it would seem if for any reason Mssrs. Anderson or Rheardon saw fit to alter the competition they could, and did.

The RACING COASTER seemed to illicit a number of humorous situations, one of which occurred during the summer of 1954. As the crew shift changed (the schedule was twenty minutes on and twenty off), two of the relief men watched the ride as two trains were in progress traveling the course. The two men immediately observed a man riding in a standing position. They concluded that something had to be done immediately as this conduct was definitely forbidden. The train with the faultor came into the station, and the passenger was immediately confronted as one who was recklessly infracting the rules of safety. The gentleman stood, revealing that he was indeed seven and a half feet plus tall and had been properly sitting throughout the ride. Perhaps the crew's comment was, "Have a nice ride?"

As was basic procedure, each day before the park opened for business all the rides were checked, and the coasters were tested by having empty trains with sand bags in them sent out to verify the condition of the tracks and structure. One day, recalls Al Schuessler (summer worker in the '50's), an empty set of trains was sent out on the RACING COASTER. The first run was done before the cars had been lubricated. One train traveled the entire ride without any problem, but the other, in need of oil, lost momentum and failed to mount the hill above the loading station. *(Illus. 82.)* The only way the unwilling train could be recovered and prepared for the day was for the crew to push it up the hill with the hope that gravity would bring it around the remainder of the course. The whole three-car train was far too heavy for the crew (Roller coaster cars weigh more than most people realize, approximately two tons each). So the difficult process of uncoupling was accomplished, and each car was pushed up the incline individually. As each was sent on its way, one of the crew climbed aboard to ride back to the station. As a result, the individual cars moved around the course much faster than they did as a train. Al felt the thrill was akin to

74

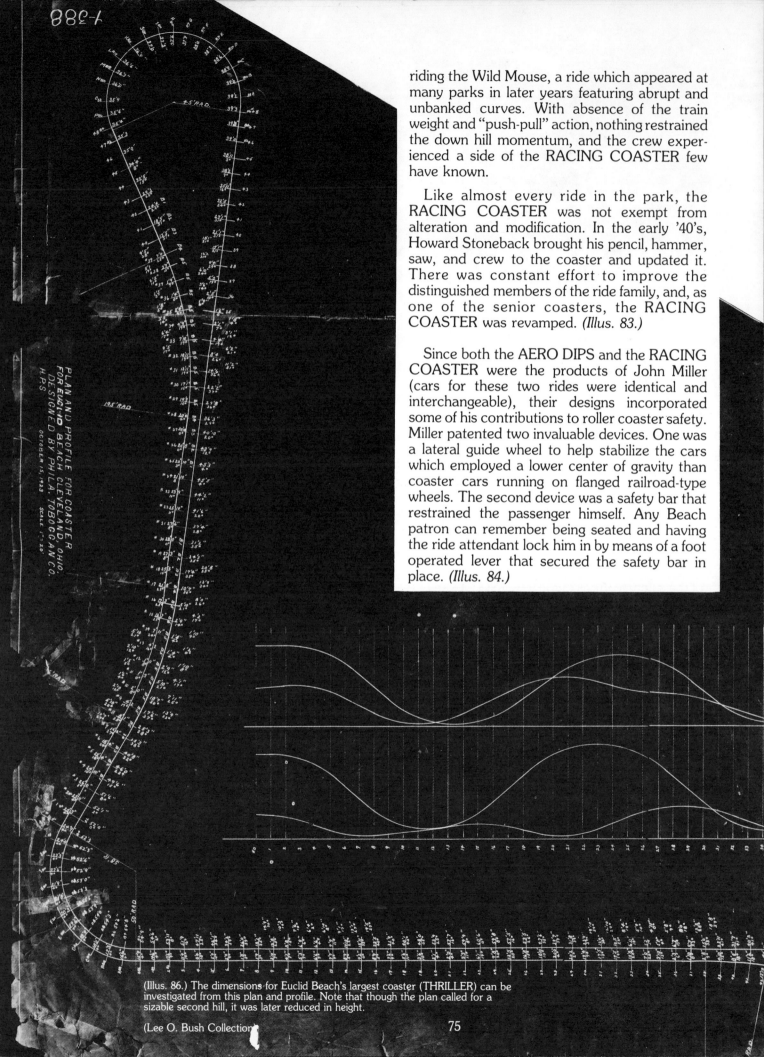

4-388

PLAN AND PROFILE FOR COASTER
FOR EUCLID BEACH CLEVELAND, OHIO.
DESIGNED BY PHILA. TOBOGGAN CO.
H. P. S.
OCTOBER 15, 1923   SCALE 1" = 20'

riding the Wild Mouse, a ride which appeared at many parks in later years featuring abrupt and unbanked curves. With absence of the train weight and "push-pull" action, nothing restrained the down hill momentum, and the crew experienced a side of the RACING COASTER few have known.

Like almost every ride in the park, the RACING COASTER was not exempt from alteration and modification. In the early '40's, Howard Stoneback brought his pencil, hammer, saw, and crew to the coaster and updated it. There was constant effort to improve the distinguished members of the ride family, and, as one of the senior coasters, the RACING COASTER was revamped. (Illus. 83.)

Since both the AERO DIPS and the RACING COASTER were the products of John Miller (cars for these two rides were identical and interchangeable), their designs incorporated some of his contributions to roller coaster safety. Miller patented two invaluable devices. One was a lateral guide wheel to help stabilize the cars which employed a lower center of gravity than coaster cars running on flanged railroad-type wheels. The second device was a safety bar that restrained the passenger himself. Any Beach patron can remember being seated and having the ride attendant lock him in by means of a foot operated lever that secured the safety bar in place. (Illus. 84.)

(Illus. 86.) The dimensions for Euclid Beach's largest coaster (THRILLER) can be investigated from this plan and profile. Note that though the plan called for a sizable second hill, it was later reduced in height.

(Lee O. Bush Collection)

(Illus. 84.) Safety Bar Mechanism on RACING COASTER (APB).

(Illus. 85.) 1924 view of the THRILLER loading platform and its first incline.   (Kekic Collection)

Although there could be many coasters enumerated that would be rated as much more fierce and stupendous than the THRILLER, few were more popular or patronized in a more dedicated manner. *(Illus. 85.)* Because it was a classic example of the American roller coaster, because it was not modest in height or speed, and because it occupied a central and important location in this most respected and respectable of parks, it was a proud ride. The THRILLER, perhaps, in fact, the most patronized of any attraction in the park, contributed significantly to the success of the park throughout its career.

The THRILLER was designed by the Philadelphia Toboggan Company in October of 1923, and erected during the winter of 1923-24, under the supervision of Howard Stoneback. *(Illus. 86.)* The highest summit measured seventy-one feet, five inches in height. Passengers were whirled away in a train of three cars of four seats each which was proclaimed by the Philadelphia Toboggan Company as being "designed for speed and safety."[36] *(Illus. 87.)* During busy days, the THRILLER operated three trains. While one train was loading, one was out on the course, and one was nearing the station to unload. Busy days, known as "three train days", placed considerable responsibility on the crew to keep the pace and proper distance among the trains. The price tag for this proud ride was $90,000 in 1923. Because of its capacity and popularity, it is claimed that it paid for itself in that first season. By the early '60's, two trains became the maximum due to overhead and safety considerations.

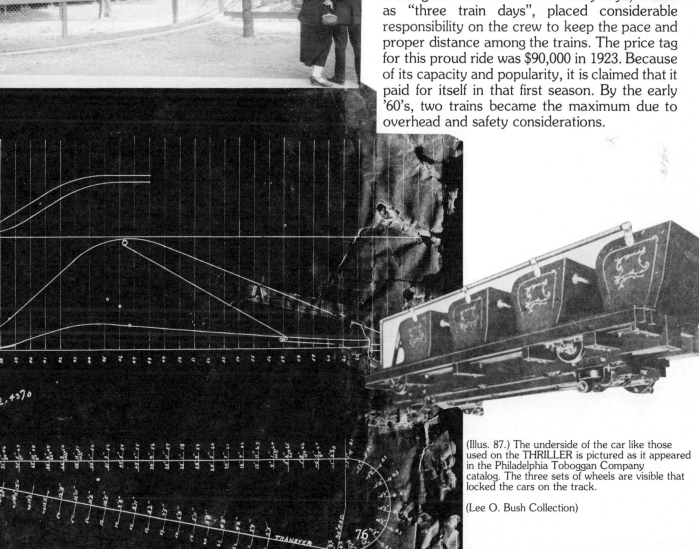

(Illus. 87.) The underside of the car like those used on the THRILLER is pictured as it appeared in the Philadelphia Toboggan Company catalog. The three sets of wheels are visible that locked the cars on the track.

(Lee O. Bush Collection)

Again the Euclid Beach alterations would not skip the THRILLER. Soon after the ride opened, the second hill was brought down from its original sixty and a half feet to nearly a third of that. *(Illus. 88, 89.)* Some have forwarded the opinion that the second hill was too high, others that it slowed the ride down. Whatever the ultimate reason, it provided a phenomena found on a number of Philadelphia Toboggan Co. Coasters. After the initial plunge, which was, of course, from the highest incline, the greatest speed and gravitational force was experienced. Instead of this momentum being somewhat reduced by the train mounting a relatively tall second hill, the cars attempted to take flight as they flew over the shortened second elevation. The riders delighted in the full effect of temporary weightlessness. There is also divided opion on the reasons for the alterations of the last series of short, choppy dips which made up the homeward leg of the journey. Some felt the coaster was providing too rough and violent a finale, while others felt the last group of hills were too tame. Whatever the ultimate reasons for these modifications, the result was a fast, smooth, but exhilarating ride that never failed to effect the special area that once was a stomach but became a butterfly den about halfway down the first dip. The THRILLER had all the characteristics of the best Philadelphia Toboggan coasters of later years, but it delivered the punch so peculiar to those built in the '20's.

(Illus. 87a.) A typical scene on the Lake Shore Boulevard side of the THRILLER'S course. A full capacity load enjoys the ride.

(The Cleveland Plain Dealer)

(Illus. 88.) The magnificent THRILLER with the higher second hill (as originally planned and built). The encroaching trailer park is absent. This ride represented a prominent feature of the Beach's countenance.

77

The cars used on the THRILLER all had three sets of wheels: the usual load-carrying vertical ones, the lateral friction wheels for direction, and "under-friction" wheels that literally locked the train onto the track construction. There is no record of a THRILLER car ever derailing. *(Illus. 90.)*

At the time of its opening, the THRILLER was advertised in Humphrey understated fashion as "safe but strenuous."[37] D.S. Humphrey found his coaster a good daily tonic as he rode it every morning. His claim was that no ride was too fast for him.[38] However, some found it a little too fast. One occasion, on a rainy July day in 1962, brought the presence of water on the braking mechanism. This caused a supreme lack of friction; that is to say, the crew could not stop the train as it went through the station. After completing three circuits, the pull chain which took the train up the first incline had to be stopped. Workmen climbed the hill and rescued the somewhat unnerved riders. "It was a Thriller."[39]

(Illus. 89.) Revised and lowered second hill of the THRILLER 1969.

(Joel Warren)

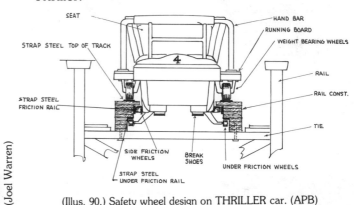

(Illus. 90.) Safety wheel design on THRILLER car. (APB)

(Kekic Collection)

A progression became evident as a line up of great "high-rides" at the southeastern part of the amusement area presented a parade, moving from the SCENIC RAILWAY, to the RACING COASTER, to its next-door neighbor the THRILLER, and then the final and highest member of the distinguished assemblage, the FLYING TURNS. (*Illus. 91.*) The FLYING TURNS was the zenith of a crescendo formed by these coasters as one moved eastward along the series of loading stations. This line up was a sort of "murderers' row" for the rider who would challenge this grand avenue of coasters.

The FLYING TURNS was designed for Euclid Beach in November of 1929 under the partner-ship of John Miller and J.N. Bartlett. (*Illus. 92.*) This unique ride was the brain child of Bartlett and was constructed in 1930 for that summer season.

Bartlett was an Englishman and had been a flyer in the First World War, and the intended aim of the FLYING TURNS was to deliver the thrill and sensation of flying in a nimble airplane. While in Europe, he had experienced the bob-sled, and it was the channel in which the sled traveled that gave Bartlett the idea for his desired effect. The train of three articulated cars employed by the FLYING TURNS ran in a "barrel" that bore a resemblance to a bob-sled course. Each of the three small cars moved on six casters that could rotate three hundred and sixty degrees. In essence, the train was "free wheeling." The barrel was constructed of one and one half inch cypress wood laid on bows made of "T" shaped steel. (*Illus. 93.*) Passengers rode two to a car, one rider seated on a cushion and the second seated on his lap or wedged between his legs, their head against the first person's chest. The ride had an appeal for obvious reasons.

(Illus. 93.) Long pieces of Cypress wood, one and one half inch square, were laid onto the metal framework which in turn rested on the timbered structure. This "barrel" was the "track" for the three car trains. Construction moved forward for the 1930 season.

(John L. Cobb Collection)

(Illus. 92.) Mr. Bartlett's idea was brought to life at the park in 1930. This most original ride is seen at its conception on this plan.

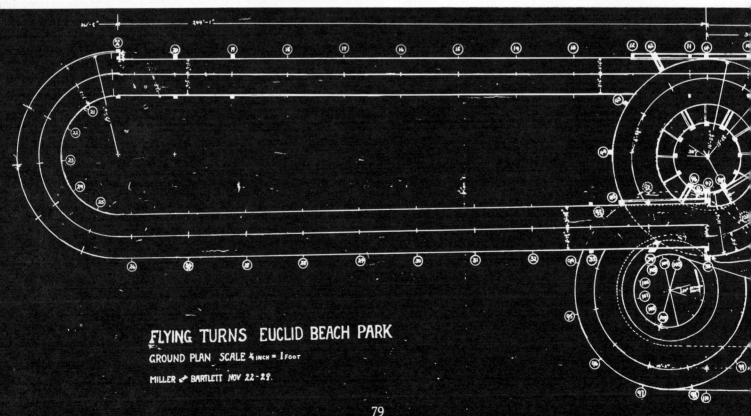

FLYING TURNS EUCLID BEACH PARK

GROUND PLAN SCALE ¼ INCH = 1 FOOT

MILLER & BARTLETT NOV 22-29.

(The Humphrey Company)

(The Humphrey Company)

(Above)

(Illus. 91.) Euclid Beach in its fullest glory - the old "Scenic",
the FLYING TURNS, and all that was the park in its finest state. c. 1933.
The biplanes are on the CIRCLE SWING, and the familiar FOUNTAIN on the
BEACH. The upper portion shows the HUMPHREY FIELD and DRIVING RANGE.

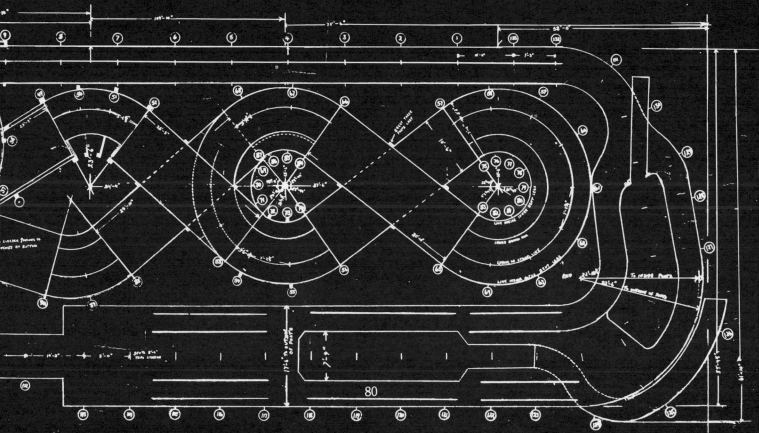

80

Each train was pulled up to a height slightly higher than the first and highest hill of its next-door neighbor, the THRILLER. *(Illus. 94.)* The ratchet that prevented the cars from sliding back down that first incline was considerably louder than those of the other coasters and resounded with an unnerving clatter. After reaching the top of the structure, the passengers experienced a series of gentle dips, only a few feet in height. Then without warning, the course began in earnest as the cars ran up on the sides of the barrel, sometimes beyond the vertical position. *(Illus. 95.)* Direction was changed quickly and constantly as gravity and centrifugal force were combined to delightfully punish the victimized rider. Of course, if a young man's riding companion was his favorite girl, the punishment was significantly lessened. During its first few seasons, the FLYING TURNS awarded many of its riders, mostly women, with fainting spells, and the ride attendants were properly equipped with smelling salts. Walter Williams verified that as the FLYING TURNS became established this phenomena decreased. However, Dave Scott related that the crew always remained agile at removing newly moistened cushions due to the unexpected sensation which this ride could furnish. The dampened seat could be removed and replaced from the ample supply of dry cushions, and the quick pace of operation which the ride demanded was never broken.

(The Cleveland Press)

(Lee O. Bush Collection)

(Illus. 94.) The three highest inclines of the RACING COASTER (left), the THRILLER (center), and the FLYING TURNS (right).

(Illus. 95.) The cars of the FLYING TURNS negotiating the barrel, testing the equilibrium of the riders.

Although Bartlett had constructed a previous model of the FLYING TURNS at Dayton's Lakeside Park, it was of much smaller stature than the example that appeared at Euclid Beach, which was built in co-operation with the Humphrey Company. *(Illus. 96.)* Bartlett felt that a FLYING TURNS of larger dimensions would deliver the thrill he wished to provide. The construction procedure was somewhat different from that of a tracked coaster. The scaffolding was built progressively from the ground up, and the barrel was then laid on the framework along the course from the top to the bottom. As construction of the barrel reached the course's midpoint, Bartlett's anticipation overcame him, and he announced he would ride the course as far as it was completed. The Beach crew advised against it, but Bartlett had a cable drawn across the top of the barrel near the last completed section. An arresting hook was fitted to the car to catch on that cable, and, in addition, a sand bag barricade was placed where the barrel's construction had stopped. Bartlett proceeded with his trial run, mounted one of the cars, and ventured down the course. Even though the barricade was a final precautionary measure, it proved necessary since the cable did not meet the hook, and Bartlett and car met the sand bag wall head on. Williams recalls that Bartlett was only dazed, but the car was heavily damaged. The experience must have provided Bartlett with encouragement. The ride was opened for the summer of 1930 and became the favorite of the heartiest park patrons. In addition to the Euclid

(Illus. 96.) The wooden framework and barrel construction of the FLYING TURNS.

(Kekic Collection)

Beach FLYING TURNS, Bartlett built examples at Riverview Park in Chicago and in numerous locations in the United States and Europe. (Fred Greenway, ride manager of the beach's FLYING TURNS, went to Chicago's Riverview Park for one year to open that park's version of the ride).

Every ride, especially a new design, had certain rough spots to be remedied. Bill Parker illuminated a classic example of a "rough" spot on the FLYING TURNS. It was during a Grotto picnic when a tall portly gentleman boarded the ride. He presented a humorous picture as he sat quite regally by himself in the lead car. About half way through the course, one of the casters jammed, caught on the cypress-constructed side of the barrel, and proceded to gouge a hole through the siding. Fortunately, the train stopped, but a portion of the first car was left dangling in space thirty-five feet above the ground. The passengers were rescued. The gentleman who had occupied the first car stayed and observed for a number of hours as the barrel was carefully repaired and the caster malfunction remedied. Harvey Humphrey and the crew he supervised began to fear the announcement of an impending law suit. When the ride was again functional, the gentleman informed Humphrey and his crew that he did not receive a complete ride. With great relief, Harvey informed the customer he could ride anything he wished in the park for the rest of the day. Parker recalled that this gentleman promptly boarded the FLYING TURNS, rode the entire course, and seemed to thoroughly enjoy it.

(Illus. 96a.) A train about to start its descent through the twists and turns.

(Kekic Collection)

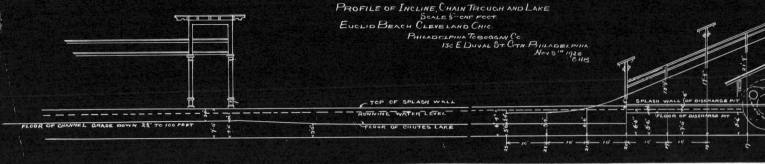

PROFILE OF INCLINE, CHAIN TROUGH AND LAKE
SCALE ⅛" = ONE FOOT.
EUCLID BEACH CLEVELAND OHIO.
PHILADELPHIA TOBOGGAN Co.
130 E. DUVAL ST. G.TN. PHILADELPHIA.
Nov 5ᵗᴴ 1920
C.H.B.

(Illus. 97.) The MILL CHUTE was a product of the Philadelphia Toboggan Company and a number of examples like the one at Euclid Beach appeared around the country. Note the incline of the hill leading into the lagoon.

(The Humphrey Company)

(Illus. 99.) OVER-THE-FALLS was designed and built as a Humphrey Company/Euclid Beach Park Product. The 1937 ride, revised from the MILL CHUTE, had a hill of 37 feet, increased from the MILL CHUTE elevation of 30 feet. The degree of descent was increased from 20° to 50°, making considerably more of a splash. (Plans for OVER-THE-FALLS were purchased by Sea Breeze Park in Rochester, New York where a version was constructed.)

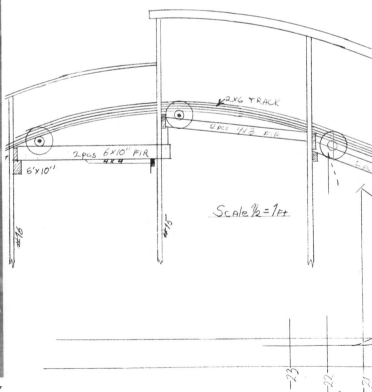

(Illus. 98.) Into the water with a splash. The SCENIC RAILWAY can be seen on the left.

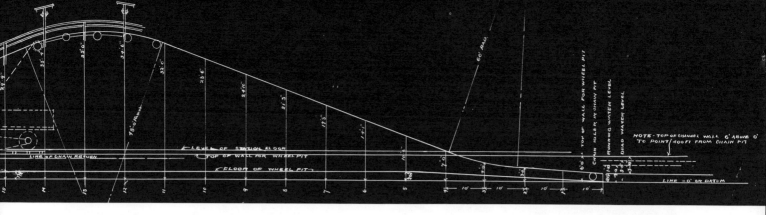

Descending a hill rapidly was a principle applied to amusement devices other than roller coasters. A rapid slide into a waiting body of water was recognized in the late 1800's as great fun. The earliest example was the CHUTE-THE-CHUTES, a ride which appeared at Captain Paul Boyton's Sea Lion Park at Coney Island in 1895. Euclid Beach, in 1896, had a slide located at the water's edge for bathers to glide into Lake Erie. The first real water-gravity ride at Euclid Beach was not built until 1921. The MILL CHUTE was yet another of the Philadelphia Toboggan Company's successful patents. It featured a darkened tunnel through which boats carrying up to six passengers floated. The current that moved the boats through the channel was generated by a paddle wheel. This was powered by the same electric motor that pulled the boats up the thirty-five foot incline. *(Illus. 97.)* The slide down this incline into a small lake was the climax of the ride. *(Illus. 98.)* Rides such as the MILL CHUTE classify as both "dark rides" and, in part, "high rides." The architecture of the MILL CHUTE, its lighted posts over the descent, and detailed loading station reflect a golden age of ride design and park style.

In 1937, the MILL CHUTE (often called OLD MILL) underwent extensive rejuvination. A drawing of a new channel route bears the name of P. Killaly, this new course being made possible by the removal of the SCENIC RAILWAY. *(Illus. 99.)* Another series of drawings bear the mark of Howard Stoneback. The new features made this attraction the equivalent of a new ride, and thus it was renamed OVER THE FALLS. This ride was, by and large, a product of the staff of Euclid Beach Park. A prominent new feature was a very severely angled incline, thirty-seven feet high, that sent the boat into the waiting water at breathtaking velocity. *(Illus. 100.)*

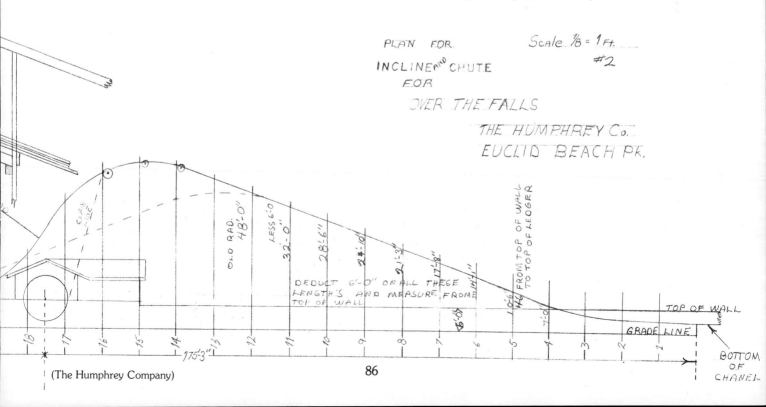

(The Humphrey Company)

(The Cleveland Plain Dealer)

(Illus. 99a.) A MILL CHUTE boat loaded with anticipating passengers rushes toward its meeting with the water.

Dark rides and fun houses are natural places for humorous occurrences. One feature of the tunnel was a "water curtain." Water poured into the channel from overhead, and it seemed unavoidable that it would fall into the boat. With a series of levers located underwater the rush of water was stopped as the passing boat activated a switch. After the boat passed over the site, the lever allowed the switch to start the water curtain once again. Due to the corroding process of water, the levers and switches had to be repaired in the OVER THE FALLS channel periodically. Consequently, the levers and switches were removed, along with the appropriate fuses which were placed on top of the fuse box. On one occasion, the ride manager was late, perhaps for the first time in years, and he scurried about making sure all the features of the ride were working. He spotted the fuses and put them back into the box, thus activating the water curtain. Of course, unknown to him, there were no means of turning it off. Since he was late, he neglected to send a trial boat through the ride. It can only be conjectured what the passengers' reactions were upon nearing the water flowing from overhead across the width of the channel. They were sure it would mysteriously stop. It did not. Besides

drenching the passengers, the overhead flow awarded the boat an ample amount of water, and it nearly sank as it entered the lake after coming down the incline. Then the manager realized the fault, but he had already sent four boats into the channel. He was not credited with developing the prototype of a new submarine ride.

The darkness of the channel not only suggested the obvious intimacy to be enjoyed while traveling the course, but in some of the young boys, it illicited a vandalizing tendency. Now and then these boys would pelt the scenery with rocks. It became sport for employees on relief shift to hide and wait near these scenes. When a wayward youth attempted destruction, an employee would reach out from the darkness and in an alarming manner, warn the lads to curtail such activities. Perhaps there was some effect. If trouble persisted the attendant who worked the "hole," the station at the base of the incline, could collect any wrong doer and have him expelled from the park. The refinement of the MILL CHUTE, that was developed into OVER THE FALLS, was popular with all age groups. Besides accumulating its share of humorous incidents, it demonstrated the technical ability and resourcefulness of the Park's staff.

(The Cleveland Plain Dealer)

(Illus. 100.) OVER-THE-FALLS boat . . . witness the splash.

(The Humphrey Company)

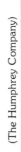

THE CARVED HORSE

The assemblage of attractions in any amusement park is incomplete if there exists no carousel on the grounds. Like the roller coaster, the merry-go-round is basic to what we know as an amusement park.

The Euclid Beach Company prepared for their second season, 1896, by installing a number of rides. Among them was the park's first merry-go-round. This machine was an early "track" type carousel; that is, the platform that carried the carved figures and carriages ran on a track under the mechanism. (Later machines were suspended; that is, the platform and attendant figures hung from radial arms.) This first MERRY-GO-ROUND was a Herschell product, possibly built by the Allan Herschell Company or under the Armitage-Herschell banner. (Illus. 13.) The park boasted that the MERRY-GO-ROUND had many fine "carriages and hobbies."[40] In addition, the machine was fitted with a splendid organ "capable of producing the sounds of any known musical instrument."[41] This band-organ was an entertainment attraction in itself and advertised as having been built at the cost of $2,000.

After the Humphrey purchase of Euclid Beach Park, the JAPANESE FLYING PONIES or FLYING PONIES, as it was commonly called, was erected for the summer of 1903 by Herschell-Spillman. (Illus. 101.) This was a unique device which featured the circular rotating structure pitched at an angle to the ground. The small horses were hung from overhead and were allowed to swing outwardly under the influence of centrifugal motion. The practice of improving and revamping came to this carousel just as it did to most of the attractions in the park. The hand-carved horses were replaced by newer pieces, and a new band organ was added in 1909. The power source which turned the structure was located on the upper floor of a building behind the ride which housed a PHOTO GALLERY at ground level. Although the revolutions of the FLYING PONIES were not dizzying, this unusual merry-go-round was popular and added to the Beach's image. (Illus. 102.)

(Illus. 101.) The FLYING PONIES, set at an angle (approx. 10°), with its suspended, free-swinging horses, was an early Euclid Beach landmark. The early track MERRY-GO-ROUND is in the background, the powerhouse for the "PONIES" is at the left. The costume, indeed, was proper.

(Illus. 102.) Although the horses on the FLYING PONIES were thought to have been changed periodically, this photo shows one of the most handsome examples.

(The Humphrey Company)

(The Humphrey Company)

(Illus. 101b.) View looking to the east, the SCENIC RAILWAY station is behind the FLYING PONIES.

(Illus. 101a.) The detail of construction is visible in this postcard view of the FLYING PONIES. The view is looking west.

(Russell Allon Hehr Collection)

The records of the Philadelphia Toboggan Company show that another carousel, NO. 9, was brought to Euclid Beach in 1905. This machine was described as having had three rows of figures. After its turn at the Beach, it was moved to Laurel Springs, Hartford, Connecticut. This carousel could have well replaced the old Herschell track machine when the CHESTNUT GROVE was established and the TROLLEY STATION was moved closer to Lake Shore Boulevard. In turn, Philadelphia Toboggan machine NO.9 was repalced in 1910 by No. 19, a large CARROUSEL of four rows.[41a] This grand machine was known to many who patronized the Beach. The Philadelphia Toboggan Company CARROUSEL was in a central location between the SCENIC RAILWAY/MILL CHUTE stations and the DANCE PAVILION, also close to the MAIN POPCORN STAND. Its placement put it at the "hub" of the park's activity. (Illus. 103.)

(The Humphrey Company)

(The Humphrey Company)

above

(Illus. 103.) The "grand" CARROUSEL (Philadelphia Toboggan Co.) with the PHOTO STAND on the left. The visitors in gentile dress stroll the boarded path. The crown-like cupola is on the CARROUSEL building.

(Illus. 103a.) The CARROUSEL surrounded by children . . . the way it was meant to be. The sign on the right points the way to the BARBER SHOP. The building that housed the CARROUSEL was altered a number of times throughout its existence.

(Frederick Fried Collection)

(Illus. 104.) The stately CARROUSEL (1910).

(Illus. 105a, b, c.) Examples of the mangificent horses from the CARROUSEL as they stood immediately after the park's closing.

(Joel Warren)

106a. (Eric Beheim Collection)

(Illus. 106a, b.) The CARROUSEL (the manufacturer's particular spelling) was decorated with two imposing chariots - a trademark of the Philadelphia Toboggan Company.

106b. (Joel Warren)

(The Humphrey Company)

The proud horses, the detailing, and fantastic chariots represented the epitome of the art and demonstrated the significance of the Philadelphia-based manufacturer. *(Illus. 104.)* The horses on the outside row were claimed to have been replicas of famous mounts such as those of Sitting Bull and Lady Godiva. *(Illus. 105.)* In company with the forty-four graceful horses, two magnificent chariots graced the ride's circling platform.[42] *(Illus. 106.)*

(Illus. 106c.) Chariot sitting on the CARROUSEL shows Art-Deco applied to the ride. Note the cornice, inner panels, and the horses painted white.

(The Humphrey Company)

(Illus. 107.) Still 2 tickets . . . what a bargain! The Art-Deco and a white picket fence (a questionable combination) did detract from the aesthetic quality of this great ride.

George Reinhard, Jr., recalls his fascination with this wonderful CARROUSEL as a boy in the early Twenties. He spent so much time at the site of the machine that Jimmy Johnson, who then ran the ride, gave him a job. George recalls that his initial duty was to maintain the supply of brass rings. Lancing the brass ring disappeared at the Euclid Beach CARROUSEL after George, Jr., went on to work on the SCENIC RAILWAY, or at least he had no recollection of anyone else following to replentish the basket of rings.

Music for the CARROUSEL was provided by a band organ of fifty-two keys. This instrument was style #188, built by the North Tonawanda Musical Instrument Works, North Tonawanda, New York. Its familiar white enamel front was an integral part of the merry-go-round. It had five registers: trumpets, trombones, clarionettes, open bass, and stopped bass. It also had painted cloth panels in the center.

Decor for the CARROUSEL and its building was changed in the Thirties as the look of "Art Deco" came into vogue. (Illus. 107.) This alteration in style was particularly evident on the upper cornice with the elimination of the BAROQUE details, mirrors, cupids, and swags. To many it was a loss of the elegant spirit of the CARROUSEL. In later years, the color scheme of the horses was also changed with the basic body of each horse painted white and the trappings, saddles, and other detailing painted in rich colors.

Immediately to the east of the CARROUSEL was a very special type of merry-go-round. Built in 1921, the GREAT AMERICAN RACING DERBY was a product of Piror and Church. (Illus. 108.) The home office of that company was in Venice, California, with an East Coast representative, H.C. Middleton, at Steeplechase Park, Coney Island, New York. This unusual ride featured rows of four horses that moved forward and backward as well as up and down. (Illus. 109.)

(The Humphrey Company)

(Illus. 108.) Looking east toward the GREAT AMERICAN RACING DERBY amid the ever-present trees.

(The Humphrey Company)

(Illus. 109.) Four abreast, these steeds competed to win the flag. This ride now operates at Cedar Point Amusement Land.

(Kekic Collection)

(Illus. 110.) Members of a family astride their mounts.

As the platform on which the horses were mounted revolved, the horses competed. *(Illus. 110.)* At a given point in the course of a ride, the up and back movement ceased, and a winner of each group of four was declared. During many of the seasons of operation, it was customary for a ride attendant to place a small American flag in a hole provided at the head of the horse signifying the winner, and thus awarding the rider a free second trip.

Walter Williams recalls how the construction company supervisor of the GREAT AMERICAN RACING DERBY carefully watched members of the Euclid Beach crew at their various park tasks and decided which members of the crew were best suited for the specific jobs of constructing the 1921 merry-go-round. Williams asserted that the installation was completed in record time.

Just as the whirling lights, brightly colored horses, and characteristic band-organ music were memorable traits of the CARROUSEL, the GREAT AMERICAN RACING DERBY had its own peculiar features. In the manner of a race track, there was a round infield open to the sun and the stars. Peculiar also, was the starting bell and the deep rumble as the platform moved at a very respectable speed. There was the flair with which the attendants got off and on the whirling platform. In the Thirties, ride workers like Norm Johnson would gracefully step on and off the ride, leaning at precarious angles to compensate for the effect of centrifugal force, and in so doing, they drew a crowd of their own fans. *(Illus. 111.)* An unusual and short-lived idea was the replacement of some of the horses with bicycles. That questionable innovation did not persist but succeeded in giving the RACING DERBY a somewhat incongruous image. *(Illus. 112.)* The RACING DERBY, as it was also called, whirled riders at Euclid Beach Park from 1921 until 1965; it now is at Cedar Point Amusement Land in Sandusky, Ohio.

The carved horse, fashioned by the hands of a supreme craftsman, was well represented at Euclid Beach. The pride of workmanship so evident in the beautiful figures was at home in such a proud park.

(Kekic Collection)

(Illus. 110a.) A full house readies to urge their horse to a win. The open infield and lattice work are evident.

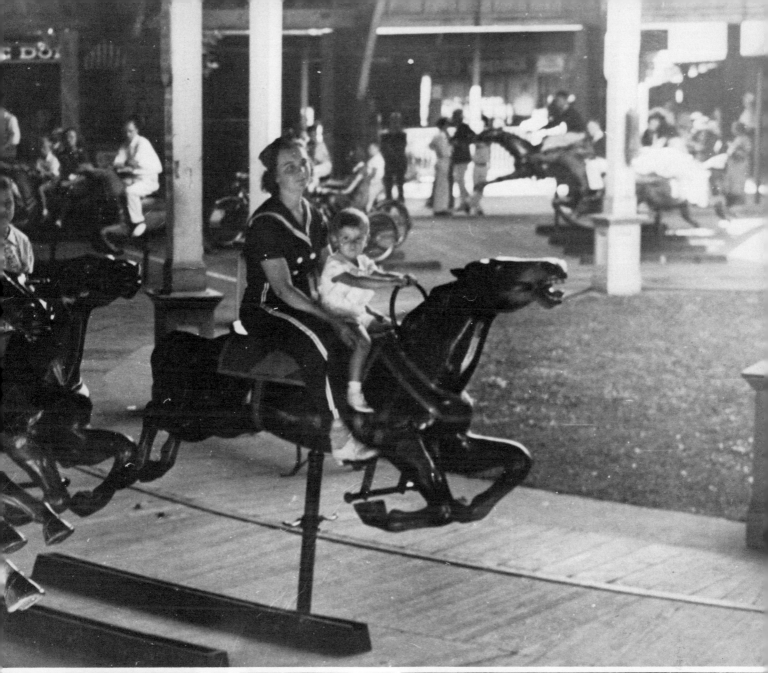

(Illus. 112.) The presence of bicycles in the place of some horses presented an unusual scene - a shortlived feature. (Also Illus. 110.)

(Kekic Collection)

(Illus. 111.) Gracefully, Bob Boyce moves onto the revolving platform. Small American flags for the winners can be seen in his back pocket.

(Bob Boyce)

A DIFFERENT TURN

Traveling in circles was always popular at the Beach, be it on one of the carousels or one of the many other circular devices. An unusual member of the revolving attraction family was an early ride called the OCEAN WAVE. *(Illus. 113.)* It was a predecessor of what is now called the octapus. The OCEAN WAVE was described by its manufacturer as a "costly" large machine, intended for park use only.[43] The OCEAN WAVE at Euclid Beach was built to the northwest of the FIGURE EIGHT loading station and operated in the early 1900's.

(Illus. 113.) Manufacturer's catalog illustration of the OCEAN WAVE by Herschell-Spillman. (1911)

(Richard F. Hershey Collection)

(Illus. 114.) An original Gondola of the CIRCLE SWING (later ROCKET SHIPS).

(The Humphrey Company)

Aviation had not only grown dramatically in the first half of the Twentieth Century, but it was an interest of importance to the Humphreys. D.S. II, his son Harvey, and, in turn, Harvey's son, Dudley S. III, were all aviation enthusiasts. The CIRCLE SWING, or AERIAL SWING, basically emulated trends of flight. The passenger carriers, changed from time to time, reflected the history of aviation. When the ride was installed in 1902, the patrons rode in wicker gondolas similar to those found under a dirigible. *(Illus. 114.)* In 1927, the builders, the Traver Engineering Company of Beaver Falls, Pennsylvania installed "deluxe cars," which were designed to look like airplanes (biplanes).[44] With the advent of Charles Lindberg and his 1927 Atlantic crossing, the airplane became a national preoccupation, and with that, the ride was renamed the AEROPLANES. *(Illus. 115.)*

(Illus. 115.) The AEROPLANES replaced the earlier wicker gondolas in 1927. The elevated loading platform was a Humphrey innovation later adopted on Circle Swings across the country.

(The Humphrey Company)

(The Humphrey Company)

(Illus. 117.) Glistening stainless steel ships floated overhead amid the lake breezes. The Artizen band organ provided melodies for the flight.

The Thirties brought the manifestation of technilogical fantasies. Buck Rogers and Flash Gordon were two such examples. Euclid Beach made use of these trends and sent Dud Scott, Howard Stoneback, Bill Parker, and the shop crew to work. After hours of interpreting comic strip versions of rocket ships, the Beach produced its own, unlike any ever to appear on circle swings elsewhere. The huge stainless steel rockets were designed, engineered, and manufactured in the park's very own shops. *(Illus. 116.)* The ride was renamed the ROCKET SHIPS. *(Illus. 117.)* (Smaller versions of the rocket ships were later copied by other parks.)

Another feature that made the Beach's CIRCLE SWING different from others was its strength. When the ride was first installed, the tower twisted slightly due to the torque of the revolving load. To be doubly safe, D.S. Humphrey had an additional tower built right over the original, thus making it a very substantial structure. In this way, the ride could easily handle the larger "ships" finally installed.

Another unique achievement was the changing of the loading platform. Originally all passengers boarded directly from the ground. *(Illus. 118.)* The Humphreys decided to elevate this platform nearly ten feet above. This construction allowed the use of the ground around the ride, eliminated the fence surrounding the boarding area, and prevented the danger of persons on the ground from being struck by the ride while in motion. *(Illus. 115.)*

Sometimes all the improvements in the world will not forestall events that are momentarily frightening. During one June evening in 1963, the operator of the ROCKET SHIPS fainted. The parents of two young children watched the ships travel on, and on, and on. Finally, panic set in, and the parents had to summon aid. The ride was a little too generous. Even if the ride had continued, the parents were assured there was no danger involved.

There is yet another myth to be dispelled. In Cleveland, and among those familiar with the

park, a tale circulates that has become a legend. Supposedly on a crowded summer day, one of the Gondolas/Aeroplanes/Rockets broke loose of its cables, and the passengers and their conveyance were flung into nearby Lake Erie. However, this myth is not true. It has been substantiated by those who worked there and knew the park that no such event ever transpired.

While the ROCKET SHIPS spun above the heads of park visitors, the air was filled with music from a band organ placed on the ground near the steps that led to the loading platform. Familiar tunes eminated from style "A" Artizan Band Organ of forty-six keys.

(Bill Parker)

(Illus. 116.) Bill Parker welded the frames of the ROCKET SHIPS, designed and built in the Park's own shops.

(Illus. 118.) The CIRCLE SWING in its original form - wicker gondolas and ground level boarding, c. 1915. Note the "Buster Keaton" look in men's hats.

(The Humphrey Company)

(Kekic Collection)

(Illus. 119.) The ever popular BUG, always fun. A product of the Traver Engineering Company.

Just south of the ROCKET SHIPS was a ride familiar to many, the BUG, also a product of the Traver Engineering Company. It was brought to Euclid Beach in the late Twenties and was claimed to have paid for itself before the Fourth of July of its initial season. It was managed under the watchful eye of Bill Parker for much of its career. Bill, who also cared for the ROCKET SHIPS, never let the slightest problem develop. This took a great deal of attention since these devices developed countless "bugs" which, unattended, would grow into costly safety hazards. The BUG was always fun to ride since passengers were first jostled one way, then another. *(Illus. 119.)* Its chain drive always gave the proper insect-like overtones. Another insect-inspired ride also appeared earlier on the same site as the BUG. It was called the CATERPILLAR. During the course of the ride the passengers were covered by a mechanical canvas hood. The presence of this ride lasted a very short time.

William F. Mangels was known both as a manufacturer of major attractions (such as carousels, dark rides, and penny arcade devices) and a noted historian of the amusement park business. One of his most popular rides was the WHIP. Patented in 1914 and 1915, this ride was a favorite at the Beach in the late Teens of this century.

The Mangels WHIP enjoyed a position just west of the SCENIC RAILWAY. This first appearance of the WHIP at the Beach was that of an open air ride; there was no enclosure. *(Illus. 120.)* Mangels designated the device built at the Beach as the "stationary WHIP." He also was the manufacturer of a portable model, which, like the stationary WHIP, had 12 cars to carry the riders on their eccentric course.

A later model of the WHIP (renamed the DIPPY WHIP) appeared in the building that had housed the AVENUE THEATRE (1938). *(Illus. 121).* After that building's use for the presentation of vaudeville, then for showing motion pictures was concluded, it became an ideal location for an indoor ride. Few who rode the DIPPY WHIP forgot the huge painting over the stage opening depicting a BALLERINA RIDING A RUNAWAY HORSE. *(Illus. 122.)*

The final ride to be considered in this lineage was the COFFEE BREAK. This attraction replaced the later WHIP in the old AVENUE THEATRE building. Passengers rode in cars fashioned after coffee cups. During the ride, these cars appeared to be on collision courses.

103

(Kekic Collection)

(Illus. 120.) The outdoor WHIP was the first of its kind at Euclid Beach. This was designer Mangel's very successful attraction. Each WHIP car had ornate, decorative scenes and scroll work on it. The SCENIC RAILWAY is to the left.

The four circular paths were designed to give this illusion. The COFFEE BREAK was one in a series of newer small rides to appear at the Beach during the last few seasons.

(Illus. 121.) The DIPPY WHIP occupied the old AVENUE THEATRE. A smaller ride than the outdoor WHIP, it had dipped turns at the ends.

(Illus. 120a.) Overhead of the outdoor WHIP.   (Kekic Collection)

(The Humphrey Company)

(Illus. 122.) The galloping ballerina was the subject of a mural on the proscenium covering the old AVENUE THEATRE.

(Lee O. Bush Collection)

(Illus. 123.) The water-going merry-go-round called the SEA SWING in the circular pool that later held the familiar FOUNTAIN.

(Bob Legan)

(Kekic Collection)

(Illus. 124.) Frolicking in the pool splashed by the FOUNTAIN provided enjoyment for many years.

(Kekic Collection)

(Illus. 125.) An unusual ride that was shortlived. Even when motors were introduced on the cars (domes had previously housed the motors), it failed to last. The building later housed the LAFF-IN-THE-DARK, which utilized the same cars.

The AVENUE THEATRE was near the walk that bordered the bathing beach. If a route was taken along this walk to the East, the PIER would be passed, and immediately to the East of it was the circular pool. As has already been noted, there appeared in that pool the SEA SWING during the Teens of the century, a somewhat different and moist way to get around. This water-bound merry-go-round featured rubber seats suspended from the overhead revolving frame-work on which bathers could splash and skim across the water as they whirled about *(Illus. 123.)* The SEA SWING was replaced by a fountain, set in the middle of the pool. *(Illus. 124.)* Swimmers were permitted to bathe in the pool and play in the cascading water. At night the FOUNTAIN featured various colored lights under the tiers over which the water fell. It became a landmark that fascinated visitors to the Beach, and, in particular, the romantically in-clined.

Many unusual and strange amusement devices were designed in the Twenties and the Thirties. One such example was the WITCHING WAVES, brought to the park by Dudley H. Scott. Scott had a fondness for attractions that featured interesting and intricate engineering. Installed in the Twenties, this ride anticipated the surfing craze of the Fifties. Designed as an oval track, the floor was an undulating, sheet-metal surface. By a series of cam-like devices operating under this floor, the surface of steel moved up and down in sequence, like the waves of an ocean. Riders attempted to "catch a wave" and were moved around the course on the crest of that wave. *(Illus. 125.)* Sometimes this was difficult, and one of the ride attendants had to lend a hand. The use of many hands to help get the ride going was a shortcoming Scott recognized. He therefore designed a small battery-operated motor fitted to the front of each car which drove the front wheel and thus allowed the riders to pursue their own wave. The WITCHING WAVES survived until 1931 when it was replaced by the LAFF-IN-THE-DARK on the same foundation.

(Kekic Collection)

(Illus. 126.) To each his own - this ride had loyal riders or was widely skirted during a visit to Euclid Beach. The detailed decor reflected the care the Humphreys took in running their park.

The BUBBLE BOUNCE was a ride that was either loved or avoided; it either delighted the riders with a dizzying whirl, or tended to deprive its victims of their most recent meal. It appeared on the scene in 1939 and occupied the area between the SURPRISE HOUSE and OVER THE FALLS. This delightfully infernal device was a product of the Custer Specialties Company of Dayton, Ohio. It featured a merry-go-round-type platform which not only rotated but rose and fell on an angle to the ground. (Illus. 126.) On this platform were located eight bubble-shaped passenger compartments or cars. These cars could be rotated by the rider by means of a wheel located in the middle of the seating area. The wheel was fastened to a shaft which was then fastened to the platform. The wheel was fixed, and the bubble was free to turn. With this arrangement, the rider could compound the circular, up and down motion with the rotation of

each of the bubbles. Some became expert at attaining such speeds of rotation that it became difficult to lift their heads due to centrifugal force or even realize when the ride had ended.

The BUBBLE BOUNCE was also subject to Euclid Beach modification. The original 7/8" shaft was not of the dimension that the Beach's crew felt was sufficient. After a trial run the shaft broke. Walt Williams remembers that he and Bill Parker fitted a two inch shaft to the BUBBLE BOUNCE and experienced no more problems. Bill Parker also instituted improvements of the air pressure system, thus strengthening the ride and furnishing more dependable service.

There were a number of new rides of a circular nature installed at the Beach during its last decade of service. The area at the eastern end of the park between the FLYING TURNS and the LAFF IN THE DARK was a site that seemingly

(The Humphrey Company)

(Illus. 127.) The HURRICANE was an example of one of the smaller rides that occupied the area at the eastern end of the park.

(Illus. 128.) The TILT-A-WHIRL and FERRIS WHEEL operated on the GREAT AMERICAN RACING DERBY site. (1969).

(Dr. Philip J. Kaplow Collection)

never found an appropriate ride. Among the rides to be placed there were examples that can now be found at many amusement parks. *(Illus. 127.)* There were the HURRICANE, OCTOPUS, ROCK-O-PLANE, and SCRAMBLER. On the site of the BUBBLE BOUNCE (formerly outdoor WHIP site) the ROTOR was placed. Also, southeast of the DANCE PAVILION a spiral GIANT SLIDE was erected (1962). Another modern ride, very popular today, is the TILT-A-WHIRL, which was introduced on the former site of the GREAT AMERICAN RACING DERBY. At this same location a small FERRIS WHEEL was placed.

The FERRIS WHEEL provides a beginning and an end in circular rides at Euclid Beach Park. The first such pleasure wheel was installed at the park in 1896, as the Euclid Beach Park Company introduced a number of rides to its patrons. This

(The Cleveland Press)

(Illus. 128a.) Small FERRIS WHEEL that appeared in the 1960's.

(The Humphrey Company)

(Illus. 128b.) ROCK-O-PLANE, an occupant of the "east end."

wheel, built by the Buckeye Observation Wheel Company, stood at the eastern end of the park, approximately where the ROLLER RINK'S east wall would be in later years. It disappeared by 1902 when the ROLLER RINK was constructed. Unlike many parks, Euclid Beach felt a FERRIS WHEEL was not essential. Not until 1963 was a FERRIS WHEEL to reappear at the park. The plans for this final wheel were submitted by the Eli Bridge Company of Jacksonville, Illinois. The FERRIS WHEEL and the TILT-A-WHIRL (a Sellner Mfg. Co. product) shared the position where the GREAT AMERICAN RACING DERBY had once spun. *(Illus. 128.)*

(Illus. 129.) The FLYING SCOOTERS, brought from the Great Lakes Expo. From 1938 on, this ride was one of the first to be seen upon entering the park from the MAIN PARKING LOT.

(The Cleveland Press)

ON THE WING ON THE HOOF

Although the FLYING SCOOTER (built by Bisch-Rocco of Chicago, Ill.) shared qualities with those rides that were circular, its greatest feature was the feeling of controlled flight. *(Illus. 129.)* Introduced in 1938, the brightly colored spinning figures were familiar first glimpses of action as patrons entered the amusement area from the MAIN PARKING LOT. Many tried to take leave of the earth's bounds by skimming over the COLONNADE in free flight - at least in fantasy.

Aviation was indeed a popular subject with the Humphreys, and this interest was reflected in many of the attractions in the park. From the time of the Curtiss (1910) and Atwood (1911) flights, the airplane and its relatives would be common sights at the park. Thus, the FLYING SCOOTER proved to be a popular attraction, giving the rider the chance to contribute to the events that would take place during the ride. It is present in most major parks now in operation.

110

An interesting but short-lived device, championed by Dudley Scott, was the ZOOMER. This was a unique product of Custer Specialties and was based on the effects of flight. A stubby replica of an airplane fuselage (body) was suspended by sprung shafts from a dolly-like mechanism which ran freely on an overhead steel beam or rail much in the manner of a monorail. *(Illus. 130.)* Propulsion was provided by the propeller of each individual unit as the prop, in turn, was rotated by an electric motor. *(Illus. 131.)* It has been recalled that the prop made quite a racket as it pounded the air. There also was another short coming. It seemed that after a rain, the units were not capable of self-propulsion; therefore, plans were made by Scott to power the dolly and furnish the needed energy. The ZOOMER only zoomed for a short while in the late Twenties.

As world wide interest in manned flight grew, so did the accompanying technology. Another such example was the LINK TRAINER. John Stoneback recalls his days of running this device in the late Twenties. Located east of the MAIN OFFICE and just south of the BUG, it attracted those who saw the romance of flight. The LINK TRAINER simulated flight as the would-be trainee manipulated the stick, rudder pedals, and other instrumentation found in airplanes of the era. John also recalls being taken in by some of the noted flyers of the day. Not recognizing them, Stoneback would explain how to handle the machine and then find the gentleman could control the device more expertly than he himself. LINK TRAINERS also appeared at Euclid Beach Park during World War II. The later model demonstrated night- and blind-instrument flying.

(Frederick Fried Collection)

(Illus. 130.) The unusual and short lived ZOOMER here seen winding its way by the ROLLER SKATING RINK and the BARBER SHOP.

(Illus. 131.) Two ladies "zooming" on the ZOOMER.

(Kekic Collection)

Certainly travel by horse differed greatly from travel by plane, but for some reason, children found both very absorbing. The wooden horse was, of course, richly represented at Euclid Beach, but no child's voyage through the park could be considered complete without a ride in a cart behind a real pony. The PONY TRACK, though occasionally changed in shape, occupied basically the same land throughout the history of the park. It was immediately south of the COLONNADE. *(Illus. 132.)*

(Illus. 132a.) An early scene of the PONY RIDE, (c. 1910). The globe of the WORLD THEATRE can be seen in the background.

(Russell Allon Hehr Collection)

(Kekic Collection)

(Illus. 132c.) Children rode the ponies on the inside track while ponies pulled wicker buggies on the outside track.

(Kekic Collection)

(Illus. 132.) A popular attraction for the kiddies, the PONY RIDE. This was a typical scene in the 1940's.

(Kekic Collection)

(Illus. 132b.) To the youngsters, this was a highlight.

(Kekic Collection)

(Illus. 132d.) A strange sight to later patrons of Euclid Beach, this OSTRICH FARM dates from 1912. The SCENIC RAILWAY can be faintly discerned in the background.

SURPRISE!

Perhaps illusion was present in every corner of the park, but it showed itself clearly in a number of buildings dedicated to deceiving the senses. Even if these attractions were not rides in the ordinary sense, they certainly took their visitors on a trip. Euclid Beach presented the CRYSTAL MAZE in 1896, as the park introduced a respectable number of new attractions. Little is known of its particulars, but it is assumed that it was a labyrinth of mirrored walls. In 1926 a CRYSTAL MAZE was once again present at the Beach. Billed as a "Hall of Mirrors," the reflections would show visitors as grotesquely fat, misshapen, or pathetically skinny. Not only that, but finding one's way through the attraction demonstrated the real meaning of a "maze." The CRYSTAL MAZE was housed on the southwest corner of the PENNY ARCADE BUILDING.

The urge to innovate brought a significant increase in the inventory of surprises for Euclid Beach visitors for the summer of 1935. Harvey Humphrey was well aware of the past competition presented by Luna Park, which had been located just a short trolley ride away on Cleveland's East side. He planned a FUN-SCIENCE HALL (later renamed the SURPRISE HOUSE), which was due to open that spring and would be in a class all by itself — and certainly surpassing the Fun House previously found at Luna, at least according to Harvey.[45] (Illus. 133.) Indeed, Harvey and electrician-radio enthusiast, George Lister had some innovative plans for the new house of surprises. Together with Howard Stoneback, the Euclid Beach crew had designed quite a few new ways to elicit laughs besides the usual air holes and sliding floors, wobbling staircases and tilted rooms, designed to disorient the senses. (Illus. 134.)

(Illus. 133:) The FUN SCIENCE HALL (later the SURPIRSE HOUSE) design prepared for Euclid Beach Park by the Humphrey Company. Another drawing by Howard Stoneback.

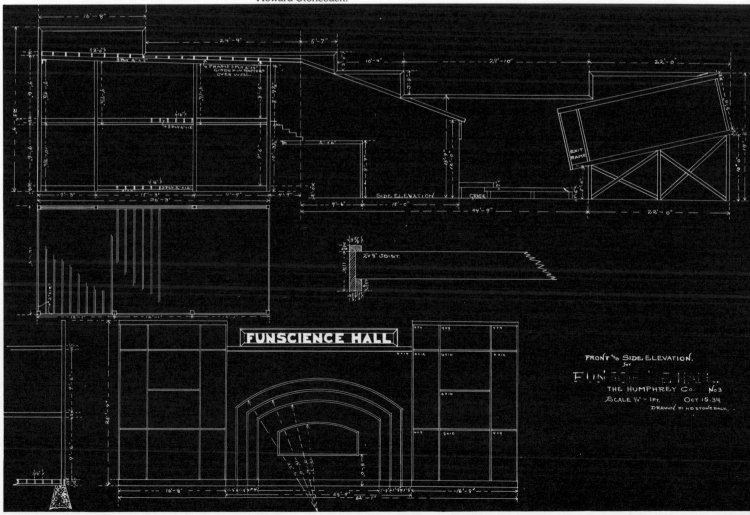

(The Humphrey Company)

A feature never to be realized was a "camera obscura." There was to be a room on the second floor of the SURPRISE HOUSE building in which patrons could see scenes from different areas of the park through means of an early television device. Bill Parker remembers that "you could actually see faint images in this remarkable [pre-T.V.] set."[46] Unfortunately, the enterprise was never completed.

Despite the omission of the television-like apparatus, there were other significant techniques utilized to delight and befuddle those who braved FUNSCIENCE HALL. Most of the displays in the Fun Houses of the period ('20's and '30's) which jumped out at mystified guests, blew up their skirts, shot water at them, or in some way moved to frighten them were triggered by a loose board or, later, an electric eye. Harvey Humphrey had devised a trip-switch based on the body's capacity to conduct electricity. This device did not require a very large flow of current. With the width of the passageway carefully calculated, this switch mechanism could be hidden in the walls at a predetermined height. As each person passed on his perilous way, his body would conduct the necessary modest amount of current and thus set off whatever scare was in store. In the midst of those who visit amusement parks and the Fun Houses within them, are those

with technological aptitudes who try to figure out how everything works. One gentleman was indeed fascinated by the lack of observable switches, electric eyes, and the like. He scoured the entire SURPRISE HOUSE for the secret but was dumbfounded. Near the exit of the wandering pathway was a tree with a hole in it facing the oncoming walkers. As they came by the tree, a large owl darted out at the passers-by, giving them a "hooting" start. By this time in the course of his visit, the inquisitive gentleman was beside himself with curiosity. He witnessed the darting owl and decided to investigate more thoroughly. He climbed up the plaster tree and stuck his head in the opening in an attempt to discover what tripped the darting owl. Unfortunately, as he peered into the hole, a following passer-by tripped the owl mechanism, and the 19 pound plaster bird darted right into the investigating visitor, broke his nose, and sent him sprawling. He never did discern the principle of the switch.

Euclid Beach was indeed free from having any major fires in its seventy-four year history, but there were occasions of near disaster. One such instance comically involved the SURPRISE HOUSE. Bill Parker and another welder had just completed some work on the metal structures at the building's site. Bill, always alert to the danger of wayward sparks, watched and waited until he

(The Humphrey Company)

(Illus. 134a.) The entrance and exit to the SURPRISE HOUSE.

(The Cleveland Press)

(Illus. 134b.) The slanted room, an interesting study in disorienting the senses.

(Illus. 135.) "Laughing Sal" enticed passers-by to come into the SURPRISE HOUSE and join in the laughter.

(The James N. Worgull Collection)

was sure there was no danger of fire. He and his helper then retired to the other side of the SURPRISE HOUSE for some refreshment. In a few short minutes, there was the cry that the SURPRISE HOUSE was on fire. A spark had indeed strayed, and in a short time, black smoke was evident, pouring from a fire escape doorway. The fire department and its accompanying gear arrived in a short period of time. The "warriors against the flame" took up their weapons to quell the blaze. However, as two of the first fire fighters on the scene neared the smokey passageway, they stopped, frozen in their tracks. They turned to Parker for aid — "just what's in there?"[47] Hose at the ready, ax in hand, the "improbable" lay inside — not a preferred path for a smoky Sunday stroll. Bill Parker described the innards of the walkways; the firemen entered and extinguished small, but smoky kindling. The "silent movie" event was over.

Some will remember another SURPRISE HOUSE scene of two portly figures of the laughing lady and the laughing man, tottering up and back in their enclosures at the front of the building. They just stood there laughing away, suggesting the state to be enjoyed upon entering the SURPRISE HOUSE. The guffawing lady was known as "LAUGHING SAL" while the gentleman, who was removed earlier, had remained nameless. *(Illus. 135.)*

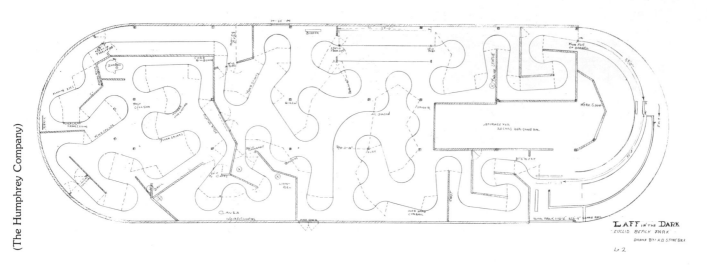

(The Humphrey Company)

(Illus. 136.) The ground plan and layout of Euclid Beach's LAFF-IN-THE-DARK. Remember the ghoul that scared you most?

The facade of the LAFF IN THE DARK pictured an array of goulish figures and monster types. The effect of this painting would stand up under today's most rigid horror standards and was indicative of the ride inside. It was a classic dark ride full of the unexpected and frightening that continued to be effective after repeated visits. The passenger cars were those used on the former WITCHING WAVES remodeled to follow a center track laid on the floor of the building. The motor was fed current from the single track and was housed under an attractive facade at the car's front, decorated with fancy guilded designs. Many will remember these jerking, lurching cars as they wound their way around the meandering path, bumping into doors, monsters, and nearly hitting all sorts of beasts, and, through the use of mirrors, almost hitting themselves. There were the barrel of stars, the enormous sliding spider, and many more such fiendish surprises. (Illus. 136.)

Some persons experienced an unusual visit to the confines of this "horrible" ride. A group was stranded within the building when the ride simply stopped because of mechanical difficulties. House lighting had to be turned on while the imperiled riders were rescued by the ride crew. Sitting motionless in the absolute darkness might have been considered more effective than the displays within the ride.

Special lighting effects incorporating ultraviolet rays and the so-called "black light" were developed by Dudley Humphrey Scott. The ride layout and details of construction were again the result of Stoneback's pencil.

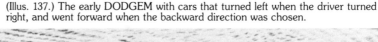

(Illus. 137.) The early DODGEM with cars that turned left when the driver turned right, and went forward when the backward direction was chosen.

(Robert Legan)

117

BEHIND THE WHEEL

Many of the joys found at Euclid Beach Park were based on the premise of participation by the rider. A person could, and would, get directly involved with entertaining himself on the rides and other attractions that functioned as tools or aids in providing pleasure. (Yes, you could sit and observe, but that particular brand of sitting is, also, a lost art.) As most visitors would leave the park at closing time, they would experience the satisfaction of exhaustion due to being an active rather than a passive audience.

The DODGEM provided an excellent example. It did nothing to or for the drivers; the drivers did things with the ride and to each other. The DODGEM sang its own song: the sound of the wheels on the steel floor; the scrape of the trolley on the wire mesh ceiling; the smell of electricity; and, of course, the bump, bang, and thud of rubber padded cars as they veered off one another, the sides of the course, and the center island. Some timid drivers averted collision at all

costs; others aimed for anything near; and yet others stalked an unsuspecting victim in a wily fashion. Oh, if only the streets could have been driven so freely, harmlessly, and so safely.

From 1921 to 1929 the DODGEM used the most unwieldly of cars. They were rather cumbersome-looking affairs which turned left when the driver turned the steering wheel to the right, and went backwards when he attempted to go forward. (Illus. 137.) Indeed everything was backward. These early cars were replaced by new front wheel drive machines in 1930. (Illus. 138.) That summer Euclid Beach featured sixty of the new models from the Dodgem Corporation of Lawrence, Massachusetts. These cars reacted in the expected manner; that is, they went in the direction the drivers wished them to go. Perhaps you remember a voice instructing through a tinny public address system, "Traffic moves one way and one way only, no head on collisions please!" [Sic!].

(Illus. 138.) The later version of the DODGEM which had conventional directional habits. The traffic scene on the back wall mural will be familiar to some.

(Kapel Collection)

(Kekic Collection)

(Illus. 139.) The RED BUG BOULEVARD had battery powered cars that were steered over a wooden course that wound between the SCENIC RAILWAY and the RACING COASTER.

(Illus. 140.) Little drivers maneuvered their cars on RED BUG BOULEVARD.

(Russell Allon Hehr Collection)

119

Even though driving wheeled vehicles was more a part of daily life than flying in various air conveyances, sitting behind the wheel of a car-like mechanism was perenially popular. This popularity was reflected in the aforementioned DODGEM and a number of other Beach favorites. The RED BUG BOULEVARD was a device born of the Custer Specialty Company, authors of the ZOOMER and the BUBBLE BOUNCE. *(Illus. 139.)* This ride featured small battery-driven cars manned usually by one person. The ride had some interesting limitations. The batteries and their frequent recharging (done some distance from the RED BUG BOULE-VARD site) were the source of some consternation. In addition, the cars as originally designed had no front or hood. When ladies in their skirts mounted the vehicles, they were positioned in somewhat of an unladylike posture. This had to be remedied, and Bill Parker set to work. He fashioned a hood piece which not only solved the problem endured by the lady drivers, but made a somewhat innocuous looking vehicle considerably more attractive. *(Illus. 140.)* The RED BUG BOULEVARD lasted until the Thirties when its raised wooden road, which wound through the framework of the RACING COASTER, was replaced by grass. *(Illus. 83.)*

During the last decade of operation, Euclid Beach introduced two more wheeled vehicle rides. The ROLLER RINK was closed and subsequently filled with antique cars in 1962. This attraction, also popular at many parks today, was called ANTIQUE CARS. The Beach's version presented the drivers of these early 1900 type autos with scenes developed in the style of turn-of-the-century architecture.

Another driving ride that indicated the mode of travel popular in the '60's and today was one called the TURNPIKE, installed in 1962 and based on an Arrow Development Corp. design. It was equipped with sports car-like automobiles which traveled over a winding course. It is interesting to note the course was laid out and poured of cement based on a plan by Howard Stoneback for a ride featuring Jeeps as the vehicles. The design was never successfully completed and was adapted for the TURNPIKE. One of the bridge structures survives today in front of a high rise apartment built on the acreage of the former Euclid Beach Park.

RIDING THE RAILS

Transportation of all types was reflected by the ride attractions at the Beach. Trains were very much a part of that reflection. The earliest appearance of a rail-born vehicle was in the early 1900's. *(Illus. 141.)* The train was a product of the Herschell-Spillman works, famous ride builders. (Herschell began his venture into business building boilers and then small locomotives, many of which were used in mining. It was only natural with this background and his amusement device interests that miniature trains would be a product.) The early oval course of the first railroad was south of the CARROUSEL-SCENIC RAILWAY area.

Due to the park's development, the original miniature railroad was phased out. In 1926, Euclid Beach once again had its own railroad. *(Illus. 142.)* This line was stationed across the walkway from the southeastern corner of the COLON-NADE. The SLEEPY HOLLOW LINE, as it was called, traveled around the south end of the MILL CHUTE tunnel, wound in and out among the SCENIC RAILWAY and RACING COASTER timber supports, and turned back to the station at the sight of the RED BUG BOULEVARD'S wooden road. This train, and in particular its locomotive, bore a unique Euclid Beach stamp. Dudley Humphrey Scott designed an alternative to the usual steam power; compressed air. Bill Parker then executed the design and successfully produced a one-of-a-kind attraction. The locomotive, again originally a Herschell-Spillman product, was completely re-engineered by the Beach's shop. Parker built the locomotive so that, if desired, it could also be run by conventional steam power. The compressed air version got its air supply from a tender (made to look like a baggage car) which contained a large air tank and trailed directly behind the engine. This tank held enough compressed air to power the train around its half mile course. The compressor and main tank, located in the MILL CHUTE power house, passed the air through a buried pipe line running to the train station. The engineer merely refilled the tender after each trip, a novelty which brought many riders.

(Illus. 141.) The earliest of the miniature trains at Euclid Beach. The engine bears the mark of the Herschell-Spillman works, who were noted ride builders.

(Kapel Collection)

121

(Robert Legan Collection)

(Illus. 142.) This later remodeled version of the miniature railroad had an engine capable of running on compressed air as well as steam. (c. 1928)

All trains must have some place to go. Where else would the SLEEPY HOLLOW RAILROAD go but the village of Sleepy Hollow? *(Illus. 143.)* After departing the station, the train ran through a tunnel which pierced a "range of mountains." Upon emerging, the passengers witnessed the quiet little village. The details of the village were sculpted, as it were, by Christian Meuer, a wizard with concrete. He fashioned the buildings of Sleepy Hollow village from cement along with many of the other featured details that delighted young and old.

Safety, too, was a prime consideration for the Euclid Beach railroad. An outside rail was fitted on the main rails. On this extra rail ran a set of flanges connected to the locomotive and each car. Although these flanges did not ordinarily touch this safety rail, they prevented derailment before it could occur. This principle was tested on occasion by Bill Parker and his "railroad" crew. After the park closed for the night, explains Bill, they would stoke up the engine and let it run the course at full throttle, unmanned. One night the speed seemed unusually high, and as the train rounded the final curve, they saw the locomotive tottering wildly. Parker thought to himself, "There it goes."[48] It did not jump the track, but it was close. That concluded these somewhat mischievious "trial" runs.

(Illus. 143.) A long time favorite of passengers who rode the tiny railroad was a visit to the village of SLEEPY HOLLOW.

(Kekic Collection)

(Kekic Collection)

(Illus. 144.) The final version of the miniature railroad was the EUCLID BEACH CHIEF, modeled after a modern diesel locomotive. It was the last type to run on the SLEEPY HOLLOW RAILROAD.

As the advent of the diesel came to America's railroads and steam became an enamoured thing of the past, Euclid Beach kept pace and replaced the steam like locomotive with the EUCLID BEACH CHIEF, a replica of the popular diesel engines that began to appear after World War II. *(Illus. 144.)* This train operated until 1969 and was the last train for Sleepy Hollow.

Another familiar train, which, by the way, did not run on rails, was the AUTO TRAIN. *(Illus. 145.)* A product of the Fadgl Bus Company of San Francisco, California, the AUTO TRAIN was brought to the Beach after it served as a touring vehicle at the Panama-Pacific Exposition in California. It was introduced at Euclid Beach shortly after the Humphreys assumed direction of the park. Douglas L. Manning drove the AUTO TRAIN for over forty years; another member of the "Euclid Beach Family." The early train had to be started by crank, recalled Manning in a 1959 statement, and had hard rubber tires and mechanical brakes.[49] Just before World War II, the shop crew equipped the train with a Willy's Jeep engine (replacing the earlier Model T power plant), self starter, inflated tires, and hydraulic brakes. The train symbolized the Beach as it quietly and leisurely roamed the cement walkways about the park and camp grounds. The ride was a relaxing must for many of the park's visitors.

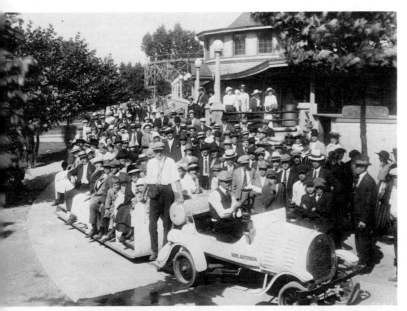

(Illus. 145.) Another train that was a trademark of Euclid Beach was the AUTO TRAIN. It lazily cruised about the park on rubber wheels, here seen about 1908. The DANCE PAVILION and the FIGURE EIGHT roller coaster are in the background.

(Kekic Collection)

SWINGIN'

The use of a suspended device for the act of swinging to and fro or even in a complete circle appeared at Euclid Beach Park in two diverse examples. With the opening of the 1896 season, the park had a set of Herschell-Spillman Park SWINGS. These devices featured a small chariot suspended from a framework by four wires or cables. For the summer of 1964, the Beach presented a set of SWINGIN' GYMS. This attraction was constructed with a number of cages in which the riders, by means of pushing and shoving, attempted to get the cages swinging up and back to such a degree that a complete circle was traversed, and the participants had the feeling of overcoming gravity, at least to an extent.

KIDDIE LAND

Many a youngster's first experience with the world of amusement parks and, in particular with Euclid Beach, started at KIDDIE LAND. *(Illus. 146.)* This feature for the youngest of patrons was housed at the south end of the COLONNADE, which, because of its concrete construction, tended to intensify the sounds of children as they squealed with delight. There was the sound of the little people's CAROUSEL, a model manufactured by W.F. Mangels Company, the KIDDY WHIP, and others. KIDDIELAND emulated the "big park" in many ways as a number of the smaller rides showed the inspiration of their larger prototypes. The KIDDIE CIRCLE SWING had smaller versions of aeroplanes to carry the young pilots. Then, as the large CIRCLE SWING assumed the Rocket Ships design, so did the smaller version in KIDDIE LAND. There was the small FERRIS WHEEL with enclosed passenger compartments that barely cleared the ceiling as the wheel turned. Young sailors steered a circular course in a small BOAT RIDE. Outside and to the

(Kekic Collection)

(Illus. 146-1) KIDDIE CAROUSEL

(Illus. 146 1-9.) For so many people, the KIDDIELAND at Euclid Beach was the beginning of a lifetime of amusement park riding. The first sensations often began with a ride on the KIDDIE CAROUSEL (Mangels), the SWAN SWING, the KIDDIE AEROPLANES (later the KIDDIE ROCKET SHIPS), the KIDDIE FERRIS WHEEL, the KIDDIE WHIP (also by Mangels), a kiddie version of the OVER-THE-FALLS, called the LITTLE MILL, and a selection of auto and horse and buggy rides for the little ones.

125

(Illus. 146-3) KIDDIE SWAN SWING

(Illus. 146-4) KIDDIE AEROPLANES

(Illus. 146-5) KIDDIE ROCKET SHIPS

(Illus. 146-6) KIDDIE PONY TRACK

(Illus. 146-7) KIDDIE AUTO'S

(Illus. 146-8) KIDDIE LITTLE MILL

127

(Illus. 146-9) KIDDIE FERRIS WHEEL

south of the COLONNADE was a Stoneback version of OVER THE FALLS. This ride had an open channel and a very small but fun-producing hill for little passengers. Also outside of the COLONNADE was the PONY TRACK which featured ponies pulling small buggies. Inside was a buggie ride designed, built, and, in part, carved, by H.D. Stoneback. The unique aspect of this ride was that as a circular attraction with small wooden horses pulling buggies, there was no center pole or radial arms. The vehicles ran on a raised wooden platform that concealed the mechanism and gave the ride a very clean appearance.

The horse was always popular at the Beach and KIDDIE LAND. Young cowboys could mount their steeds on a carousel-type ride and with electronic pistols quell the bad guys as they circled the villains.

KIDDIE LAND shared the COLONNADE with a large indoor picnic area and a number of concessions. It was the perfect place for parents to sit and sip coffee, eat a hot dog (or whatever

their favorite might be), and watch their proud offsprings delight in the marvelous devices put in KIDDIE LAND just for them.

The staff of KIDDIE LAND had in its number many golden agers who watched the youngest visitors to Euclid Beach play and ride. It seemed proper that these senior citizens (like Grace Williams, George Albright, Archibald Dick, and one-time KIDDIE LAND manager James Sheehan) should attend that part of the park dedicated to the youngest citizens.

Just as growing children progressed from the smaller rides to larger ones and finally to any the Beach had to offer, the same progression held true for employees. Many new workers were broken in at KIDDIE LAND and gradually moved into positions in the "big park"

It would seem that those joys discovered in KIDDIE LAND did not really change, but the tools used to elicit those joys merely changed in size and scope.

(The Western Reserve Historical Society)

(Illus. 147.) The SUN TAN LINKS, a miniature golf course located near the COLONNADE. The course was popular in the 1920's.

GAMES PEOPLE PLAYED

There was indeed a place for the athletically inclined to demonstrate their prowess at Euclid Beach Park. In 1926, outdoor dancing was attempted on a poured cement patio north of the DANCE PAVILION. This idea did not prove successful and was curtailed. In its place, TABLE TENNIS was instituted, and SHUFFLE BOARD COURTS were laid out. From time to time, table tennis or ping pong tournaments were hosted at the Beach. The brightly lit courts amid the Sycamores presented a picture many will remember.

Golf, too, was represented at Euclid Beach. In 1930, the SUN TAN LINKS was advertised. This miniature golf course was, at that time, operated by The Florida Landscape Company, and the course was located southeast of the COLONNADE, near the site of the later miniature railroad station and just behind the power shed of the FLYING PONIES. *(Illus. 147.)*

The SUN TAN LINKS was removed, but miniature golf persisted at the park in the form of PEE WEE miniature golf for which Stoneback drew up the plans in 1949. *(Illus. 148.)* The Humphrey Company built this attractive course located just to the east of the MAIN OFFICE front porch and to the south of the AVENUE THEATRE building and the BUG. *(Illus. 149.)* It was a delightful course featuring 18 holes, plenty of shade from trees, and cool breezes off the lake. The course was divided into two segments which were connected by a foot bridge that crossed a park walkway. From this vantage point, the whole course could be surveyed along with the adjoining parts of the park. A study could be made of the reactions of the golfers as they tallied their scores and proclaimed the champions. It was just another facet of the enjoyment available at Euclid Beach Park. (Located across Lake Shore Blvd. on the south side, was a PAR-THREE, CHIP and PUTT golf course and a DRIVING RANGE.)

129

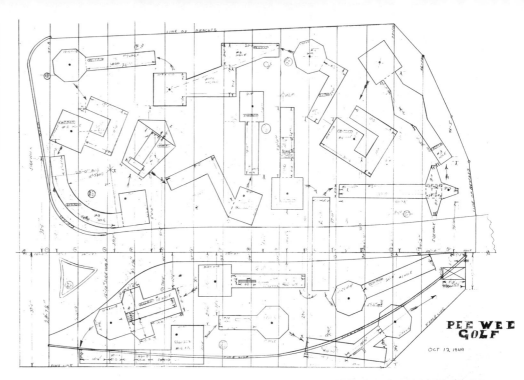

(The Humphrey Company)

PEE WEE GOLF

OCT 12 1949

(Illus. 148.) The ground plan for the PEE WEE golf course. This miniature course was popular with visitors until the park closed.

(Illus. 149b.) Trying to be below par on the miniature golf course. Even in this 1969 picture, the soft shade under the many trees is a prevalent part of the vista. The AVENUE THEATRE and ANNEX are behind the course.

(Lee O. Bush Collection)

(James P. Marcus Collection)

(Illus. 149a.) The PEE WEE golf course looking toward the OFFICE with the LAKE LUNCH on the right beyond the trees.

In buildings immediately west of the COLON-NADE were the SKEE-BALL machines, products of the National Skee-Ball Company, Coney Island, New York. Two models of the Skee-Ball machine were represented: a moderate-size example, a number of which lined the walls that ran the length of the room; and a larger example, arrayed along the entire south wall. A small change booth was situated in the center of the room where the aspiring players could obtain a supply of nickles. A careful bead was drawn on the center hole, and the game was on to register the highest score. The only danger to be found in this pavilion was addiction to playing SKEE-BALL.

(Russell Allon Hehr Collection)

(Illus. 149c.) The great American pastime, baseball, was popular at the Beach. The ball field was located near the later site of the THRILLER.

130

A PENNY FOR SOME FUN

Among the necessities of an amusement park, such as a carousel, a roller coaster, and the like, is a Penny Arcade. This special place housed the most fascinating of mechanical devices which, when grouped, created a separate and unique world. Euclid Beach had its own special corner dedicated to one-penny fun. Its PENNY ARCADE was located in the southwest corner of the cluster of adjacent buildings that housed the ROLLER RINK, the MAIN LUNCH, and the transfer platform of the AERO DIPS (previously the site of the FIGURE EIGHT). *(Illus. 150.)*

The prototype of the Penny Arcade, as it has been known over the last half century, was preceeded by "arcades" or "parlors" featuring picture-showing apparatus developed by Thomas Edison. These "drop-card" machines furnished the viewer a pictured story with accompanying music which fell into the category of "Automatic Vaudeville." The groups of picture-/sound devices comprised an attraction called "Edisonia." Plat maps of Cleveland show that a building labeled "THE EDISON" existed at Euclid Beach in 1897 on the site of the later PENNY ARCADE. Still-picture presentations, probably utilizing Edison techniques, were, in that same year, advertised at Euclid Beach Park. (The Edisonia were furnished with drop card/cylinder record machines manufactured by Edison or Mills Novelty Company of Chicago, Illinois.) Thus it would seem that a small, long rectangular building located to the southeast of the DANCE PAVILION was the predecessor of the PENNY ARCADE.

The PENNY ARCADE at the Beach was largely developed into a successful attraction by William Gent. This concession was one of the few not owned by the Humphrey Company. It was run under a long term lease. After Mr. Gent's death in the early Thirties, the PENNY ARCADE was then directed by his son William Gent, Jr., and consequently remained a leased attraction until his death in the late Fifties. At this time, it reverted to the Humphrey Company. In the spirit that pervaded the park, the PENNY ARCADE was successfully developed by the dedication of its directors, the Gents.

(Illus. 150.) On the walkway between the DANCE PAVILION and the PENNY ARCADE. The twin umbrellas shade the ARMY/NAVY SCALE.

(Kekic Collection)

131

(Illus. 151a.) A penny to witness unlimited adventure and romance. Here a group of entranced viewers patronize a line of "Iron Horses."

(The Cleveland Press)

(The Cleveland Plain Dealer)

(Illus. 151b.) A young lady views an adventure while a couple considers the prophecy of the GRANDMOTHER, William Gent's own machine.

The years 1905, 1906 and 1907 seem to have been significant times for arcade development. It was in those years that the Mills Novelty Company launched many new devices into full production. From the early part of the century on, the PENNY ARCADE at Euclid Beach was a popular gathering point for fun seekers, young and old.

By the 1930's, the arcade housed a significant selection of penny-operated machines. There were nearly thirty-five "DIGGERS" arrayed along the walls of the Arcade with some by the entrances to entice customers. A penny put into a DIGGER (known as the "Iron Claw" and built by the Exhibit and Supply Co.) gave the eager, but temporary operator the chance to procure "fabulous" treasure as the patron encouraged the claw to grasp a desired item with the derrick-type device.

132

Along the south wall of the PENNY ARCADE, near the entrance to the ROLLER RINK, were a number of hand-crank operated visual machines. Turn the crank and witness a story of love, tragedy, adventure, or comedy unfold. The devices were the product of International Mutoscope Reel Co., Inc., New York City, and were known to some as the "Iron Horse." *(Illus. 151.)*

Pictures of "untold beauty" or "fantastic treasures" were not the only items presented at the PENNY ARCADE. If one's life had been lonely and romance absent, a love letter could be procured from "Cupid's Post Office" (Mills Novelty Co.) for only a penny! With that encouragement, one could have his or her amorous ability gauged by the LOVE TESTER (Exhibit and Supply Co.). Patriots could patronize the UNCLE SAM GRIP MACHINE and grip the great Uncle's hand (A Caille Brothers machine). Mill's or Roover's PUSS-N-BOOTS could tell your future, or, if you preferred, your palm could be read by a penny machine, a product of Mutoscope. The brave and strong could withstand electric shock administered by another Mills Novelty product. (Electricity was thought to have great therapeutic qualities in the Teens and Twenties of this century.) For the sports minded, there were baseball, football, hockey, and soccer game machines, and, if your tastes ran to the more strenuous challenges, there was boxing. There were also various strikers and hand grips to test the strength of the visitor. Certainly by the time a thorough tour had been taken at the PENNY ARCADE, an individual would know all there was to know about his physical prowess, personal destiny, and ability to conduct electricity. What more could be asked?

The summer of 1930 found a line of would-be weight watchers waiting to mount the ARMY & NAVY SCALE. Henry Prekel came to work at the SCALE in that year. *(Illus. 152.)* As a scale boy (a starting position at the PENNY ARCADE) Henry remembers Mr. Gent, the director, encouraging him to move quickly. Time was money then, too, and a bit more scarce. The ARMY & NAVY SCALE was situated just outside the west door of the ARCADE, and many significant people came to be weighed. In 1935 members of the Cleveland Indians and other noted baseball teams came to Euclid Beach as the Major League All-Star game was being held in Cleveland. Mr. Preckel remembers weighing these distinguished players as being one of his greatest thrills.

Bill Gent, Sr., understood the principles of what is now called marketing. Two ingredients were his stock and trade: 1. the lure of the machines; and 2. the pennies. The machines were idle if the customers were short of the copper. Gent instituted the "penny boy" who roved the ARCADE selling pennies. With the proper chant, "Change, pennies for sale," the young boys sold the coins for a commission. Twenty-five pounds of pennies were worth forty-four dollars and forty cents. If a penny boy sold that amount, he made one dollar and eighty cents, approximately four percent commission.

(Henry Prekel)

(Illus. 152.) Henry Prekel (left) and friends at the ARMY/NAVY SCALE, located in front of the PENNY ARCADE.

In 1933, nickel games were introduced, and a legal technicality came into play. Playing the machines for prizes at the cost of a nickel constituted gambling. To circumvent this, Gent had boys circulating with modest prizes which were awarded to anyone who did not win something while playing the nickel devices. No gambling in this park!

133

One of the most aesthetic machines was called the "GRANDMOTHER." This was a product of Gent's own machine shop (Wm. Gent Vending Machine Co. 830-850 East 93rd St., Cleveland, Ohio).[50] *(Illus. 151.)* Built in the Twenties, the GRANDMOTHER featured a beautiful wax head made in Dresden, Germany, by the makers of the famous Dresden Dolls. Good old GRAND-MOTHER moved her eyes, head, bosom (to simulate breathing), passed her hand over a set of cards, and dispensed the "future" of the patron on a pre-printed card. These mechanisms are regarded as some of the most finely produced in the industry.

Gent also developed a special type of shooting gallery in the early Thirties. It featured electric-eye type guns which were aimed at figures and appliances in a kitchen scene. If the proper spot was hit by the beam, one of the figures performed a task, or an appliance performed its proper function. This gallery was never mass produced, but the prototype did have a short stay at the Beach.

The personnel of the PENNY ARCADE included the penny boys, the scale boy (who weighed the patron and wrote the weight and date on a card), and floor attendants whose duty was to aid anyone not receiving proper service and tending to recalcitrant machines. In the Thirties, a scale boy worked for seven hours a day, seven days a week. His wage was sixteen cents an hour. Floor attendants worked for twenty cents an hour and, with a little seniority, would make twenty-five cents an hour and have one day off per week.

Intrigue and mystery were also present at the PENNY ARCADE. A safe was kept in the back office for obvious reasons. For a period in the mid-Thirties, sums of money turned up missing the morning after they were placed in the safe. Surveillance went on, but no one could detect the thief. For a considerable period of time, attempts were made to solve the mystery. A custodian had noticed a number of holes drilled in the floor of the office in front of the safe. A mechanic also noted the rearrangement of some of the stock kept in the back room. Investigation was prompted when noise was detected under the office floor. A thorough search revealed a cut in the floor, an underground passage, and a room dug under the office complete with a table and chair. Apparently, the culprit observed the combination of the safe as it was opened and closed and came up to pilfer the loot. Subsequently, alarms were set to snare the thief, but he never reappeared — nor did the missing money!

(The Cleveland Plain Dealer)

(Illus. 152a.) Two young patrons about to inquire into the future with the aid of the GRANDMOTHER.

The PENNY ARCADE was yet another facet of Euclid Beach Park. A place to test your luck, watch one of the visual machines, or just listen to the interplay of sounds from these distinctive devices, it was another special world within a special world.

Euclid Beach Park offered something for everyone when it came to the rides and related attractions: from the classic roller coaster (the THRILLER) to its PENNY ARCADE; from its CRYSTAL MAZE to its DODGEM; from its collection of glorious carousels to the splash of its OVER THE FALLS. An entire family could play miniature golf while the most daring could brave the FLYING TURNS. Most of all, every visitor could participate. Each ride could be the vehicle of the individual's fantasies or just the tool of outright fun. Each ride, attraction, and its attendant mechanisms were constantly watched, and the highest safety standards were adhered to by the park's crews. It was the Beach's policy not only to present the widest array of attractions but to insure as much as possible that they were safe.

134

Chapter 5
Clean up, Paint up,
Fix up, Keep up

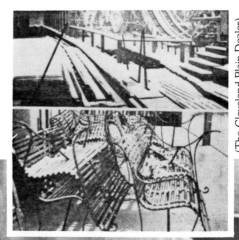

(The Cleveland Plain Dealer)

(Illus. 153.) Anticipating the next season, the horses wait patiently, covered against the snow.

Perhaps it was the best job in the world, and maybe it was not, but, of course, that would depend on one's point of view. To crawl over every inch, examine every nail, board, bolt, and section of track belonging to one of the roller coasters at Euclid Beach may seem unduly risky, or one heck of a lot of fun, depending on the priorities. To men like Fred Greenway, employed by the Humphrey Company since 1924, it was HIS job, and, like many of his fellow workers of long time standing, or even short timers, it was more than just a job. Every year each board on all the high-rides at the park was carefully examined, as great care was taken to safeguard against structural deficiencies. The cars that comprised the roller coaster trains were scrutinized and frequently spent much of the winter being completely overhauled. Carousel horses were carefully covered while others were repainted. *(Illus. 153.)* Mechanisms were examined and failing parts replaced. Everything had to be in order. The safety and enjoyment of the park visitor was at stake, and there was no compromise on that subject. The Humphreys, from the time of their initial direction of the park in 1901, were preoccupied with the priority of good maintenance.

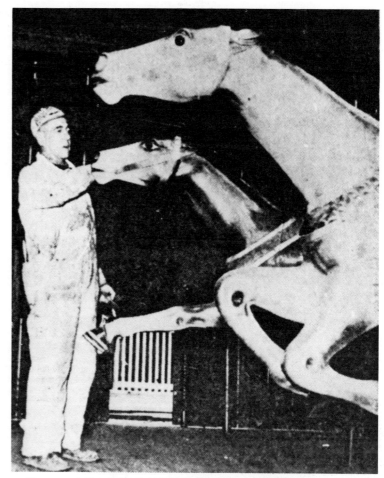

(Illus. 153a.) The GREAT AMERICAN RACING DERBY horses being painted by Edward Kent.

(The Cleveland Press)

(Illus. 153b.) Maintenance of every description kept a year-round crew constantly active.

(The Cleveland Press, The Cleveland Plain Dealer)

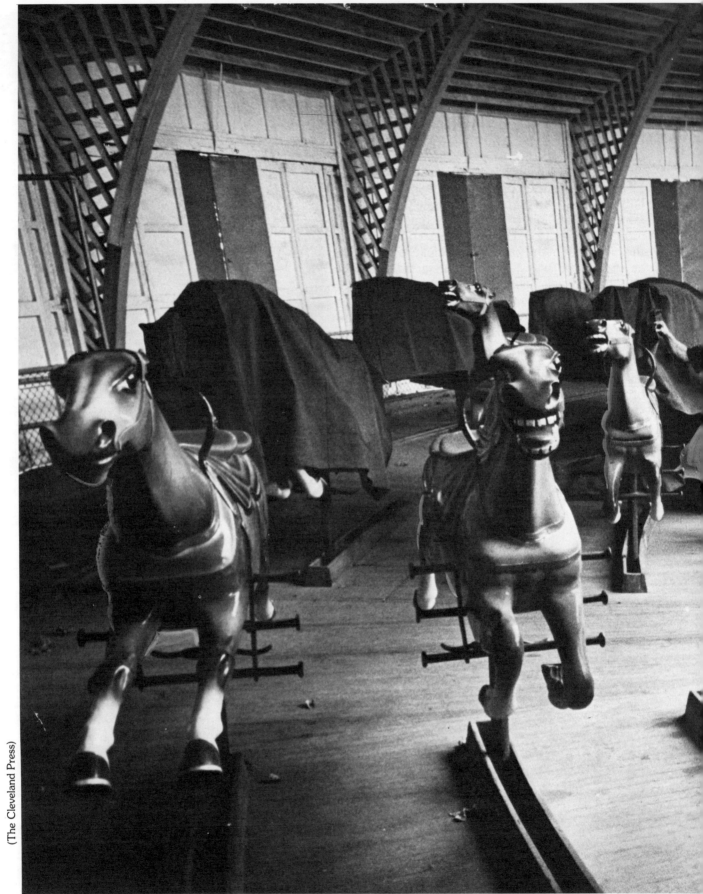

(The Cleveland Press)

137

(Illus. 153c.) Walter Williams, Euclid Beach perennial, covers the stilled racing steeds of the GREAT AMERICAN RACING DERBY in the fall of 1938. They will await the next season and the rush and whirl of the coming spring. (Inset) The brush of Mr. Kent refurbishes the proud horses.

A tradition was formed by those who were in charge of the making sure every detail was right. William J. Maclevie joined the Humphreys at Euclid Beach in 1905; then Howard Stoneback came to the park in 1923 to work with Maclevie and stayed until 1959. At that time, E.P. Hudson took over until the closing of the park. The surveillance of the cables supporting the ROCKET SHIPS was a frequent occurence, and Bill Parker went to the highest elevation of the ride to check every detail. *(Illus. 154.)* (The original cables, replaced in the early '60's, were found to be as good as new.) Every ride manager and attendant was encouraged to spend some of his relief time listening to and inspecting the rides on which they worked. The morning of each day the park was open, the tracks of each of the roller coasters were "walked" by maintenance men and carefully inspected. Before any passengers rode them, a train loaded with sandbags was sent out to make sure the structure and vehicles were in proper order. The barrel of the FLYING TURNS was "walked" by Fred Greenway and his crew, and dummy trains were then sent through the course. A familiar scene in the 1960's was Greenway and a crew made up of Al Jacklitz, Harry Krause, and Bob "Bugs" Vogel taking a test run in the THRILLER, a precaution exercised just prior to the park's daily opening.

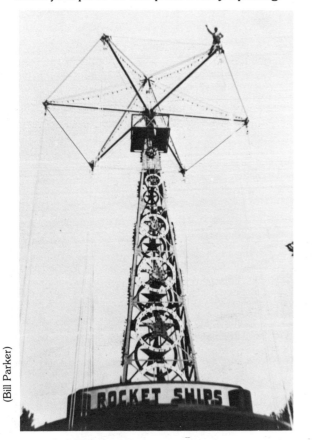

(Illus. 154.) "Wild" Bill Parker demonstrates some justification for his nickname. Here he performs his routine check of the cables on the ROCKET SHIP ride.

(Bill Parker)

There were numerous occasions when the work of the maintenance men was made more difficult than usual. During World War II, items such as steel were almost unobtainable. The strap-steel rails (1/8″ by 1″) on which the roller coaster trains ran showed signs of wear periodically and had to be replaced. The resourcefulness of the Euclid Beach personnel was present to accomplish the necessary adjustments. Howard Stoneback reasoned that the majority of wear was accumulated at the bottoms of the various dips on each of the park's coasters since it was at this point that the gravitational force was greatly multiplied. Stoneback merely suggested switching the rails from the tops of the inclines, where the amount of wear was least, to the bottoms, and vice versa. He was recognized by the National Association of Amusement Parks for his suggestion, which, more than likely, kept many a roller coaster in operation during the war.

Many seemingly simple discoveries were also made by the maintenance crew men at the Beach. Since the dawn of the roller coaster, painting the structure was common procedure. This practice was costly and time consuming. By 1930, Euclid Beach had five coasters and a great deal of regular painting to do. After a careful look at the principles involved, a basic but astounding conclusion was drawn. It was astounding in that the recommendation was simple; do no painting at all. Why? Paint on the framework was deteriorated by the forces of weather, principally rain and snow. Logic illuminated the fact that the upper surface of the paint went first, then the sides, and finally, if at all, the bottom. Obviously, the paint had acted as a containing property rather than deterent to the accumulation of moisture. The opposite of the desired effect was being accomplished. Conclusion: do not paint. The wooden structure of the FLYING TURNS was never painted and, in turn, never showed extensive signs of deterioration. *(Illus. 96.)* The only portion of the FLYING TURNS regularly painted was the course the trains followed through the barrel. Grey deck paint was applied frequently which kept deterioration of the Cypress barrel to a minimum.

High-rides, due to their massive wood construction and complexity, required a great deal of care. *(Illus. 155.)* Fortunately, coasters proved to be among the greatest money makers in any park. Besides the daily safety checks, the roller coasters of Euclid Beach demanded a good bit of special daily attention. Train No. 4 of the THRILLER was equipped with a small lubrication tank which oiled the track of the entire ride. Each day, No. 4 was sent forth to ready the course. The same procedure was applied to the other coasters also, with the exception of the SCENIC RAILWAY. (Its flanged wheel arrangement did not require an oiled track.)

Listening to the rides in operation was important since sound was often the best medium for the detection of a malfunction or its beginnings. Bill Parker reiterated such an example. Upon entering his home (located near the back stretch of the THRILLER) at lunch time, his wife greeted him with the opinion that the coaster had an unusual sound. Bill listened and hurriedly made his way to the ride. Indeed, part of the track on which the friction wheels ran was beginning to work loose. Many instances of would-be danger were averted by the detection of sounds which were not usual.

Even though the running season of Euclid Beach Park was basically three months long with week-ends and a few assorted special days before and after the primary season, the wear and tear on the rides can be easily understood in terms of their capacity. The THRILLER could carry up to 800 riders per hour; the LAFF IN THE DARK up to 300 per hour; the RACING COASTER 72 passengers per trip; while the DODGEM could handle 100 per ride. This represented a lot of traffic; many of the days throughout the history of the Beach there were close to capacity crowds.

(Illus. 155.) High ride maintenance performed by the Euclid Beach crews on the RACING COASTER. (Inset) Fred Greenway at the top of the THRILLER'S first hill.

(The Cleveland Plain Dealer / The Cleveland Press)

(The Cleveland Press / The Cleveland Plain Dealer)

(Illus. 155a.) The most demanding maintenance was to be found on the high rides. Not only did the crews climb the many structures, but they tested them personally. This was not always unpleasant. Seen here are: Bob Vogel, Harry Krause, Fred Greenway, and Al Jacklitz.

Sometimes the functional peculiarities of one ride would provide maintenance men with aggravating recurrences. The GREAT AMERICAN RACING DERBY could rotate at a very stimulating speed, which was proper, since the ride emulated the fastest of steeds. However, on occasion, there was a failing. The large circular platform was driven by a cable which ran on the edge of the platform under ground level which fit into a slot cut in the maple edge of the revolving platform. As the ride whirled, the lubricant which was present in all cables would work into this slot causing slippage and, consequently, slowing of the ride. Walter Williams remembered that tightening that cable was an all-too-frequent duty.

With the massive numbers of possible malfunctions and routine maintenance, the job of keeping up the park was a twenty-four-hour-a-day responsibility during the operating season. The task of upkeep was also a matter of pride. Bill Parker watched the BUG constantly and would not allow a gap to exist between the rail and its supporting framework such as he had witnessed at other parks he visited. *(Illus. 156.)* Every step was taken to keep supports and foundations secure.

Ironically, the pursuance of safety often led to being pursued by danger. On one occasion, the FLYING TURNS was being serviced, and one of the cars became lodged at the top of the chain-

141

pull. A crew of men including Bob "Bugs" Vogel went aloft to remedy the fault. The train was dislodged, and the men proceeded to push it down the barrel. The first few hills were very shallow, and the train loped gently over these smaller hills. As speed was gained, the crew members bade the train on its way. An inexperienced member of that crew neglected to free himself and now clung to the outside of the accelerating group of cars. Observing this and the possible result, Vogel chased the train and caught it at the last possible instant. As the cars moved along the course, the twists and turns became quite violent. Carefully moving from the last of the three cars to the first, where the endangered worker clung to the gyrating vehicle, Vogel got close enough to pull the alienated rider into the seat. This required a great deal of strength and was accomplished none too soon. In another instant, the train would have reached the "crowd brake" that stopped the momentum of the ride, and the threatened worker would have been bashed to death. Even after the harrowing experience, the neophyte had not realized the extent of his peril. His inappropriate comment was that Vogel need not have bothered.

Not only did every mechanical device have to be in top form, but the appearance of the park had to reflect the mood of the Humphrey policy: clean, neat, conservative. One former employee stated that no matter what color was to be applied to a structure, the result would probably be green. No gaudy look insulted the eyes at Euclid Beach Park; the soft and quiet atmosphere that spread throughout the park was, in part, due to the lack of garish color schemes. Paint shop men such as Jim Burton, Ted Kent, and Gene Vehr kept things preened properly. Whether it be a park bench or a magnificent Philadelphia Toboggan horse on the CARROUSEL, it was a reflection of the pride the Humphrey Company and its crews took in "their" park.

There were instances, though, which showed that fine maintenance, a beautiful facility, and constant warning were not sufficient to avert disaster. Over the seventy-four years of operation, and in particular those years since 1901, a very small number of accidents took place. The THRILLER, because of its speed, height, and popularity, received the Lion's share of mishaps.

Some of the problems that were attributed to the THRILLER were humorous. A group of young lads from a boys club in Detroit came to the park and were very taken with the big coaster. After each trip they would gather, exchange impressions, and gallop back on the ride. After one particular ride, a boy riding near the front of the train yelled to the attendant that his companion fell out of the coaster car. At first, the crew man felt he was being fooled, but the boy quickly drew his attention to the vanished rider's shoes. There they were, side by side on the floor, without an occupant. Park men and the Beach's police went to the supposed scene of the tragedy. There, somewhat shaken, lay a battered young man whose first words to the policeman were, "What happened?" What had indeed happened was that this rider stood up as the THRILLER train rounded the far turn near the front of the park. A rider behind him gave the standing lad a healthy jab in the ribs and literally tickled the boy out of the train, over the guard rail and three high tension wires, and into a Sycamore where he bounced from branch to branch until he reached the ground. This broke his fall and saved his life.

Others who ignored the "Do Not Stand Up" signs were not so lucky. One gentleman decided to flaunt gravity and centrifugal force at the last curve of the THRILLER as the train turned for home. He fell from the car, his head hit the posts that hold up the guard rail, and he was killed. Another accident at the same location furnished a foolish rider with a humiliating experience. By standing up, he fell out of the car and skidded along the guard rail for some distance. He was not

(Illus. 156.) Bill Parker tends to another of his charges, the BUG. No structural defect would be permitted on this popular ride.

(Bill Parker)

142

seriously injured but accumulated a substantial collection of slivers. To his sorrow he discovered it was considerably easier and more comfortable to remain seated - and more fun, too.

The RACING COASTER also had its share of those who were skeptical of safety precautions. John Stoneback related an incident which occurred during a Collinwood Picnic in the 20's. Two recent high school graduates, occupying each of the two RACING COASTER trains, decided to stand, reach out, and clasp hands as the trains vied for position. The proximity of the trains was not always close. One of the boys fell from his seat, was dragged a distance by the cars, and then fell down through the framework of the coaster. He died soon afterwards. Most accidents which occur at amusement parks and which did occur at Euclid Beach were the fault of the patrons - people who find it impossible to abide by rules, even if those rules mean their lives.

It was the policy of the Humphrey Company to keep public attention paid to accidents to a minimum. One July day in 1943 the Beach experienced two accidents, one on the THRILLER, and one near closing time at the AERO DIPS. A fully loaded train of the small AERO DIPS coaster rushed through the loading station unbraked and failed to negotiate the sharp turn as the ride's course commenced again. The cars were derailed, and there were numerous injuries. Despite the lateness of the hour, the park was quite crowded, and the realization that an accident had occurred brought the curious to inspect the scene. Before a crowd could gather, the area was cordoned off, the injured were removed, and the reassembling of the platform and damaged train began. Bill Parker, Dave Scott, and other crew members worked throughout the night. The toppled fence the careening train had flattened was made upright, the platform restored, and repairs to the wayward train applied. A bit of dust was added to the cement, and a special batch of faded paint was mixed. Therefore, the concrete work looked as if it had not been recently done, and the repainted surfaces did not have a fresh look. By 9:00 A.M. the following morning, the area at the AERO DIPS loading zone appeared undisturbed. Curious visitors had begun to gravitate to the accident site quite early the next day but were confounded by what they found — nothing irregular. The principle was simple: stories circulated freely about one ride or another, this catastrophy or that tragedy. A factual story of a roller coaster accident involving more than a few people could progress by irrational stages to: "twenty deaths as the whole coaster train fell

from the highest elevation and hundreds were crushed while the entire park burst into flames and the dawn of the world's end was upon us." (Exaggerated rumors grow more quickly than weeds in a vegetable garden. The fact that fewer accidents occur on amusement park rides than happen in the kitchens of private homes means nothing. For the patron to fully enjoy the park and have confidence in the extensive safety precautions means a deemphasis by park management of the infrequent mishaps that are, by and large, unavoidable.)

Keeping a busy facility like the Beach neat and clean was no mean task. To aid in this consideration, a huge vacuum cleaner to clean the park was introduced by Dudley Scott in the late Twenties. *(Illus. 157.)* The details were executed by Bill Parker — one of his first assignments. When the dirt-greedy vehicle was finished, it picked up

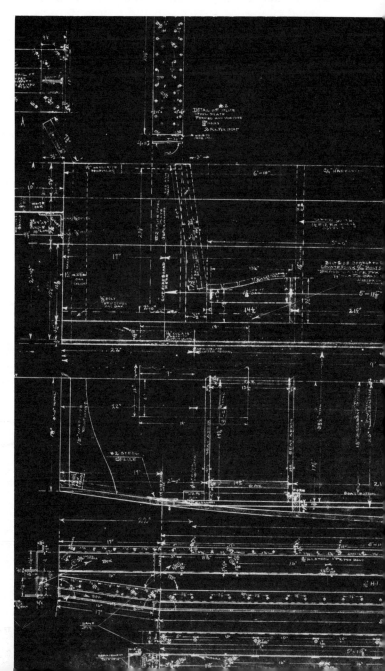

everything from a loose hair to good sized stones. Having an appearance not at all reminiscent of an Italian sports car, the monsterish machine was effective, but complicated to operate. Unfortunately, Bill was relegated the exclusive task of driving the vacuum since he was the only one who could handle the eleven levers required to manipulate it.

(Illus. 157.)
The big vacuum cleaner was one of Bill Parker's first projects when he came to the park. It was designed by Dudley Scott and built with the expertise of Mr. Parker.

(Amusement Park Management - National Association of Amusement Parks)

(The Humphrey Company)

(Illus. 158.) The depth of detail can be seen on the working drawing of the new OVER-THE-FALLS boat as designed by Howard Stoneback.

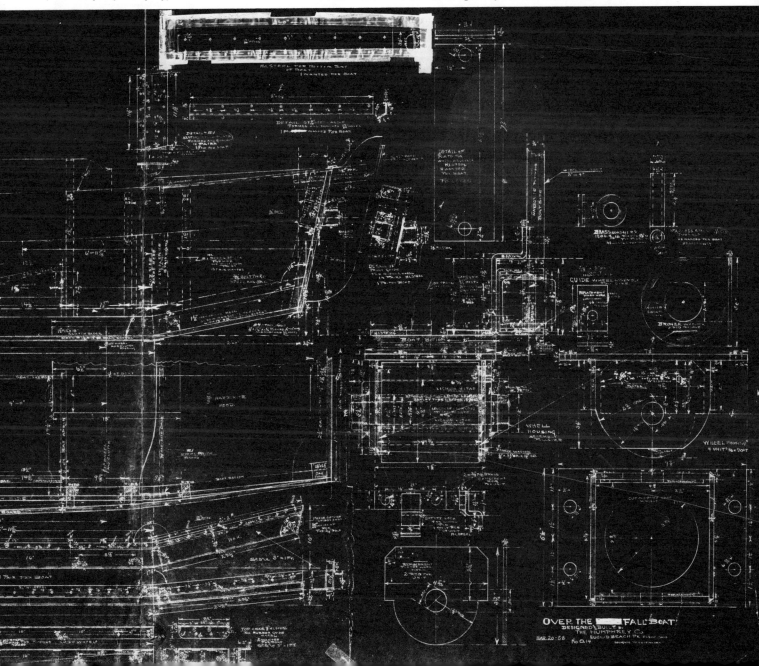

Keeping up meant not only maintaining status quo, but keeping up with the progress of the industry and, if possible, setting trends. The Beach excelled in both of these. The FLYING TURNS was a revolutionary ride and was, in part, a Humphrey venture. The compressed air miniature locomotive, the redesigned platform on the ROCKET SHIPS, not to mention the gleaming silver ships themselves, were highly innovative and superbly executed additions to the amusement park industry.

The MILL CHUTE was a popular ride throughout its history, but the crew and management of Euclid Beach redesigned it into a water ride that would deliver more excitement. The resulting OVER THE FALLS (1937) was almost completely a Euclid Beach product. The initial layout was by Perce Killaly, the fine design and execution by Howard Stoneback. In 1959, it was decided that new boats should be designed for OVER THE FALLS. The drawings for these boats are remarkable in themselves and reflect Stoneback's scope and knowledge. *(Illus. 158.)* Every detail of design was carefully considered except one. As a perfectionist, he wanted the boats to move through the channel with the slightest possible tolerance. As the crews readied the park for the spring of 1959, the cracks in the concrete channel caused by winter temperatures were patched, which at some points narrowed the path by too great a margin. The newly constructed boats were tested, and the very first one jammed. The patched cracks restricted its course. This failure was probably one of Stoneback's greatest disappointments. As a perfectionist, it was an unthinkable and intolerable event. He died shortly thereafter and was succeeded by Ed Hudson, a former assistant. The boats were subsequently reduced in width which then allowed them to clear the channel and carry passengers until their last voyage in 1969.

During the summers, the manpower of Euclid Beach Park stood at more than 400 employees. The winter put 70 full time men to work, while primping for the spring opening called for 30 additional employees as the park would prepare for yet another season. This primping process took about six weeks to insure the proper spring opening and furnish the public with what it took for granted inside the gates of Euclid Beach.

(Illus. 158a-1)   (Lee O. Bush Collection)

(Illus. 158a-2)   (Dr. Philip J. Kaplow Collection)

(Illus. 158a-3)   (Dr. Philip J. Kaplow Collection)

(Illus. 158a. 1-7) The alumni of workers from the Beach will remember many of the ride controls and mechanisms, from the FLYING TURNS brake station (A1), ROCKET SHIP controls (A2), and gears (A4), to the BUG operating switches (A3), to the BUBBLE BOUNCE elevating pumps (A5). Of course there was Josephine Walter to tend to human maintenance (A6). The ROCK-O-PLANE receives its share of attention (A7).

(Illus. 158a-4)   (Richard F. Hershey Collection)

(Illus. 158a-5)   (Bill Parker)

(Illus. 158a-6)   (Russell Allon Hehr Collection)

(The Cleveland Press)

(Illus. 158a-7)

**"On with the dance! Let joy be uncon-
fined."**[51]

The joy was indeed unconfined as couples
swayed and shuffled to the sweet sounds of their
favorite bands; the era of ballroom dancing was
richly represented at Euclid Beach Park. Perhaps
no single attraction holds more memories than
the DANCE PAVILION, even though the cool
lake breezes that swept across it are but a faint
remembrance and the dance orchestra's
rhythms a mere echo. *(Illus. 159.)*

Chapter 6
A light fantastic trip

(Russell Allon Hehr Collection)

(Illus. 159.) Early scene showing the DANCE PAVILION as depicted on a postcard,
looking to the Northeast. This picture pre-dates the installation of the BUG.

(The Humphrey Company)

(Illus. 159a.) The expansive dance floor that hosted many a "light-fantastic trip."
Note the north bandstand area and the enlarged east-end orchestra area. Note the
"drum" shaped lighting, mirrored balls, and painted ceiling. (c. 1927)

The DANCE PAVILION was one of the few buildings on the park's acreage to remain throughout its history from 1895 to 1969. The revered BALLROOM stood as a center for park activity during much of its existence. Apart from being a major attraction at Euclid Beach, it held somewhat of an autonomous position, in that many patrons came to the park for only one reason, to dance. It was a landmark within a landmark.

A park booklet of 1899 tells of the early PAVILION DANCE HALL:

> The dancing Hall in the main Pavilion is one of the most attractive and interesting places in Euclid Beach Park. The dimensions are 90 x 190 feet and will accommodate 2,000 dancers and spectators. Hard wood and well waxed floor invites the young and old to join the merry dance, keeping time to the stirring music rendered by the orchestra on the stage. Commodious balconies entirely surrounding the pavilion give a pleasant promenade and resting place from which to watch the dancers.[52] *(Illus. 8.)*

It is interesting to note that the stage, or "bandstand," of the PAVILION DANCE HALL during the early seasons was originally constructed near floor level at the west end of the building. *(Illus. 8 - 159a.)* The location of the orchestra's "stage" was consequently shifted a number of times. It finally was located back at its original position.

148

(The Humphrey Company)

(Illus. 160.) Dancing to the melodies of John Kirk's Orchestra. The band is on the balcony level on the north side of the PAVILION. Early lighting is evident. (pre-1907)

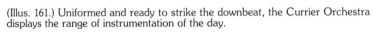

(Illus. 161.) Uniformed and ready to strike the downbeat, the Currier Orchestra displays the range of instrumentation of the day.

(The Humphrey Company)

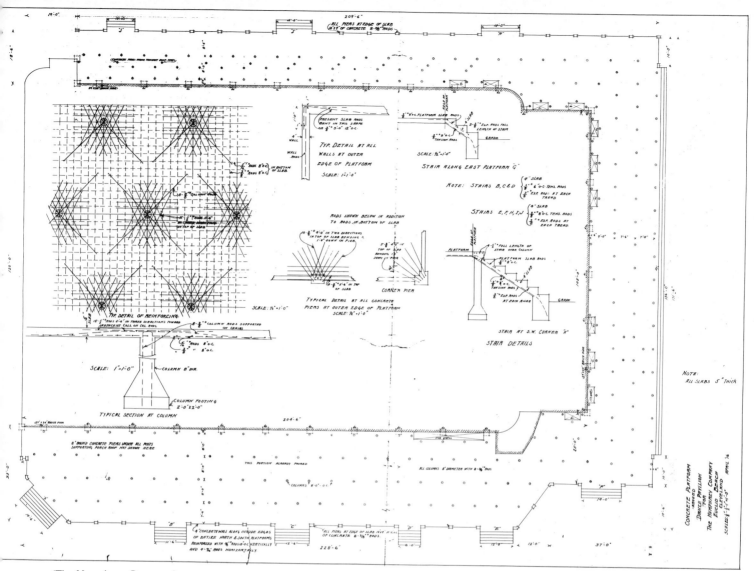

(The Humphrey Company)

(Illus. 162.) The knowhow provided a platform around the DANCE PAVILION made by the Humphrey Company's own cement pouring technique. Here is a working drawing detailing the construction.

The DANCE PAVILION, like numerous other structures on the grounds, was altered after the park was acquired by the Humphrey Company. The interior was also enlarged significantly soon after the Humphreys acquired the park. The floor boasted an area of 18,000 square feet. The earlier open interior with exposed beam work was enclosed, and a ceiling with decorative light fixtures was installed. The bandstand was moved to the balcony on the north side of the PAVILION. It was from this balcony vantage point that band leader John Kirk and his ensemble played for dancing in the years preceding 1907. (Illus. 160.)

The year 1907 brought a prominent name in Cleveland's music circles for a long stay at the DANCE PAVILION of Euclid Beach Park. Louie J. Currier and his orchestra played the park from 1907 thru 1924 — the longest engagement of any single orchestra. The dance

orchestras of this era wore band uniforms. (Illus. 161.) The instrumentation was more like a chamber ensemble than that which evolved as the "dance band" instrumentation of the Thirties. Currier's band included violins, bass viol, reeds (clarinet and flute), cornets, French horns, trombones, percussion and piano. A noted family name among Cleveland's music professionals to play at the beach in its early days was Sholle. Frank and George Sholle, along with Emil, played with the Louis Currier Orchestra in the Teens and early Twenties. (Emil Sholle was a former percussionist with the Cleveland Orchestra.)

Dancers delighted to perennial favorites at the Beach's DANCE HALL; the two-step, Shottische (featured two tempos), the waltz, and the Cuban Waltz (similar to the Viennese Waltz but with broad sweeps on the first beat of each four measures).

The Humphrey Company employed a way of handling the volume of dancers which was known as "park plan" dancing. At the end of each "dance set" two men with ropes attached to the corners of the east end moved from the center of the ballroom. As they moved westward to the opposite end, their ropes formed a "V". Those outside the "V" left by the side exits while those inside the "V" became the group of dancers to enjoy the next "set".[53]

The late Charlie Avellone (Avellone is another well known musical name in Cleveland) recalled that playing "park plan" dancing was hard work. Charlie, clarinetist with Currier, related, "The first night, my lower lip actually stuck to my bottom teeth from playing so much."[54] In addition to the marathon playing schedule, there were none of the modern aids that later bands enjoyed such as a public address system. Currier's band played on the balcony stand (North side) and Avellone recounted that while playing "Narcissus", a favorite of the day, he could hardly hear the clarinet's low register above the shuffle of the dancers. It was question in Charlie's mind whether the dancers ever heard that register of his instrument.[55] The musicians (side men) played for $75 a week, and despite the amount of playing (seven days a week, afternoons and evenings), the engagement at the Euclid Beach DANCE PAVILION was one of the most prestigious and sought after engagements in the area at that time.

It was during this period that members of Currier's orchestra were called upon to play solos from the THEATRE balcony to announce to the crowds the beginning of a new show. (Illus. 40.) Currier and his side men, Joe Heidenreich (baritone horn) and Eddie Purcell (piano), were among those to perform this duty. Currier's ensemble also performed at the ELYSIUM during the winter season for ice skating.

It was also during the stay of the Currier Ensemble that another significant alteration was made to the "grand" PAVILION. In 1916, the Humphreys utilized their skill and development of cement pouring and constructed a concrete outdoor promenade which bordered all but the west end of the PAVILION. (Illus. 162.)

Frank Wilson, saxaphonist and band leader, brought his orchestra to the park for the seasons of 1925-26. During his stay, the bandstand was relocated on the balcony at the east wall, and the area for the musical ensembles was increased. In addition, the instrumentation of the orchestras began to assume the form of a "dance band." Wilson's aggregation featured three saxaphones (doubling on other reeds), two trumpets, one trombone, banjo (double on guitar), tuba (double on string bass), percussion (traps and various percussion instruments), and piano. (Illus. 163.)

During the summer of 1926, The Humphrey Company experimented with outdoor dancing after a dance floor of concrete was poured to the north of the DANCE PAVILION. (Illus. 164.) However, this surface did not seem to be satisfactory to the dancers. Also, moving inside and out was not popular with the musicians. Subsequently, the practice was dropped after only two seasons, and the area became the site of SHUFFLE BOARD COURTS and TABLE TENNIS.

In 1927, the sign above the bandstand on the balcony of the east end conspicuously read, "Joe Smith's Euclid Beach Orchestra," and an array of loud speaker horns was installed thus helping the musicians to be heard. (Illus. 165.) The Joe Smith aggregation, which employed two saxaphones (with doubles), two trumpets, a trombone, piano, banjo, string bass (doubling on tuba), and drums, worked at the Beach from 1927 to 1931, playing seven days a week, 2:00 P.M. — 5:00 P.M. each

(Russell Allon Hehr Collection)

(Illus. 164.) The short-lived outdoor dance floor lasted only a short time. Later, this area was filled with ping pong tables and shuffle board courts.

(Dave Hyman)

(Illus 163.) The Frank Wilson Euclid Beach Orchestra on the east-end BANDSTAND. Members include: William Frankel (piano), Dave Hyman (banjo), George Sholle (drums), Frank Wilson (leader, clarinet and saxophone), Art Gerlach (bass), Otto Kopel (coronet), Frank Emde (saxophone and cello), Eddie Moore (trumpet), Lee Roth (Rothapel) (violin and saxophone), Bob Austin (trombone). The decor of the BANDSTAND features Renaissance detailing as opposed to the later Art Deco. The obvious presence of the white shoe poses an interesting contrast in style. (1925)

(Jerry Borden)

(Illus. 165.) Joe Smith's Euclid Beach Orchestra followed the Wilson aggregation as house band. Art Deco began to appear on the BANDSTAND background. The public address system is apparent overhead.

Joe Smith's Orchestra: Front Row - Left to Right: Joe Smith, George Arnold (Banjo), Ernie White (Sax), Frank Nealson (Sax), Second Row: Jerry Borden (Drums), Art Kozlik (Piano), S. Klein (Trumpet), Joe Toth (Trumpet), Earl (Dock) Chatham (Bass), Ernie Emma (Trombone).

afternoon and 8:00 P.M. to 12:00 midnight each evening. Sidemen with the Smith orchestra were paid $70 to $90 a week, which was over the pay scale established at the time. Working musicians had come a long way from the times when Frank Hruby (the Hrubys being another distinguished musical Cleveland family) played the Beach for $17 a week with his father's band (1901).[55 a]

Joe Smith's Euclid Beach Orchestra was also the first ensemble to broadcast from the DANCE PAVILION. The broadcasts were made over radio station WTAM and were announced by Tom Manning, a long time favorite Cleveland radio personality. Broadcasts occurred whenever afternoon baseball games were not aired. Smith's band also played the OUTDOOR DANCE FLOOR just before the idea was abandoned. Also, it should be noted that the members of his band held the distinction of being the first orchestra to ride the FLYING TURNS after it opened in 1930.

Joe Smith was a colorful person who drove a Pierce-Arrow and flew his own airplane. Occasionally he would "buzz" either the park or friends on the golf course much to the aggravation of the "buzzed." On one occasion, Smith coerced a friend, Otto Horn, to take a plane ride (Otto's first), and Smith unintentionally wound up ditching the plane in the lake off Euclid Beach.

Playing for continuous dancing was hard work for the musicians. The members of the orchestra did not take an intermission, but one or two at a time would leave to take a brief rest. Some years, to keep the sound of music moving in an uninterrupted flow, records were played while the floor was being cleared.

(Illus. 166.) Art Deco arrives in full bloom as the DANCE PAVI-LION reflects the spirit of the 1930's. The dancers swayed before the mirror-lined walls and pillars.

153

(Alden Armstrong / The Humphrey Company)

(Illus. 167.) The Larry Revell Orchestra on the floor level BANDSTAND. (Inset) Left to right: Alden Armstrong (percussion), Walter Bergner (piano), Harold Coplin (guitar), Hank Schneider (trombone), John Tierney (violin), Howard Moran (violin), Dick O'Heron (vocal), Larry Revell (leader), Cyrilla Truitt (vocal), Frank (Doc) Nealon (saxophone), Otto Kubat (bass), Harold Fessenmeyer (saxophone), Del Goris (trumpet), Elgin "Izzy" George (trumpet). The collective sense of humor of the band members is depicted in the larger picture which shows the personnel with instruments switched among the members.

(The Humphrey Company)

(Illus. 167a.) The picture shows dancers in the 1950's.

In addition to the radio broadcasts, the music played in the PAVILION was piped out into the park. Undoubtedly, George Lister, the Beach's radio/electronic wizard, had much to do with this feature. (Lister along with Harvey Humphrey operated a "Ham" radio station at the park — W8NV.) Once again the members of the "Euclid Beach Family" added innovations to the format of the park's attractions and allowed the park visitors to enjoy the music that the dancers found so delightful.

As the Thirties progressed, the look of "Art Deco" came to the Beach. Not only was this style evident on the facades of the RACING COASTER, THRILLER, and FLYING TURNS, but it came to the DANCE PAVILION. The bandstand was moved from the east end balcony down to the floor level at the west end of the dance floor. Inverted pyramid-like lighting fixtures hung from the ceiling while matching but larger, upright pyramid-like fixtures flanked the bandstand proper. Two large mirror-facetted globes also hung from the ceiling and projected many star-like glistenings around the DANCE HALL as various colored spot lights played on them as they revolved. (Ah, the romantic setting of a "MOONLIGHT WALTZ.") Mirrors also lined the walls that were on each side of the band stand as well as on all the pillars around the dance floor. *(Illus. 166.)*

Larry Revell's Orchestra was the first park ensemble to perform on the relocated floor level stand. *(Illus. 167.)* This accommodation also proved advantageous when visiting bands came to the park. Besides the established instrumentation of two trumpets, one trombone, three reeds (saxes, clarinets, etc.), piano, bass, drums, and guitar, Revell featured a string section, known as the "Three Irish Fiddlers." (Tierney, Moran, and

Revell).[56] Two vocalists were also presented with the orchestra, Cecillia Truitt and Dick O'Heren. When Arthur Murray chose the nine best dance bands, the Humphreys publicized their feeling that Revell and his band should have been included in the list.

The "park plan" dance format was strictly observed and placed a considerable challenge on the band leader and his orchestra. The format demanded twelve dance sets per hour, each five minutes in length. There were two dances per set, each two and a half minutes in duration. The Larry Revell Orchestra had the five minute double-dance set well under control. The band was often observed by management to make sure the proper amount of sets were performed per hour.

It was in 1932 that guest name bands began to appear at the Park with such names as Archie Bleyer, Eddie Duchin, Ishan Jones, Vincent Lopez, Ozzie Nelson, and Red Nichols, along with Larry Revell's Euclid Beach Orchestra. The visiting bands appeared at the park on Sundays and alternated every two hours with Revell. During this period the WTAM (a NBC affiliate) radio broadcasts continued to air two to three fifteen minute programs each week. Gene Hamilton was the announcer for these Euclid Beach/Larry Revell broadcasts which opened with the theme, "By the Sea, by the Sea, by the Beautiful Sea."[57]

Musicians sometimes show a sarcastic sense of humor combined with delight in the practical joke. Often the vocalists with the band enjoyed playing the maracas during a Latin number. Unfortunately, they sometimes had difficulty "feeling" a steady tempo. This brought a good deal of frustration to the members of the orchestra, and on one occasion, steps were taken to seek revenge on the tempo-wandering vocalists. The usual maracas were replaced with an extremely large, heavy, and unweildly pair which were almost impossible to manipulate. When the singer reached below her chair and could hardly lift them, the members of the band could scarcely contain themselves.

Larry Revell died in 1935, a young man of 35 years, overcome by asthmatic bronchitis. A rising career was cut short, and Euclid Beach lost another noted and popular name. After Revell's passing, the baton of the Euclid Beach Orchestra went to his successor, Austin Wylie.

Wylie conscientiously spent four days a week from 9 A.M. until 2 P.M. arranging and rearranging music for the seven-day-a-week afternoon and evening dance sessions. Twenty new pieces of material were introduced each week, and by the week's end, 140 arrangements had been played. (Approximately twenty less popular arrangements were eliminated each week.) While the park bands handled the "park plan" dance set format, many of the traveling bands had considerable difficulty fitting their highly stylized orchestrations into the five minute double-dance scheme. In addition, the two hours of continuous play was, in many cases, a considerable departure from the usual schedules these "road" bands had kept.

During 1935, Eddie Duchin, renowned pianist and band leader, came to the park. Along with him was Frankie Carl, playing second piano. Carl had a great many friends in the northeastern Ohio area who faithfully came to see the "second" pianist. During the course of an evening, Carl had a number of solos which were met with enthusiastic applause by his ardent followers. Duchin received little or none. It can only be speculated that Euclid Beach was not one of Eddie Duchin's favorite engagements.

The period from 1936 until 1943 found the absence of a resident orchestra so a parade of local and traveling ensembles inhabited the bandstand in the great DANCE PAVILION, frequently booked for two or three week engagements. (Illus. 167a.) This era heard the sounds of local bands such as Jimmy Joy, Clint Noble, Hal Lynn, Paul Burton, Aud King, and Gene Beecher. Likewise, traveling bands under the batons of Lawrence Welk and Blue Baron brought their prominence to Cleveland and the Beach. (see appendix for extensive band listings.)

World War II boomed on, and George Duffy brought his beat for dancing to the PAVILION in 1943. His orchestra stayed for two years, occasionally alternating with other bands. Dancing was held from 8:30 in the evening until 12:30 A.M. Afternoon dancing was featured during special functions (major picnics such as the Goodyear outing reserved the ball room). However, dancing was conducted on Sunday afternoons from 3:00 P.M. until 5:00 P.M.

Vic Stuart and his orchestra took over the bandstand in 1945 and remained there until 1959. (Illus. 168.) Since the public's taste in dancing was changing rapidly and extensively, the ballroom dancing format at the Beach was reduced to weekends in the later years of the PAVILION'S operation. Stuart's ensemble assumed the form

(Illus. 168.) Vic Stuart's Orchestra, the Beach's last house band. Personnel included:

Robert Tayek (Piano), Phil Nelson (Bass), Kenny Whale (Drums), (Back Row) Bill Burkhardt (Trumpet), Art Cairns (Trombone), (Front Row) John Staurt, Erv Wahl, Erich Christiansen (Saxes), (Front) Les Adair (Vocal) and Vic Stuart (Leader.)

(Vic Stuart)

known as a "Tenor band." This compliment included three tenor saxophones (with doubles), two trumpets, one trombone, piano, bass, and drums. The two vocalists to appear with the band were Les Adair and Jackie Lynn. Euclid Beach tried to provide the ballroom dancers with their favorite bands, and throughout the PAVILION'S history, bands such as Vic Stuart's proved to be very successful.

The DANCE PAVILION was run by a private dance club from 1947 to 1959 and for the last ten years was only open to private functions. The thirst for the two-step, waltz, Cuban Waltz and other perennials had all but evaporated. Times and tastes changed rapidly from the end of World War II to the end of the park's existence. The period from 1938 to 1958 was acknowledged by the American Society of Composers, Authors and Publishers (ASCAP) with a plaque commemorating twenty years of "providing its (Euclid Beach's) patrons with America's finest music." (Illus. 169.)

Cleveland emerged during the Fifties as a center of ethnic music, in particular, the polka. This trend, too, was registered at the Beach while Polka bands such as Frankie Yankovic, Johnny Vadnal, and Johnny Pecon appeared on the bandstand for the Wednesday "Polka Night."

Other trends were evident too, as rock stars Jan and Dean, and the Beach Boys came to Euclid Beach. Still, from time to time, larger ensembles resembling the bygone era of the "dance band" would mount the stand for a special occasion and tempt some of the forgotten echoes absorbed by the very fiber of the great DANCE PAVILION. There are those who are sure that those days of swaying dancers and lilting melodies are gone, and they know we are all just a little poorer for it.

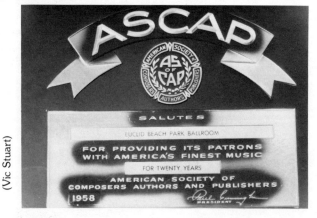

(Vic Stuart)

(Illus. 169.) The American Society of Composers, Authors and Publishers' salute to the Euclid Beach Park Ballroom.

Few areas in the park exemplified the concern for proper behavior more than the DANCE PAVILION. Proper dress, gentlemanly and ladylike conduct were required at all times, or the result would be expulsion from the hall or perhaps the park. Some will remember that these rigid rules were implemented by Dave Swank, long time manager of the DANCE PAVILION.

One attraction that rivaled the DANCE PAVILION in popularity was the ROLLER RINK. Countless numbers of patrons came to the park to roller skate regularly. The ROLLER RINK building was constructed in 1904, along with the FIGURE "8", on the site formerly occupied by the SWITCHBACK RAILWAY. The original 1904 building was enlarged for the season of 1909.

A feature which will seem unfamiliar to those who skated at the RINK in its later days was the original method of providing music. Melodies for skating were played on two sets of chimes of thirty bells each. A set was placed at each end of the skating rink floor, and each was operated by a mechanical device attached to the orchestrette or controlling mechanism located in the center of the rink. (Illus. 170.)

More familiar to those who skated at Euclid Beach after 1910 was a classic band organ, an instrument now world famous among collectors of mechanical music making devices. (Illus. 171.) It was manufactured by the firm of Gavioli et Cie. It is recorded that the instrument was built for an unknown purchaser who decided not to buy it when it was brought to America. Dudley S. Humphrey, II, went to New York City and purchased the organ from the New York branch of the Gavioli firm. Though valued at more than what the Humphrey Company paid for it, it was reported to have sold for $15,000. Originally installed at the ELYSIUM for ice skating, the organ did not prove popular. In 1910, it was moved to the ROLLER RINK and registered an immediate success. The Gavioli remained there to delight skaters until the close of the rink in 1962. Its sound and beauty became a trademark of Euclid Beach Park.

(Illus. 170.) The inside of the ROLLER RINK with its early attendant chimes and Orchestrette. This postcard view was taken before the installation of the Gavioli Organ.

(Kapel Collection)

(Illus. 171.) The magnificent Gavioli with its Rococo facade held a popular place in the memories of thousands of skaters that visited the park's rink each season.

(Kapel Collection)

The Gavioli organ featured 110 keys with which to produce an extensive ensemble of registration such as violins, piccolos, basses and contra-basses, saxophones, baritones, hooded trumpets, clarinets, and a percussion compliment including xylophone, bass drum, cymbal, bell, snare drum, castanets, triangle, and bell. Indeed this magnificent band organ presented an impressive array. During much of its stay at the Beach, it was cared for by Steve Dossa.

The organ's Rococo facade of carved wood in high relief featured three automatons in a large center panel in front of the exposed pipes. The bottom of the center panel exhibited a large painting of putti framed by a huge shell motif in relief. Two smaller panels on either side displayed drums in their upper sections while the outside edges of their lower sections sported high relief griffins. All was heavily gilded and painted. A visual delight thus provided the shell for this magnificent audial barrage.

The requirements for the highest form of behavior, which the Humphreys insisted upon, were also demanded of those who patronized the ROLLER RINK. The activities of the rink were under the direction of its manager, Frank Kilby, for many years. Kilby, a man of record, informs us clearly of the ROLLER RINK'S popularity Throughout his thorough diary which logged the rink's attendance and the sales of the two refreshment stands under his management, it can be seen that the rink was seldom empty. For example, Monday, July fourth of 1927, 546 persons attended the afternoon skating session while 517 skated that evening.[58] For non-holiday days, the ROLLER RINK attracted numbers usually in excess of 100. The evidence shows that it was among the most popular attractions in the area and the park, and that its patronage was consistently heavy throughout its history. In the later years of its operation, the rink was leased to a private skating club, the Cavaliers. After the RINK closed in 1962, the building became the foundation for a ride called the ANTIQUE CARS.

Humphrey resourcefulness, innovative skill, and ability to develop popular attractions (even if in an embryonic state) was clearly exemplified by the ELYSIUM. This structure was built by the Humphreys in 1907, after the liquidation of Forest City Park the year before. It was the second largest indoor ice skating facility built in the country and the second to appear in the United States. *(Illus. 172.)* The ice of the ELYSIUM hosted thousands of skaters, Cleveland's first professional ice hockey team, and gave encouragement to the art of figure skating. The technology required to develop and maintain such a facility is yet another credit to the skill and intelligence of the Humphrey family. The ELYSIUM set the trend which was followed by the Cleveland Arena and the present Coliseum in Richfield, Ohio. Although it was not directly part of Euclid Beach Park, it employed many of the summer workers and enabled them, as well as many of the bands which performed at the DANCE PAVILION, to be kept busy year round. This indoor ice skating rink was yet another contribution to the community until its close at the beginning of World War II.

Be it the desire to "trip the light fantastic," roller skate around the great Gavioli organ at the ROLLER RINK, or cut a neat figure eight on the ice, the Humphrey Company provided visitors from far and near with the most wholesome means to take "a light fantastic trip."

(Kekic Collection)

(Illus. 172.) The ELYSIUM (outside view) East 107th and Euclid Avenue on Cleveland's east side.

(Illus. 172-1.) Inside the ELYSIUM.

(Kekic Collection)

(Kekic Collection)

(Illus. 172-2.) Inside the ELYSIUM with decoration.

Chapter 7

A taster's choice

popcorn,
custard,
and a kiss

(Kekic Collection)

"Ode To D.S.H."

"Oh soul of tact! Who when he finds himself
Columbus bound reserves his "kisses" not
for ONE but passes them around."

The only fault I can find with the popcorn
and taffy is: "They taste like more."
Many times THANK YOU![59]

The sight of a large field of corn about to be harvested might not normally give rise to thoughts of roller coasters, merry-go-round music, and the lilt of a dance band as dancers float across the floor. However, corn, more specifically popcorn, was indeed the medium that brought the Humphreys to Euclid Beach. Their method of preparing and growing popcorn provided this notable family with a base from which a skyrocketing success was accomplished out of the dregs of poverty. While the Humphrey wagons sold the bags of popcorn delight, Euclid Beach Park under the founding company (1895-1900) provided anything but a menu of tastes similar to those the Humphreys would bring to the Beach.

In the manner of many parks during the late '90's, and especially Coney Island, New York, beer and attendant alcoholic beverages ran in a constant stream. It could be said of those early days at the Beach that the flavor of the park was hardly dry! The GERMAN GARDEN (beer garden) existed in "A very merry, dancing, drinking, laughing, quaffing and unthinking time."[60] *(Illus. 172a.)* It might have been an unthinking time, but the Humphreys saw this manner of conduct in a public amusement park as unthinkable.

The summer of 1901 brought sobriety and restraint to Euclid Beach as the Humphrey family leased, then purchased, Euclid Beach Park. The spirits that had flowed were dammed/damned, but the taste buds would not suffer. From the Humphrey's earliest days to the end of the park, lemonade, vanilla ice cream, ham sandwiches, and pies meant that the visitor to the Beach never wanted for an amusement park's "gourmet" menu.

Just as visitors to the park had memories of favorite rides, edible delectables were etched on their taste buds. The TAFFY, called "pull candy," was originally sold by the Humphreys' "hole-in-the-wall," [60]a store on Cleveland's Public Square. *(Illus. 22.)* It was a sought after treat whenever families came to the park. In its early days they saw Russ Ramsey pulling the candy by hand. *(Illus. 172b.)* David Humphrey subsequently invented a candy cooling machine which was patented in 1915. Many a park visitor stood mesmerized by the fascinating "fingers" of the machine as it pulled the candy until it was ready to be cut, wrapped, and displayed. *(Illus. 172c.)* This confection (made at the refreshment stand area between the DANCE PAVILION and the CHESTNUT GROVE) was made of only the

(Amusement Park Books, Inc.)

(Illus. 172a.) The GERMAN GARDEN (VILLAGE) where beer and spirits flowed before the Humphreys stemmed the flow.

(Amusement Park Management Magazine)

(Illus. 172b-1.) A comparison view showing the site of the downtown Humphry store (1905) and the later (1930) occupant; the main Higbee Compnay store.

1905   **1939**

(Illus. 172b.) The Humphrey Company POPCORN STAND at Euclid Beach Pa[rk] before the family acquired the Park.

(Illus. 172c.) Above and below, another child of invention from the Humphrey Company, their own candy making machine. Park visitors could watch the delectables being produced.

(Kekic Collection)

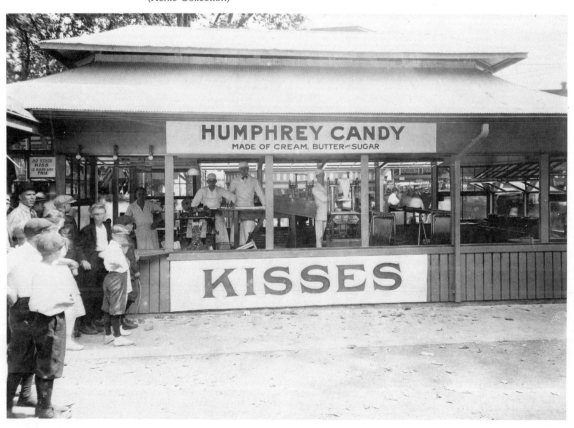

164

(Kekic Collection)

(Illus. 173.) LOGANBERRY JUICE by Phez featured at this popular stand was a center for tasters with a summer thirst. (c. 1920)

(The Humphrey Company)

(Illus. 174.) CASTLE INN where a home cooked meal could be enjoyed. The INN later became the home of D.S. Humphrey II and his family.

purest of ingredients: cream, butter, and sugar. The sweet taste of these candy "KISSES" would linger in the mouth and present any sweet tooth with the highest form of satisfaction.

Among the treats offered by the refreshment stand in the Teens were: PHOSPHATES, ICE CREAM SODA, the perennial Vernors GINGER ALE and Hires ROOT BEER, and, of course, Phez LOGANBERRY JUICE. *(Illus. 173.)* This favorite is remembered by many as an indiginous item of the Beach. It was pointed out by Louise Lambie that in one of the years during World War One the sale of LOGANBERRY JUICE grossed approximately $42,000.00.[61] Many a summer worker at the MAIN REFRESHMENT STAND by the DANCE PAVILION can recall Bill Blauty crawling down into the basement under this stand and adjusting the soft drink mixture. (The dispensed soft drinks utilized another of David Humphrey's inventions in their mixing and carbonation.)

No visit to Euclid Beach would be complete without a HOT DOG or two. Some indication of this staple delight can be seen from the count kept by Frank Kilby, manager of two of the park's refreshment stands. For the season of 1943, the two stands under Kilby sold a remarkable 43,237 dozen wiener rolls and 50,722 lbs. of weiners. The traffic in the '40's can be seen as significantly increased as reflected in a comparison to the 20,270 dozen rolls sold in 1929. However, many items moved in volume as the year 1929 saw the dispensing of 348 gallons of horseradish. The American Recreational Equipment Association lauded Kilby for his efforts in promoting the sale of the HOT DOG (Sylvana Brand supplied by the Hildebrandt Provision Co. of Cleveland.), and the business reflected over $42,000 for the 1942 season while the 1943 summer reflected an increase to $62,000 in income.[62]

If the desires of the visitors were for a more conventional meal served in restaurant style, the Beach featured CASTLE INN for awhile. *(Illus. 174.)* Also, a cafeteria on the lake was in operation during the early part of the century. In 1931, a familiar Cleveland restauranteur took over the CAFETERIA in the BATH HOUSE building, naming it CROSBY'S-ON-THE-LAKE. *(Illus. 175.)* This also was a cafeteria sytle restaurant and was capable of serving a variety of meals at tables or counter, while providing a view of the lake, bathing beach, and PIER. For some visitors, eating dinner at CROSBY'S was a highlight during a day's outing.

Another restaurant was proposed, but the planned facility was never realized.[63] *(Illus. 55.)* The design of the COLONNADE reveals accommodations for a second floor for that purpose.

(Kekic Collection)

(Illus. 175.) CROSBY'S-ON-THE-LAKE, a popular cafeteria-style restaurant, located on the upper floor of the BATHHOUSE.

(Kekic Collection)

(Illus. 175a.) Tables set for visitors at CROSBY'S-ON-THE-LAKE.

(Kekic Collection)

(Illus. 175b.) The atmosphere was that of a clean and pleasant place which was in keeping with the rest of the park.

During the '20's in the MAIN LUNCH area (between the AERO DIPS and PENNY ARCADE), a SODA FOUNTAIN flourished serving visitors cooling sodas and ice cream dishes as the patrons sought to elude the summer heat. (Illus. 176.) Such cooling refreshments were augmented by another Euclid Beach treat called FROZEN WHIP or CREAMY WHIP FREEZE. (Illus. 177.) This treat dwells in the memory as one of the real Beach trademarks. The original supplier of the creamy delight was Soeder's, and later the mixture was delivered by Euclid-Race Dairies of Euclid, Ohio. The sugar cones to hold the FROZEN WHIP were made at the park in the '30's at a location near the FROZEN WHIP stand (northeast corner of the COLONNADE). It was managed by the Purity Cone Co. of Cleveland. The smooth, creamy texture and superb flavor and crispness of the cones were and still are hard to match.

In the early spring and again in the waning days of warm weather, or whenever the taste for coffee emerged, everyone familiar with Euclid Beach knew the coffee served at the many stands in the park was excellent. The brand used was a special urn blend by Widlar. Many will remember sitting by the ROLLER RINK, COLONNADE, or the BOULEVARD STAND and sipping a steaming cup of coffee. The refreshment stands always had fresh sandwiches or pies to go with that delicious coffee.

(Illus. 177.) A highlight of any visit to Euclid Beach was a cone filled with the distinctive flavor of CREAMY WHIP FREEZE (FROZEN WHIP) - a taste that has lingered in the memories of many.

(Kekic Collection)

(Illus. 176.) Cooling drinks and ice cream treats flowed at the SODA GRILL. (c. 1920)

(Kekic Collection)

(William Terrett)

(Kekic Collection)

(Illus. 178.) The LAKE LUNCH with crew outside the building. Pictured in this 1925 scene are: (back row) Walter Okowski, William Light, William Terrett, Enos Peterson, Jr., Frank Zgontz, Lefty. (front row) Harold Guy, Albert Smith, Theodore Okowski, Robert Jennings, and Enos S. Peterson.

(Illus. 178b.) LAKE LUNCH, outside view.

The LAKE LUNCH, occupying an area west of the AVENUE THEATRE near the beach bluff, served 300 to 500 gallons of coffee daily. *(Illus. 178.)* Such was the flow of coffee that 500 new mugs were ordered in the 1920's. When these began to disappear, the employees put a small chip in each to lessen the desire to "borrow" them. The LAKE LUNCH building formerly housed a BOWLING ALLEY. This subsequent eating facility had tables and benches made from the flooring of the alleys. This stout furniture wore well until the last mug of coffee was poured in 1969.

Perhaps the most noteworthy of all the treats were the popcorn products. During much of the history of Euclid Beach Park, the Humphreys grew their own popcorn on one-hundred and fifty acres of their own land. In the Twenties, the Humphrey family repurchased the Wakeman-Townsend farm which they had so painfully lost in the 1800's. *(Illus. 19.)* On this land, a hybrid called Japanese hulless baby rice popcorn was grown.[64]

It was reported in 1949 that 200 tons of corn were raised annually for Euclid Beach.[64] Although it did not have a large kernel, it was quite tender and had very little hull when popped. The POPCORN BALLS were also a unique product of the Hymphrey method, and there are few who knew the park who did not know that flavor and texture as a basic ingredient of the Beach.

Often in the cold of winter those waiting to make bus or trolley connections would retreat to the BOULEVARD STAND on Lake Shore Boulevard and preview the flavors of the next season, or recall the ones of the seasons past. *(Illus. 179.)* At this stand where Otto Price spent so many years, and "Es" Judd and his brothers became so closely associated with the Beach, is where there was a year-round reminder of the park via the TAFFY KISSES, the magnificent and welcome COFFEE, the HOT DOGS, POPCORN, POPCORN BALLS, and PEANUTS IN THE SHELL that were basic identifying qualities of Euclid Beach Park's "Taster's choice."

(William Terrett)

(Illus. 178a.) Inside the LAKE LUNCH with the crew ready to serve hungry and thirsty patrons. Pictured are: Lefty, Frank Zgontz, Harold Guy, Theodore Okowski, William Light, Albert Smith, Enos Peterson, William Terrett, and Walter Okowski.

(Illus. 178c.) Attacking their thirst, park visitors enjoy the Orange and Root Beer drinks. The compressor for drink dispensing is visible - part of another Humphrey innovation.

(Kekic Collection)

(Illus. 179.) The BOULEVARD STAND was a familiar sight to those who passed the park on Lake Shore Boulevard. Open year round, the stand served many of the park's favorites. Today (1977) the building is a fruit and vegetable stand.

(James P. Marcus Collection)

Chapter 8

A tent for rent
by the BEACH at the beach

(Illus. 180.) The promotional booklet published by the Euclid Beach Park Company for the 1899 season pictured the BATHHOUSE with towels flying. The original FERRIS PLEASURE WHEEL is located just behind the building.

(Amusement Park Books, Inc.)

The city dweller and his family came to flee the heat and congestion of the city. These urbanites were drawn to the water's edge where cool breezes blew and refreshing waves met the sand. The organizers of the Euclid Beach Park Company recognized the appeal of the sand and surf (Lake Erie variety), and when they chose the acres between Collamer (later E. 156th St.) and Ursuline Avenue, bordered on the south by Lake Shore Boulevard, they were sure that the 1700 foot beach forming the northern boundry would be an element to entice many patrons to come to Euclid Beach Park.

The BATH HOUSE was one of the original buildings erected on the property for the park's opening in 1895. The two story building built into the BLUFF overlooking the beach was equipped with two hundred and fifty private rooms in which the bather changed his or her attire. *(Illus. 180.)* The BATH HOUSE also offered "the most inviting and beautiful bathing suits."[65] The beach was of "pure" sand sloping gently into the water, and to add to the fun, the "bathing grounds are supplied with diving platforms, horizontal bars, and cable swings."[66] The BATH HOUSE also housed a restaurant on the second floor from which those who were dining could watch the bathers frolic in the water or play on the sand.

Also, the original Euclid Beach Park Company installed a "Toboggan" SLIDE or CHUTE on which bathers could descend into the waves. The tower stood on the BEACH east of the BATH HOUSE, and the use of this SLIDE is rumored to have been very dependent upon the calmness of the lake. (The tower structure, and chute, remained for several years.)

For those who would rather be on the water than in it, the early park offered a BOAT LIVERY with rowboats to rent. *(Illus. 181.)* A young man could not only demonstrate his prowess as a seaman but could also have some privacy with his lady fair. The beach and the water were, indeed, two of the basic qualities on which the park was developed.

(Tom Oldham Collection)

(Illus. 181.) These lovely ladies of 1910 prepare to cast off into Lake Erie from the area of the BOAT LIVERY. The early Humphrey Company PIER construction is evident.

(Illus. 181a.) The BOAT LIVERY and PIER before the Park came into Humphrey hands.

(Kapel Collection)

(Illus. 182.) The CAMP GROUNDS as pictured in the 1899 booklet. Beyond the tents is the row of Poplar trees running from east to west.

Another popular area of Euclid Beach Park for many seasons was the CAMP GROUNDS. The lake front and the joy of camping naturally went together. Advertising for the season of 1899 boasted of: "New clean tents. Smooth lawns. High grounds. Fresh water. Good Fishing. Fine drainage. Fine boats." *(Illus. 182.)* Undoubtedly, many of these new clean tents were made by the Wagner Manufacturing Company, later to be known as the Wagner Awning Co. A new tent could be purchased for the nominal sum of $4.95.[67] (It should be noted that it was at this part of the park that the Humphreys stayed while they ran the popcorn concession at the Beach during the late 1890's.)

One of the significant additions the Humphrey Company made to the CAMP GROUNDS was the creation of a series of CONCRETE COTTAGES built in 1915. *(Illus. 183.)* Again, the Humphreys, through their skill, brought summer visitors greater comfort for a vacation stay.

(Amusement Park Books, Inc.)

(Illus. 183. 1-6) Many of these concrete summer cottages, constructed in 1915, still stand in the surviving trailer park. They are a testament to the Humphrey ingenuity. Two types are shown.

(Kekic Collection)

During this same period (mid-Teens), the grounds hosted a working-girls camp called CAMP LAKE BREEZE. This facility offered working girls a place to spend a couple of days when a substantial vacation was impossible. This camp was under the auspices of the park and the employment bureau.

Euclid Beach Park became a name known throughout the country as well as in countries around the world. In part, some of the reputation that the park gathered was spread by the numerous visitors that came to the park's CAMP GROUNDS for vacation. The peaceful landscape, the (then) clean lake, boating and fishing, and a major amusement park drew vacationers from many areas across America and a share of foreign visitors. The lake breeze, the ever-shading Poplars and Sycamores made a tented stay as pleasant as could be found anywhere during the 1890's and the first half of the twentieth century. *(Illus. 184.)*

(Illus. 184.) Above and below, Quiet lanes, rows of tents and trees give an idea of a time (early 1900's) very different from our own (1977).

(Kapel Collection)

Accommodations at the CAMP GROUNDS were reasonable in cost which made a visit to the grounds even more attractive. A stay at the Beach's CAMP GROUNDS, even as late as the Fifties, was modest in cost. A four room tent was $4.00 a day, $25.00 a week, or $220.00 a season and was equipped with two double beds, camp chairs, clothes tree, etc. The cement cottages cost $300.00 to $325.00 per six month period. The rate was dependent on the size of the dwelling.[68]

The Thirties marked the appearance of a phenomenon now familiar to the American scene; the house trailer or mobile home appeared. At the Euclid Beach CAMP GROUNDS a TRAILER "PARK" was established (which still stands) with many such vehicles forming a veritable community. Seventy families called the trailer park "home" in the year 1948. Previous to World War II, the trailer camp facilities were open only during the summer season, but as the war

(Illus. 185-1)

(Kekic Collection)

(Illus. 185-2)

(Kekic Collection)

progressed and housing was needed in industrial communities, the Humphrey Company announced that the trailer park would remain open year round providing additional living space for war workers. In 1948, there were one hundred sixty tent dwellings which, together with the permanent citizens, increased the summertime population to fifteen hundred people.[69]

Through the years there would be numerous scenes with campers in small tents, trailer-born tents, large and elaborate tents, cottage dwellers, and those with the house trailers. For the tenters, there was a TOURIST'S KITCHEN provided for added comfort and convenience as well as a gathering place. A number of log cottages were also available for those wishing to vacation in a more rustic fashion. *(Illus. 185.)*

Despite the wooded acreage, the pleasant breezes, and the warmth of summer, there was some evidence of imperfection; every scheme has a flaw. It would seem that the camp visitors of 1939 endured a fate that many before and after them might well have shared. The problem was that of noise — noise from hundreds of starlings that dropped by nightly to join in the festivities. Unfortunately, the birds' contribution was a din of squawking and screeching that was in no way appreciated by the tenters. A variety of technique were employed to encourage the uninvited callers to leave: hoses placed under the trees, ringing cymbals, clattering pots and pans, and any other item which produced noise. At first this scheme of out-noising the starlings from the area brought some success, but it would seem that after a short time the birds interpreted the noise as encouragement and returned en masse. No historic documentation is available to report whether an effective means of "dismissing" the birds was ever found, but it did show that nature could produce some unexpected diversions for those who wished to spend part of their summer(s) out-of-doors and in communion with it.

(Illus. 185-3)

(Kekic Collection)

177

(Illus. 185-4)

(Illus. 185-5)

(Illus. 185-6)

(Illus. 185. 1-7) The TOURIST KITCHEN was the social center for the CAMPGROUNDS. Some of the tents were modest, like these pitched near the 1912 Model T. Some tents were elaborately personalized with gneerous space. For others, there were the more permanent log cabins, while still other campers brought trailer tents or those which could be ttached to the family car. In any case, it was a great way to spend all or part of the summer.

(Kekic Collection)

(Illus. 185-7)

(Kekic Collection)

(Illus. 186.) The PIER in 1901, after the dividing rail was removed and before the installation of the CIRCLE SWING (1902) to the west (here on the right) of the PAVILION.

(Kekic Collection)

(Illus. 187.) The Park at its zenith. The BEACH is crowded, and many can be seen strolling the PIER. Cars fill the MAIN PARKING LOT and much of Humphrey's Field across Lake Shore Boulevard. A golden era.

179

Just as the CAMP GROUNDS was a feature at the Beach from the first season, the PIER was also there when the park opened in 1895 and was a familiar characteristic of the Euclid Beach vista until the final closing in 1969. Transportational service to and from the park (1895-1900) was not only provided by the street railway and interurban lines (from the areas farther west and east) but by the two steamers "Superior" and "Duluth", sometimes with extra ships used to handle larger crowds. *(Illus. 6.)* The two Euclid Beach "TUBS" landed the fun-seeking visitors at the PIER. The PIER as it appeared during the first five years of the park's existence was divided down the middle by a railing so that incoming and outgoing travelers could be separated and have a clear way to and from the boats. *(Illus. 4.)* When the Humphreys took over direction of Euclid Beach, they agreed to discontinue boat service in return for one street car fare charge to the Beach. At this point, the PIER was remodeled and the dividing rail removed. *(Illus. 186.)* In addition, the Humphreys put their inventiveness to work as they used their cement pouring process to put an attractive ramp at the land end of the PIER. *(Illus. 187.)*

Anyone familiar with the habits of Lake Erie can attest to the manner in which its waters attack the south shore. (Because Erie is the shallowest of the Great Lakes, it tends to have many furious storms which develop with little notice. Also, heavy pounding conditions happen frequently during such storms. The Toll on the shore lines, docks, and piers is heavy.) The PIER at Euclid Beach presented the Humphrey Company with a major maintenance problem. Each winter extensive damage was done to the pilings and deck. Keeping the PIER intact took more than its share of the park's maintenance budget. *(Illus. 188.)*

The BEACH itself also fell victim to the effect of the lake's eroding action. Many square miles of land had been washed away, but the Humphreys were alone in actively and effectively doing something about it. During the '30's, Harvey Humphrey invented and developed a new kind of permeable jetty construction. Jetties at right angles and parallel to the shoreline were installed along the shore. Not only did they check the erosion but they regained the lost beach. The basic principle was the permeability of the structure which reduced the force of water flowing through it and so caused the sand in suspension to be dropped. This invention saved the pool beside the pier, and the bathhouse building, and the grass banks running along the entire northern boundary of the park.

(Illus. 188.) The PIER demanded constant maintenance and frequent overhauling.
(c. 1910.)

The BEACH facilities had already suffered other damage at the hands of Erie's waters. For many years bathers had enjoyed a concrete WADING POOL which was located on the beach just east of the BATH HOUSE. The POOL was fun for the young and old and was equipped with a SLIDE to increase the enjoyment. *(Illus. 189.)* During the late '20's, a severe winter storm brought violent, pounding waves well up onto the beach area. Water rapidly scooped sand out from under the pool, leaving much of it unsupported, and, coupled with freezing temperatures, cracked the concrete, thus destroying the usefulness of the facility. The effects of a rampaging Lake Erie had to be checked, and the concept of the jetties was developed.

(Illus. 189.) The WADING POOL on the BEACH was a great place for the children and timid bathers to splash. The SLIDE was ever popular.

(Kekic Collection)

BEACH at the turn of the century

(Kekic Collection)

The lake shore frontage was an important and attractive quality of Euclid Beach Park. *(Illus. 190.)* Early visitors knew that walk along the BLUFF as "LOVERS LANE." *(Illus. 191.)* The shade of the trees, the breezes off the water, and the warmth of summer, indeed, made the scene a romantic one. The popularity of the wooded CAMP GROUNDS made the Beach an important summer resort with hundreds of visitors coming to stay on the grounds each season representing every corner of the world. Vast numbers of these vacationers would return year after year as regular patrons of Euclid Beach Park.

Even in 1899, some sought to express their view of the Beach. Although in poetry of another era, it was said:

"Come unto these yellow sands
And then take hands —
Court'sied when you have, and kissed —
The wild waves whist."[70]

The behind the scenes functions of preparation and maintenance of a major amusement park such as Euclid Beach required attending to an endless amount of details. However, as in producing a stage play, the sets were designed and constructed, the rehearsals conducted, the curtain was rung up and, indeed, as the sign announced at the MAIN GATE, Euclid Beach Park was open for the season.

(Illus. 190) The BEACH during the early years of the century was the scene of many aviation events. Here, a tent pitched on the sand became an aircraft hanger. (2.) Bathers of the 20's, with the FOUNTAIN and PIER in the background.

(3.) Oh, those bathing suits - the wild '20's - wild for Euclid Beach that is.

(1) (4) Apparel was either the bathing suit of the day, or a suit, tie, and hat.

(Illus. 190.)   (Kekic Collection)

BEACH at the turn of the century

(Kekic Collection)

(Illus. 190-1.)   (Kekic Collection)

(Illus. 190-2.)   (Kekic Collection)

(Illus. 190-3.)   (Kekic Collection)

187   Winter - 1920's   (Kekic Collection)

OVERLAY LOCATION OF RIDES, BUILDINGS AND
STRUCTURES AT VARIOUS TIMES FROM 1895-1969

1. East 156th Street
1. Collamer
2. Lake Shore Blvd.
3. Auto Exit Gate
3. Exit Gate for Autos
4. Cottage
5. House
6. House
7. West Gate (1895)
8. Stables (1895)
9. Cobb Farmhouse
9. Office: first:
9. Dudley S. Humphrey, III House
10. Bowling Alley
10. Lake Lunch
11. Ravine (later covered over)
12. Bridge across Ravine
13. Beach of Euclid Beach Park
14. Turnpike (ride)
15. Parking lot - main
15. Main Parking Lot
16. Outdoor Theatre
17. Log Cabin
18. Office: second: of concrete
18. Concrete Office
18. Cement Office
19. Annex
19. Stage Housing of Avenue Theatre
20. Mural of a "Ballerina Riding a Runaway Horse"
20. "Ballerina Riding a Runaway Horse" on the covered-over stage opening of Theatre
21. Dippy Whip (ride)
22. Coffee Break (ride)
23. Theatre (Avenue Theatre)
23. Avenue Theatre
24. Pee Wee Miniature Golf
25. Bug (ride)
26. Caterpillar (ride)
27. Aerial Swing (ride)
27. Aeroplanes (ride)
27. Circle Swing (ride)
27. Rocket Ships (ride)
28. German Village
28. German Garden
29. Pier
30. Main Gate
30. Gate (main)
31. Bicycle Track
32. MacLevie Cottage
33. Shop
34. Garage
35. Skee Ball

36. Flying Scooters (ride)
37. Ballroom (inside of Dance Pavilion
37. Dance Floor
38. Dance Pavilion
38. Dance Hall
39. Promenade (concrete) around Dance Pavilion
39. Platform of concrete around Dance Pavilion
40. Men's Washroom (under northwest section of Dance Pavilion)
41. Women's Washroom (southeast section of Dance Pavilion)
42. Outdoor Dance Floor
43. Shuffleboard Courts
44. Ping Pong Tables
45. Table Tennis
46. Fountain
47. Circular Pool (near Pier)
48. Sea Swing (ride)
49. Cafeteria (Bluff level)
49. Crosby's-on-the-Lake
50. Bath House (Beach level)
51. Ocean Wave (ride)
52. Swingin' Gyms (ride)
53. Post Office
53A. Link Trainer (ride)
54. House
55. House
56. Cottage
57. Miniature Railroad (ride): #1:
58. Ostrich Farm
59. Pony Track (ride) (live)
59A. Kiddie Cars (ride)
60. Street Car Station: #2: (near later Kiddie Land)
60. Trolley Station: #2: (near later Kiddie Land)
61. Grove Lunch
62. Colonnade
63. Merry-Go-Round (ride)
64. Street Car Station: #1: (near Dance Pavilion)
64. Trolley Station: #1: (near Dance Pavilion)
65. Drink Stand
66. Candy Stand
66. Popcorn Stand
67. Hot Dog Stand
68. Sun Tan Links
69. Fun House
69. Surprise House
69. Funscience Hall
70. Photo Gallery
71. Flying Ponies (ride)
71. Japanese Flying Ponies (ride)
72. Carrousel (ride) (1910 - 1969), #19
73. Cigar Stand
74. Giant Slide (ride)
75. Crystal Maze: #2: (1926)

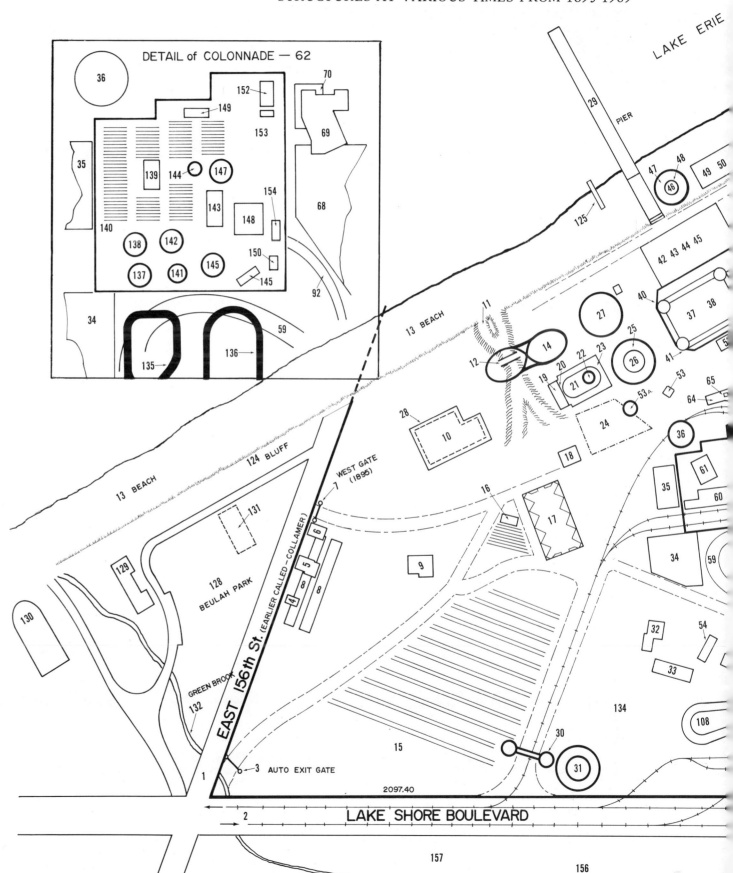

Summer - 1920's   (Kekic Collection)

(Illus. 190-4.)   (Kekic Collection)

188

MAP OF
EUCLID BEACH PARK

SCALE 1 inch = 100 ft.

Sewers shown thus
Water Pipes
Gas Pipes
Catch Basins

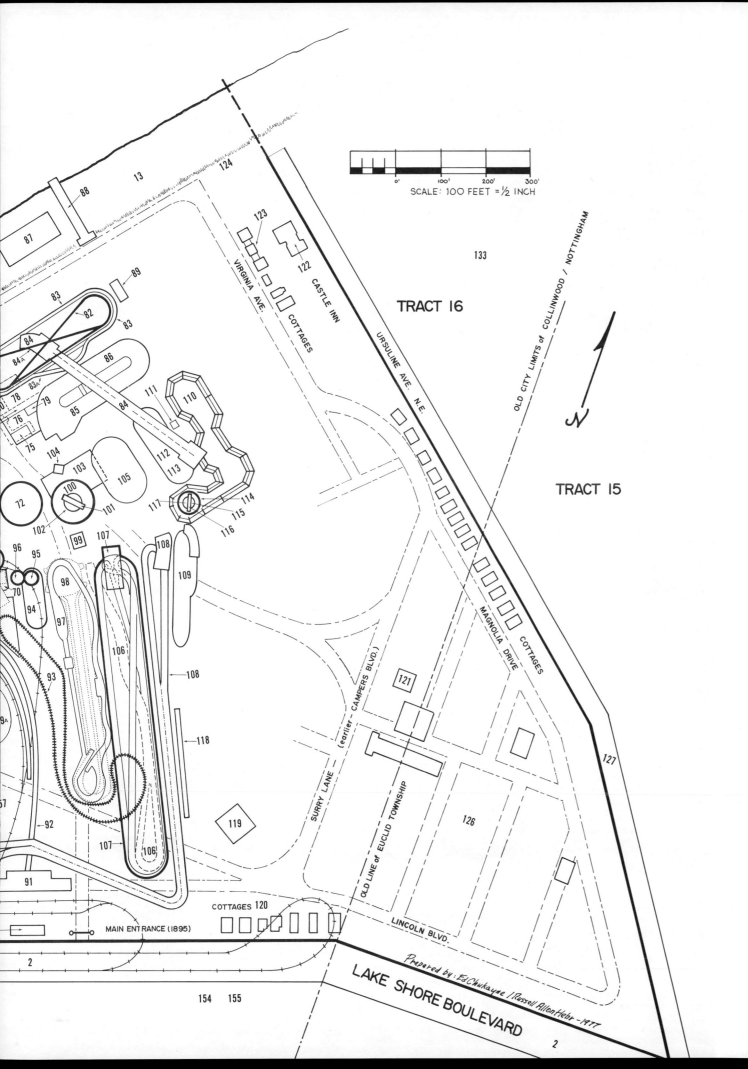

SCALE: 100 FEET = ½ INCH

TRACT 16

TRACT 15

N

OLD CITY LIMITS of COLLINWOOD / NOTTINGHAM

VIRGINIA AVE.

CASTLE INN COTTAGES

URSULINE AVE. N.E.

MAGNOLIA DRIVE

COTTAGES

SURRY LANE

(earlier — CAMPERS BLVD.)

OLD LINE of EUCLID TOWNSHIP

LINCOLN BLVD.

COTTAGES 120

MAIN ENTRANCE (1895)

Prepared by: Ed Chukayne / Russell Allon Hehr — 1977

LAKE SHORE BOULEVARD

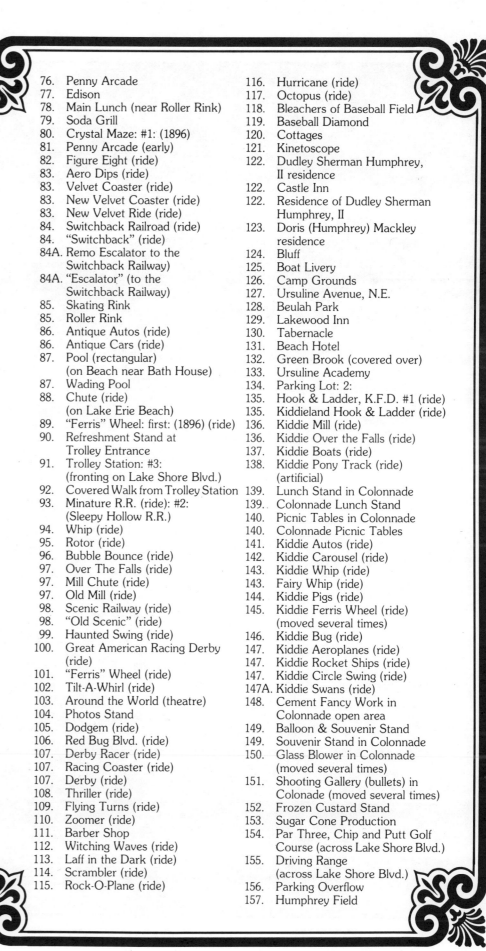

76. Penny Arcade
77. Edison
78. Main Lunch (near Roller Rink)
79. Soda Grill
80. Crystal Maze: #1: (1896)
81. Penny Arcade (early)
82. Figure Eight (ride)
83. Aero Dips (ride)
83. Velvet Coaster (ride)
83. New Velvet Coaster (ride)
83. New Velvet Ride (ride)
84. Switchback Railroad (ride)
84. "Switchback" (ride)
84A. Remo Escalator to the
     Switchback Railway)
84A. "Escalator" (to the
     Switchback Railway)
85. Skating Rink
85. Roller Rink
86. Antique Autos (ride)
86. Antique Cars (ride)
87. Pool (rectangular)
    (on Beach near Bath House)
87. Wading Pool
88. Chute (ride)
    (on Lake Erie Beach)
89. "Ferris" Wheel: first: (1896) (ride)
90. Refreshment Stand at
    Trolley Entrance
91. Trolley Station: #3:
    (fronting on Lake Shore Blvd.)
92. Covered Walk from Trolley Station
93. Minature R.R. (ride): #2:
    (Sleepy Hollow R.R.)
94. Whip (ride)
95. Rotor (ride)
96. Bubble Bounce (ride)
97. Over The Falls (ride)
97. Mill Chute (ride)
97. Old Mill (ride)
98. Scenic Railway (ride)
98. "Old Scenic" (ride)
99. Haunted Swing (ride)
100. Great American Racing Derby
     (ride)
101. "Ferris" Wheel (ride)
102. Tilt-A-Whirl (ride)
103. Around the World (theatre)
104. Photos Stand
105. Dodgem (ride)
106. Red Bug Blvd. (ride)
107. Derby Racer (ride)
107. Racing Coaster (ride)
107. Derby (ride)
108. Thriller (ride)
109. Flying Turns (ride)
110. Zoomer (ride)
111. Barber Shop
112. Witching Waves (ride)
113. Laff in the Dark (ride)
114. Scrambler (ride)
115. Rock-O-Plane (ride)

116. Hurricane (ride)
117. Octopus (ride)
118. Bleachers of Baseball Field
119. Baseball Diamond
120. Cottages
121. Kinetoscope
122. Dudley Sherman Humphrey,
     II residence
122. Castle Inn
122. Residence of Dudley Sherman
     Humphrey, II
123. Doris (Humphrey) Mackley
     residence
124. Bluff
125. Boat Livery
126. Camp Grounds
127. Ursuline Avenue, N.E.
128. Beulah Park
129. Lakewood Inn
130. Tabernacle
131. Beach Hotel
132. Green Brook (covered over)
133. Ursuline Academy
134. Parking Lot: 2:
135. Hook & Ladder, K.F.D. #1 (ride)
135. Kiddieland Hook & Ladder (ride)
136. Kiddie Mill (ride)
136. Kiddie Over the Falls (ride)
137. Kiddie Boats (ride)
138. Kiddie Pony Track (ride)
     (artificial)
139. Lunch Stand in Colonnade
139. Colonnade Lunch Stand
140. Picnic Tables in Colonnade
140. Colonnade Picnic Tables
141. Kiddie Autos (ride)
142. Kiddie Carousel (ride)
143. Kiddie Whip (ride)
143. Fairy Whip (ride)
144. Kiddie Pigs (ride)
145. Kiddie Ferris Wheel (ride)
     (moved several times)
146. Kiddie Bug (ride)
147. Kiddie Aeroplanes (ride)
147. Kiddie Rocket Ships (ride)
147. Kiddie Circle Swing (ride)
147A. Kiddie Swans (ride)
148. Cement Fancy Work in
     Colonnade open area
149. Balloon & Souvenir Stand
149. Souvenir Stand in Colonnade
150. Glass Blower in Colonnade
     (moved several times)
151. Shooting Gallery (bullets) in
     Colonade (moved several times)
152. Frozen Custard Stand
153. Sugar Cone Production
154. Par Three, Chip and Putt Golf
     Course (across Lake Shore Blvd.)
155. Driving Range
     (across Lake Shore Blvd.)
156. Parking Overflow
157. Humphrey Field

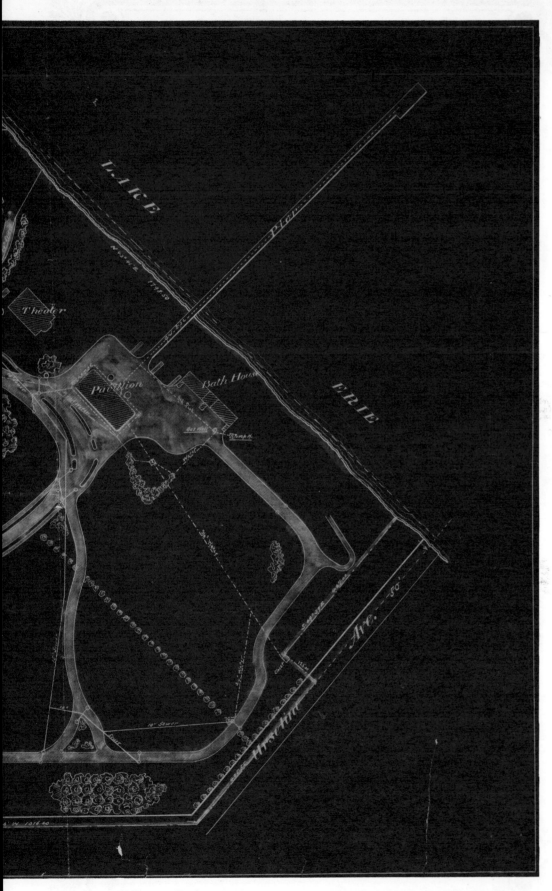

Map of Original Park, 1895. (also page 5)

(Kekic Collection)

EUCLID BEACH PARK CAMP

Situated within the park grounds, makes an ideal location for the Vacationist and Tourist. Completely furnished Tent Cottages, also sites for those with their own equipment. Hot and cold running water, Community Kitchen and Dining Hall, Showers, well lighted and police protection. Rates reasonable. Address all communications to The Humphrey Company, Euclid Beach Park, Cleveland, Ohio.

Views showing our Four-Room Tent Cottages with permanent roofs, for the vacationist

View of our Tourist Camp, showing our Two-Room Sleeping Cottages

View of our Tourist Camp, showing a Tourist with his own equipment

ORGANIZATION PICNICS

We are thoroughly equipped to handle your picnic reqirements whether large or small. For complete information address

THE HUMPHREY COMPANY · CLEVELAND, OHIO

(The Humphrey Company)

(Illus. 191.) The path along the BLUFF overlooking the BEACH and the lake was known as "Lover's Lane." The postcard view dated around the turn of the century.

(Kapel Collection)

"What the Public Wants is Clean Stuff"

A Cleveland firm has found to its profit that most people prefer to keep away from the rough

A TALL, broad-shouldered white-haired Clevelander stood up before an audience of amusement park managers in Chicago, recently, and "bawled them out" most vigorously. And they all seemed to like it!

The Clevelander was Dudley S. Humphrey, president of the D. S. Humphrey Co., which controls Euclid Beach Park, the Elysium, and a score or more pop corn and taffy stands in the city. He was telling his hearers in effect that the sooner they learned to operate summer amusement parks which contained no demoralizing concessions, the sooner would they be able to realize bigger dividends.

It was not a new note, of course. Mr. Humphrey's listeners had heard it before, but few of them really took it seriously. It may be all right for Euclid Beach Park, Cleveland, they argued, but it wouldn't do for their towns at all.

These managers believed that an amusement park, like everything else that caters to the public, must give that public what it wants. If the patrons craved gambling devices and freak concessions, the park executives felt they were compelled to install such things. Theirs not to question a man's right to throw away his nickels. Theirs the job to give him the opportunity.

But Mr. Humphrey told them they were merely fooling themselves, and that there really was no profit in such things in the long run. Good clean amusement paid better. He had seen both methods tried out at Euclid Beach Park and he knew, he insisted.

The straight-from-the-shoulder speech of the man from Cleveland gives one a glimpse into his character that nothing else could do so directly. It tells why he has succeeded. He doesn't believe in half-way measures or in beating about the bush.

The speaker told his audience the story of how he had started in the amusement park game in Cleveland, and of the plans he had formed based on his firm conviction that clean conditions would pay.

as to how amusement parks should be run, and the opinions in no way coincided with those of the men who were putting Euclid Beach Park on the market. These people had invested about $400,000 in land and improvements, and they had operated the park about five seasons at a loss. Even the Humphrey pop corn and taffy stand out there was not paying.

FOR that reason, long before they learned the park was to be sold, the Humphreys were trying to find out why the park was a losing proposition. It could not be due to inefficiency, they thought, for these behind the project were big business men and successful in their own

first crack off the bat, and everything else that contained the element of chance. Out went the liquor. And out went anything that D. S. Humphrey and his colleagues thought tended to debase the real purpose for which amusement parks are created, viz., to afford clean fun and recreation for every member of the family. The high board fence around the place went down, and with it disappeared the 10-cent admission charge. Out went all freak concessions, and with them went the fakers. The new slogan was: Free gate, no beer, no freaks, no fakes or fresh people.

The last named group was rather hard to eliminate. Its members were

such harangues in a court of law were rather extraordinary, turned to the father and informed him quietly that neither he nor his son would ever be permitted within the confines of Euclid Beach Park again.

"Huh!" blustered the father. "I'd like to see you or anybody else try to keep me out. I'm going out there tomorrow."

HE did. Mr. Humphrey was watching for him. He summoned one of his athletic guardians, walked up to the man and said:

"Mr. Blank, I've changed my mind about not letting you in. But I'm going to have my friend here look after you. You might come to some harm. He's been sworn orders to

spotted and a mark nowhere to be found at his side. Finally he gave up, telephoned Mr. Humphrey and promised to "be good" if permitted to enter and leave without an escort.

"That's fine," said Mr. Humphrey. "Why didn't you wake up your mind in that long ago? You are at perfect liberty, now, to come and go whenever you please. But I don't want your son around. He doesn't know how to behave when he comes our guest. We'll keep him out as long as we have anything to do with the park.

"And the best part of it," continued Mr. Humphrey, "is that the courts have upheld us in our contention that Euclid Beach Park is private property and that we can do what we please about keeping people out if we want to. We had several suits on this point, and we won them all.

A young woman was misbehaving one day, and she received the same treatment. Once she appeared with a man who declared he was a private detective and that he had accompanied her to see that she wasn't persecuted.

"That's good of you, I'm sure," declared Mr. Humphrey. "I'll appoint two policemen to take care of you, one for her and one for you. I want you to know that we spare no pains to keep our guests from being molested." Disconcerted, the couple left, nor did they appear again.

Another time a girl who had furnished much newspaper copy with a tale of having been kidnaped at Euclid Beach Park, and kept prisoner at a camp on the lake shore, appeared on the grounds. Mr. Humphrey was watching for her. He asked several questions and upon receiving confused and evasive answers he told her politely that he had decided the park was too dangerous for her and that she must go away and never come again. She made a great to-do about it, but he was firm. And she, too, vanished.

"I had no idea," he said, in explanation, "that the young lady was what you might call a liar. The truth was that she had remained away from home longer than was proper, and so she concocted that story in order to persuade her parents that she had been, a very good girl. But we don't want people like that around here.

"We valued the publicity she gave us, of course, but there was a disturbing element in it. If our patrons, and especially our women patrons, got the idea that our park was not safe for them or for their daughters we'd be up against it."

Residents of Cleveland may still recall the flurry when the Humphreys posted guards on the gates to prevent anyone from entering the park if he had visited a saloon across the road. Men who had left the park to get a glass of beer suddenly found themselves barred when they attempted to return.

"Why," exclaimed one man, "my wife's in there with the kids. She's not feeling very well, and she'll become hysterical if I'm not back."

"Sorry, but we can't help that," replied the guard whom the man tried to brush past. "But the regulations are plain. We don't want any drunkards in here."

"But I'm not drunk," expostulated the man.

"Not now, perhaps, but how do I know you won't be when the stuff you've been drinking begins to take effect? Maybe, if you can tell me where to find your folks I'll tell them why we won't let you in, and they can join you here."

"It's an outrage," protested the other, "and I'm going to sue the park."

"That's your privilege," returned the guard.

(The Cleveland Plain Dealer)

Chapter 9 The Family Place always clean, always dry

The Family Place —
Always Clean, Always Dry

The popularity of Euclid Beach Park was no accident. From the Humphreys' first season in 1901, and throughout the history of the park, the basic appeal was to the "decent" person who wanted wholesome recreation in a clean and positive atmosphere. The patrons of the Beach were primarily working people and their families. (There was no shortage of members of the middle/working class in the highly industrialized greater Cleveland area and the surrounding Northeastern Ohio communities.) "Nothing to depress or demoralize" is just what the hard working population wanted and supported with great enthusiasm. *(Illus. 56.)* Dudley S. Humphrey, II, knew that the principles he and his family held would meet a demand yet untouched before the 1901 season. The absence of alcoholic beverages proved only to be an advantage. Those who came by the millions with their wives, children, and relatives were confident that there would be little to offend anyone at Euclid Beach. *(Illus. 28.)* (Whenever that condition disappears — the condition of a well controlled public place — so does the facility!) The principle was elementary, and the Humphrey Company saw it as self-evident.

In essence, Euclid Beach offered a relief from the daily situations that fatigued the citizenry by offering them pleasurable diversion. The scene was that of quiet wooded land to wash away the oppression of the city stone and cement; yet within the confines of these acres was the whirl and excitement of the latest and most stimulating of attractions. The blend neared perfection, and any traveler who had visited parks across the country knew Euclid Beach was different, even if the "why" could not be explained.

There has always been an element of the population that has proven incapable of keeping their frustrations to themselves and, in turn, must express those frustrations to the dismay of those around them. These "rowdies" were the primary object of the Humphreys' policy supervision; there was never any place at the Beach for such persons. Since admission to the park was based on the "Free Gate" policy, the degree to which persons were welcome at Euclid Beach was estimated by their behavior. For many seasons the results of this estimation were enforced by the Euclid Beach Park POLICE FORCE. *(Illus. 192, 193.)* Those who were not welcome were clearly informed of this by the FORCE and often found themselves on the outside looking in with an unquestionable impression of the disdain in which they were held:

(Illus. 193.) Badge No. 29 was worn by Robert Ward.

(Robert Ward)

(Illus. 192.) The men of the Euclid Beach Park Police Force line up behind their captain, John MacDonald.

(Frank Jeran Collection)

Almost all the men employed in the park police force are deputized and have the authority to arrest. This is never done when it is possible to avoid it, however, and when a patron becomes so unruly that something must be done he is usually escorted out of the park.

That is one of the advantages of a free gate and free parking — you can eject any one and be under no obligation whatever.[71]

For a number of decades the small police force at the park (sometimes numbering less than fifteen men) was directed by Captain Mac-Donald, or Captain "Mac", as he was known to those about him. To MacDonald, there were only two modes of conduct: proper behavior, which allowed the visitor access to all the park, and improper behavior, which prompted a hasty exit from the park. The principle was simple and easy to understand.

A bond existed between the park police and the other employees. Each knew he could count on the other if any difficulty arose. A series of signals were devised between the various police and the workers. Often, if someone's conduct seemed questionable, a ride attendant would pass the word to the police by means of the park phone system and that person/s would be carefully observed as he/they would move about the park. Usually such persons were not aware they were being watched but discovered it quickly if their behavior became unacceptable. Many a would-be trouble maker viewed the outside of the wire mesh fence surrounding the park before he was aware of what had happened. If an individual policeman was in trouble, he would hit his night stick on the cement, and fellow officers would come quickly to the aid of the signaling officer. Almost every park employee was alert to possible trouble and made immediate moves to stop it. The 15th Precinct Station of the Cleveland Police Department was host to many an unwilling visitor who was transferred from the park to the station by "special" invitation.

The Humphrey Company policy was that of presenting fair and honest attractions to encourage a clientele to enjoy themselves in safety and peace. (Illus. 194.) The PARK POLICE were charged with maintaining that policy, and for most of the period from 1901 until the mid century, this type of atmosphere was energetically pursued. Disdain of any offensive behavior by the management was, in large measure, responsible for the feeling by the public that Euclid Beach was THE place to visit.

(The Humphrey Company)

EUCLID BEACH

Come Early in the Morning
Stay the Whole Day

Cleveland's Only Lake Shore Amusement Park
Delightful Lake Breezes at

Euclid Beach

"The Amusement Park With a Conscience"

At no other resort in the world are honest pleasures more promoted and enjoyed.

At no other resort in the world are rowdyism and intemperance more thoroughly eliminated.

(Illus. 194.) The Humphrey Company proclaimed the basic operating principles of Euclid Beach Park in this ad.

196

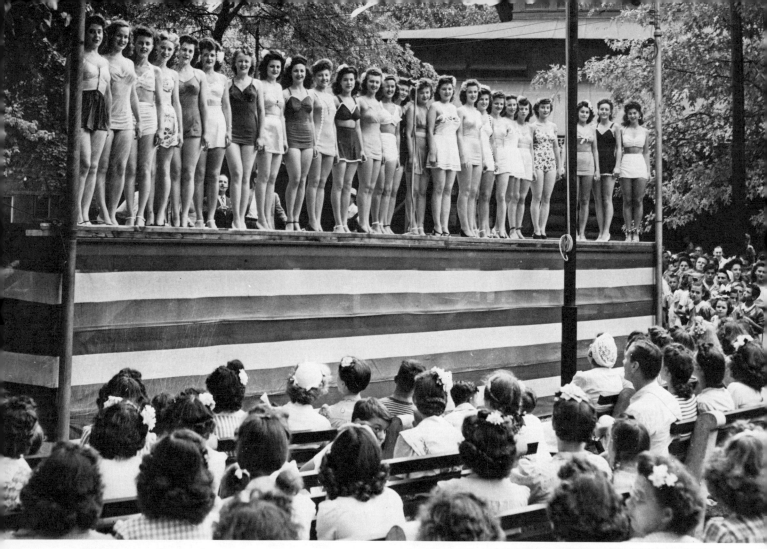

(The Humphrey Company)
(Illus. 195-1)

(Illus. 195 1-5) These views show typical events and places that were a part of the annual picnic. From the games and beauty contests to the LOG CABIN, BANDSTAND, and the ANNEX to rest under the shade trees, a thousand memories were generated for millions of Euclid Beach patrons.

The working man had a limited budget with which to provide his family special entertainment. This was true especially during the depression period of the 1930's. The company picnic or "annual" was one way the workers and their families could get out and enjoy an outing *par excellence*. These special summer events became favorites of the children who saw this event as "second only to Christmas." It would be anticipated for many weeks. The thought of all that was Euclid Beach engendered almost unbearable waiting until that day arrived. In fact, special outings were held by many different organizations including area communities, lodges, clubs, ethnic groups, and professional and trade unions; just the list of businesses alone picnicking reads like a Who's Who of American Commerce: names like the Goodyear Tire and Rubber Company, the Goodrich Rubber Company, the White Motor Company, Richman Brothers Clothes, the Cleveland Plain Dealer, and the Cleveland Press, to sight a few. *(Illus. 195.)*

From the first years of the park's operation, organizations held their annual outings at Euclid Beach, but not until the Humphrey Company's lease and purchase of the park in 1901 did this picnic trade mushroom. Even though the Woodmen, the Knights of Pythias, and the Butchers (among others) held outings at the park in the '90's, stern policies of the Humphrey management were deemed much more suitable to family entertainment.

The number of people who came to the park for the annuals would be the envy of any major league baseball team. In 1903, the Grotto Picnic, a major picnic at the Beach for decades, drew an estimated 20,000 persons while the Woodmen's function brought 15,000 guests to the park. Among the biggest picnics to travel to the Beach were those held by Goodyear. These outings, along with the Goodrich picnics, were known as the "Akron" picnics. In 1931, Goodyear's employees and families swelled the day's attendance to over 80,000. It took over 22,000 cars to

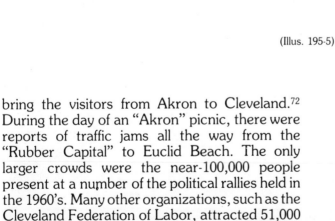

(Illus. 195-2)   (The Cleveland Press)

(Illus. 195-5)

(Kekic Collection)

bring the visitors from Akron to Cleveland.[72] During the day of an "Akron" picnic, there were reports of traffic jams all the way from the "Rubber Capital" to Euclid Beach. The only larger crowds were the near-100,000 people present at a number of the political rallies held in the 1960's. Many other organizations, such as the Cleveland Federation of Labor, attracted 51,000 as they held an "Italian Power" Day in 1969.[73]

In the 1940's, the size of the crowds traveling to the park encouraged the transit system to put additional street cars into service. The Press (Cleveland Press) outing of 1941 made it necessary to employ extra trolleys. Those arriving by street car were given free strips of Euclid Beach tickets. The public was invited. The size of the Eleventh Annual East Cleveland Community picnic necessitated the use of extra busses to handle the picnickers. Over 40,000 came to that event in 1946. Not only were the visitors numerous, but treats given away at these events sometimes approached astronomical figures. At the Fisher Brothers (grocery chain - to later become Fisher-Fazio-Costa) annual, 15,000 sticks of gum, 10,000 lollipops, and 10,000 balloons were distributed. Some unusual contests were held at these outings. One featured a "Johnny-Calling Contest" which tested a mother's strength of voice to call her child. Another picnic offered a "Milk-Drinking Handicap" to test the capacity of milk-drinking enthusiasts.

(Kekic Collection)

(Illus. 195-3)

(Kekic Collection)

(Illus. 195-4)

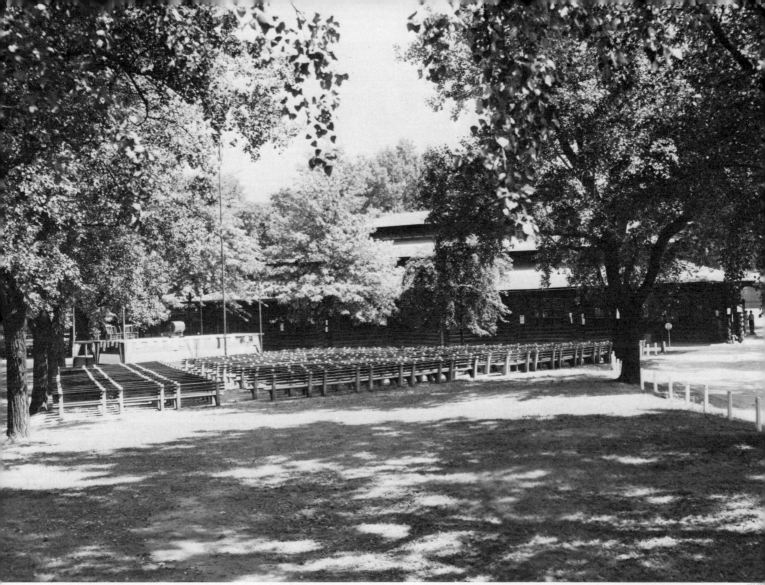

(The Humphrey Company)   (Illus. 195A.)

At some larger picnics guests registered and then had their hands stamped. The stamp on the hand became a *passe partout* at the attractions — a mere flash of it at the attendant gained entrance. One could repeat this process as often as desired depending on how long one cared to stand in line.

A beautiful summer day with the breeze blowing in off the lake, a treasure of ride tickets or a stamp on the hand, a picnic lunch under the Sycamores at the COLONNADE, the LAKE LUNCH, or CAFETERIA, a "three legged race", an egg throw, a "thousand" rides, the companionship of co-workers/friends/family, and a "delightful exhaustion" at the day's end compose a million memories of Euclid Beach. Yes, the company, community, or organization annual outing was a very close runner-up to Christmas.

The events that filled the Beach's summer schedule were significant manifestations of the park as a "family place;" an institution in the minds of millions of Clevelanders, Ohioans, and Americans.

Many organizations, such as Goodyear, planned a full day for their employees. The park opened at 9 A.M. on those days, and the rides opened at 10 A.M. The picnickers could look forward to 14 hours of riding in addition to special events scheduled throughout the day. Goodyear presented three youth-band concerts *(Illus. 195a.)* during their outing of 1961 along with contests, games, softball, a drawing, *(Illus. 195a.)* and dancing in the evening. The park closed at midnight. During the decades the DANCE PAVILION operated, the park often offered "courtesy" dances to the larger picnics, furnishing the organization with afternoon dancing exclusively for their guests. During the park's last decade many organizations utilized the LOG CABIN for evening dancing. *(Illus. 196, 197, 198.)*

(Illus. 197)

(Russell Allon Hehr Collection)

(Illus. 196.) The LOG CABIN was a Euclid Beach landmark. It served as a meeting place and headquarters for organizations holding outings at the park. This postcard picture shows the newer windows which replaced the original oval ones. The scene dated around 1915.

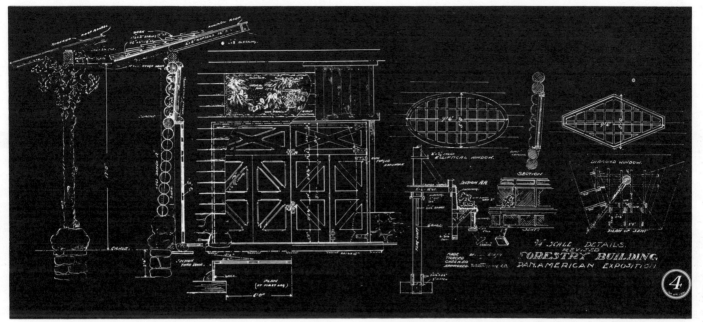

(The Humphrey Company)

(Illus. 197, 198.) Two elevations of the LOG CABIN, originally the Forestry Building at the Buffalo, New York Pan-American Exposition in 1901. The original windows were unfamiliar to later visitors to the park.

The LOG CABIN and the ANNEX (formerly the stage housing and fly gallery for the AVENUE THEATRE) functioned as headquarters for the groups holding the outing. Many will remember going to those locations to get that precious bundle of tickets that allowed them on the rides. A child with a balloon tied to his wrist determinedly clutching strips of tickets was a usual sight at Euclid Beach Park during one of the annual picnics. (Illus. 199.)

Almost all former Euclid Beach employees remember a "family" day for children who had no families — Orphans' Day. The Humphrey Company and the Automobile Club hosted this very special annual occurrence for more than SIXTY years. From the earliest days of the century, members of the club caravaned the children without families from orphanages to the park. (Illus. 200.) Euclid Beach opened at 10 A.M. just for these children, and from the opening hour until 1 P.M., the park was theirs alone. (Illus. 201.) Listening to the comments of the park employees, it is difficult to determine who found the day more special, the children or the workers. On the morning of this day, the park management and staff did everything possible to provide the orphans a great and memorable time.

(Illus. 199.) The '20's were in full swing and the kiddies loved a balloon as much then as they do now. The date is July, 1926.

(The Cleveland Press)

CLEVELAND PLAIN DEALER

CLEVELAND, MONDAY, JULY 7, 1941

Auto Club Carried Orphans to Picnic 'Way Back in 1905

(The Cleveland Plain Dealer)

(Illus. 200.) The Cleveland Automobile Club's annual Orphans Day Picnic was a special event for both the children and the park people. Here in a 1905 scene the caravan is ready to go.

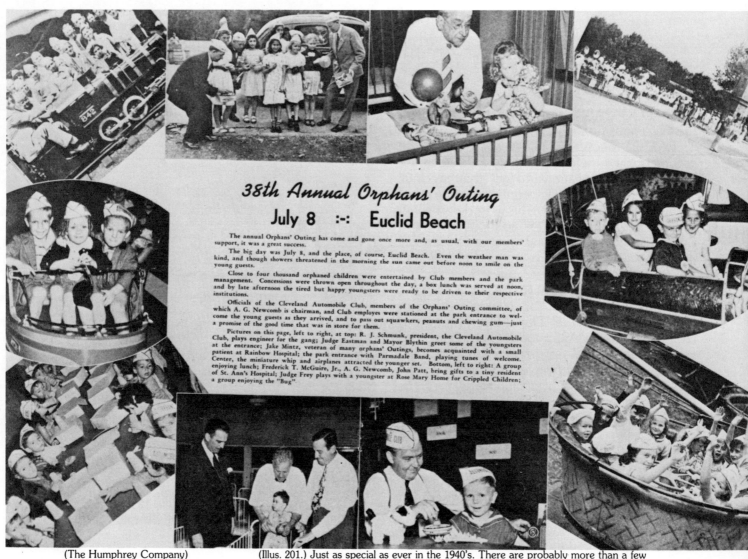

38th Annual Orphans' Outing
July 8 :-: Euclid Beach

The annual Orphans' Outing has come and gone once more and, as usual, with our members' support, it was a great success.

The big day was July 8, and the place, of course, Euclid Beach. Even the weather man was kind, and though showers threatened in the morning the sun came out before noon to smile on the young guests.

Close to four thousand orphaned children were entertained by Club members and the park management. Concessions were thrown open throughout the day, a box lunch was served at noon, and by late afternoon the tired but happy youngsters were ready to be driven to their respective institutions.

Officials of the Cleveland Automobile Club, members of the Orphans' Outing committee, of which A. G. Newcomb is chairman, and Club employes were stationed at the park entrance to welcome the young guests as they arrived, and to pass out squawkers, peanuts and chewing gum—just a promise of the good time that was in store for them.

Pictures on this page, left to right, at top: R. J. Schmunk, president, the Cleveland Automobile Club, plays engineer for the gang; Judge Eastman and Mayor Blythin greet some of the youngsters at the entrance; Jake Mintz, veteran of many orphans' Outings, becomes acquainted with a small patient at Rainbow Hospital; the park entrance with Parmadale Band, playing tunes of welcome. Center, the miniature whip and airplanes attracted the younger set. Bottom, left to right: A group enjoying lunch; Frederick T. McGuire, Jr., A. G. Newcomb, John Patt, bring gifts to a tiny resident of St. Ann's Hospital; Judge Frey plays with a youngster at Rose Mary Home for Crippled Children; a group enjoying the "Bug".

(The Humphrey Company)

(Illus. 201.) Just as special as ever in the 1940's. There are probably more than a few who look back on those outings with a wealth of memories.

On July 7, 1955, the Humphrey Company, the officers, and employees were awarded a plaque commemorating the 50th year of Orphans' Day outings. *(Illus. 202, 203.)* It read:

IN APPRECIATION
TO
THE HUMPHREY COMPANY
ITS OFFICERS AND EMPLOYEES

For the smiles you've etched on children's faces . . . For the thrills you've given youthful hearts . . . For the wholesome example of civic generosity you have so modestly set, and . . . For the splendid cooperation Euclid Beach Park has rendered to the Orphans' Outing Committee of the Cleveland Automobile Club, we commend and thank you. Your unselfish efforts for over half a century have won for you the respect and admiration of the Club membership and especially of those privileged to serve on the Outing Committee.

Signed this 7th day of July, 1955
for the
Board of Trustees
Cleveland Automobile Club
W.A. Stinchcomb
President
Frederick T. McGuire, Jr.
Vice President, and Outing Chairman[74]

Perhaps the award and what it stood for captured the overall atmosphere of Euclid Beach Park.

The park was a gathering place for families during all of its seventy-four seasons, and "dry" for its last sixty-eight. With the high priority placed on safety and maintenance, the park presented the appearance of a solid and neat (yet not anticeptic) facility filled with attractions and conveniences *(Illus. 204.)* proper to the pleasures of people.

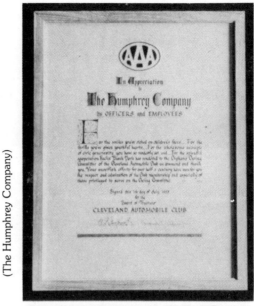

(The Humphrey Company)

(Illus. 202.) Participation in the Orphan's Day activities by the Humphrey Company is acknowledged by the Automobile Club, July, 1955.

(The Humphrey Company)

(Illus. 203.) Harvey Humphrey receives the plaque from Carl V. Weygandt, then chief justice of the Ohio Supreme Court. Two of the orphans, Steve Hahn and Constance Allen, assist.

(Kekic Collection)

(Illus. 204.) The clean and roomy men's restroom was not typical of many parks of the era. However, the Humphreys proclaimed their opinion as the sign declares, "This is a Nice Place." It seemed fitting.

Chapter 10

Great People and Great Events

(Illus. 205.) Glenn H. Curtiss, pioneer aviator on the BEACH at the "Beach." The 1910 flight was a historic event for both aviation and the park.

Some of the things that can illustrate the stature of Euclid Beach Park are the appearance there of notable people and the occurrence of significant events on the site. Throughout the history of the Beach patronage was dedicated, and, as a result of the vast number of visitors, the park became an ideal place for famous persons and special activities.

Even during Euclid Beach's earliest seasons, people of reputation came to the park. Paul Boyton, amusement park pioneer and water show producer, came to the Beach in 1896. (Boyton had devised a predecessor of the "wet suit." In this rubberized and inflatable garment he attempted to jump from an ocean steamer leaving New York harbor for Europe and then in his inflated suit swim back to America. As the ship was some distance out to sea, he attempted his self propelled voyage but was restrained by the crew. As Ireland was approached, he successfully convinced the ship's captain that he could make it to land and did, gaining wide acclaim. This lead to his venture at Coney Island.)

Clara Morris, nationally known actress, performed at the Beach in 1898. (This popular starlet's visit was made more significant by the fact that her career had started in Cleveland.)

The Humphrey's interest in things technological brought other notable persons to the Beach's Erie shore. Glenn H. Curtiss was an aviation pioneer in 1910, and the keen interest of the Humphrey brothers in the "aeroplane" (air plane) brought Curtiss to northern Ohio. On August 31, 1910, the Curtiss biplane, with Curtiss at the controls, flew from Euclid Beach to Cedar Point (Sandusky, Ohio) and back again. *(Illus. 205.)* Some of the thousands who lined the PIER and the BEACH, used by Curtiss as a runway, had never seen an "aeroplane" before. Some of these people doubted that such a thing could/did exist. Whatever the reason, the event was one which drew a multitude to the park. (Curtiss became one of the major manufacturers of aircraft in the 1930's and 1940's.)

(The Humphrey Company)

206

Almost a year later, another young aviator was invited to land at the Beach. Harry N. Atwood landed on the sands of Euclid Beach Park on August 17, 1911, as one of the stops on his St. Louis to Boston Flight.[75] His route took him from Toledo to Sandusky and then, presumably, to Cleveland and Euclid Beach. Atwood mistook Edgewater Park for Euclid Beach and made an unscheduled stop there. He then resumed his flight and successfully landed on the park's BEACH. Throngs greeted him, and on the following day, more crowds came to see Harry Atwood put on an exhibition. (Illus. 206.)

Not only were the Humphreys interested in aviation, but they understood its appeal and, in turn, its value as a show business attraction. D.S. Humphrey was present at the Atwood event, helping guide the crowds, addressing them through a large megaphone. Atwood was hosted as a visiting celebrity with a great deal of attention and a dinner at the Lake Shore Country Club. (Illus. 206.) The romance of aerial pioneering was in full bloom during the second ten years of the twentieth century.

However, not all connected with the Atwood flight was of the nature of romance. The young flyer was greeted by a baliff who immediately attached the aeroplane. Atwood owed $300 to the Standard Oil Company of New York. The practice of petroleum companies sponsoring such events had not yet come into vogue. The Humphreys came to the rescue, and "the law was satisfied" — the festivities were then allowed to proceed.

Another incident that marred the 1911 flight was the drowning of a swimmer as Atwood's aircraft approached the landing site.

Despite the distraction of the airplane and the drowing, the activities were witnessed by many curious about manned flight. The day after the landing Atwood demonstrated the craft's capabilities to thousands.

The year 1914 brought another flyer to the Beach as Lily Irvine (aviatrix) broke all existing records by flying from Cedar Point to Euclid Beach in sixty minutes.

From this early time in the history of aviation to the present, members of the Humphrey family have shown an active interest in flying. This interest was/is shown by Harvey Humphrey, Harvey's son (Dudley S. Humphrey III), and by Perce and Mabel Killaly.

Those well known for their feats of flying were not the only persons of reputation to visit Euclid Beach. August 12, 1924, found the child movie star Jackie Coogan at the park for a visit. The young screen idol agreed to a sitting in front of the camera with Dudley S. Humphrey, II, and Captain McCready of the Cleveland Police Force. (Illus. 207.)

(The Humphrey Company)

(Illus. 207.) Captain McCready of the Cleveland Police Force, Jackie Coogan, child movie star, and D.S. Humphrey II.

(Right)

(Illus. 206.) The Humphrey interest in aviation and innovative technology was evident as Harry Atwood made his flight to Euclid Beach in 1911 and proceeded to hold a flying exhibition.

THE CLEVELAND LEADER

Copperplate Pictorial Section

Copperplate Pictorial Section

CLEVELAND GREETS THE GREATEST MAN-GULL OF THE ERA

Atwood Tornadoes into Forest City While Thousands Cheer and Wonder

Photographs by Frank Smith, Leader Staff Photographer

Machinists Lemat and Lawson "Making Safe."

Hooray! Off for the Country Club at Last.

First Time in History Aeroplane Sheriff-Seized

Skimming Tree Tops Like Gulls Over Foam Crests. Off for Erie.

Landing at Euclid Beach, Where Throngs Waited Hours

Nonchalantly Smoking on the First "Getting Ready"

Society "Fancy-Working" while Atwood-Waiting

Section of Anxious Thousands at Euclid Beach.

Early Morning Crowd at Euclid Beach Inspecting Aeroplane

First Touch of Earth Since Toledo

Across the Club Links Clipping the Grass Before Rising

And Now a Minute Nearer Flight to Country Club

(The Cleveland Leader)

During his youthful days, another star of radio, television, movies, and stage visited Euclid Beach frequently. This world famous figure was Bob Hope. He and boyhood friend "Whitey" Jennings were regular competitors in the races that were held at the frequent outings at the Beach and Luna Park. The fact that this speedy duo, which almost always won, was not necessarily affiliated with the organization hosting the picnic did not detract from their competitive spirit. Many days the pair would call the two parks to inquire about the picnics of the day and the time of the races. As a result, they might compete at two different outings in a single day. The cash prizes provided incentive to compete in as many contests as possible. The street car line connecting Luna Park and the Beach was a familiar route to Hope and Jennings. Somewhere in the city there must have been more than one outing committee member who wondered who those boys were.[76]

Cleveland was the original home of many show business personalities. Besides Bob Hope, another noteworthy show business figure to call Cleveland "home" was Kaye Ballard. Her father took her and the family to the Park frequently. In fact, it was the first amusement park she ever attended. One of her favorite rides was the THRILLER, even though "it was such a scary height."[77] A practical joke which was a favorite of her brother's was to pretend they were lost in the SURPRISE HOUSE. This had an unnerving effect upon Miss Ballard. She even has recollection of singing at a special event at the DANCE PAVILION. Among her fondest memories of Euclid Beach, her favorite park, was the "delicious frozen custard."

The appearance of noted bands and band leaders was not a rarity at Euclid Beach. The bands of Lawrence Welk, Frankie Carl, Blue Baron, and Eddie Duchin were just a few of those who brought their prominence to the bandstand of the DANCE PAVILION.

Another event that many will remember from their childhood was not the appearance of a dignitary, movie star, or aviation hero, but the advent of Coca-Cola Day. This day brought thousands to the park with bundles of tickets obtained as prizes for the purchase of Coke. Many a collection of empty Coke bottles was carefully acquired as youngsters attempted to secure a treasure of prize tickets. This form of promotion was prevalant in the 1960's.

The Coca-Cola Bottling Company of Cleveland used another promotion technique in earlier times. A free ride ticket would be given to each person buying a bottle of Coke at the park for the regular 5-cent price. (Yes, that's 5-cents!)

Another "Great Event" patiently awaited by eager Beach visitors was "NICKLE DAY." On this day, usually a day during the middle of the week, almost all rides cost a nickle per ride. (The value of a nickle has significantly changed!) Needless to say, these special days were very popular.

The use of an amusement park as an arena for airing political views is not new, and many noted politicians made trips to Euclid Beach. Frank J. Lausche (at the time, Common Pleas Judge) spoke at the park in June of 1941, rebuking strikes as the nation stood on the threshhold of war. (Lausche later became governor of Ohio.)

In 1936, the year the Republican National Convention was held in Cleveland, D.S. Humphrey, II, invited the visiting delegates to come to Euclid Beach. In the years to follow, some of the most famous political leaders of the United States would appear at the park.

Perhaps one of the most popular presidents the country has ever known was John F. Kennedy. As a presidential hopeful, the Senator from Massachusetts spoke to thousands at Euclid Beach as he campaigned for the presidency. Kennedy was to speak at three of the Ohio Democratic functions held at the park. (Illus. 208.)

CUYAHOGA COUNTY

DEMOCRATIC STEER ROAST

Senator John F. Kennedy
For President

Senator Lyndon B. Johnson
For Vice President

EUCLID BEACH PARK

CLEVELAND, OHIO

September 25, 1960

(Kaselak Collection)

(Illus. 208b.) John F. Kennedy at the lectern of Euclid Beach Park. Congressman
Charles Vanik is directly behind Kennedy.

(Illus. 208a.) Kennedy and Johnson, soon to be elected, were the
focus of attention for the 1960 Democratic Steer Roast held by
the Party in Cuyahoga County.

(Kaselak Collection)

210

Others to speak at the Democratic "Steer Roasts" were Kennedy's Vice-President Lyndon B. Johnson, Senator Hubert Humphrey, *(Illus. 209.)* and Senator Ted Kennedy, brother of the President. *(Illus. 210.)*

The Democratic Party was not the only political party to utilize the Beach for rallies. Two noted Republicans to hold forth at Euclid Beach were Barry Goldwater, Jr., campaigning for his father, and Governor James Rhodes of Ohio. Political rallies were some of the functions to draw the largest crowds during the park's last decade of operation. The Steer Roasts attracted huge crowds of up to 100,000.

From the very first years of Euclid Beach Park until its close, the appearance of dignitaries, showmen, pioneers and well-known persons was not unusual. (It is even rumored that a shipwreck occurred on August 27, 1906, offshore of the Beach involving the steamship, the WM. GRANDY.) The park itself was indeed a famous name, and for famous persons to be present on these acres was truly fitting.

(Kaselak Collection)

(Illus. 209.) Hubert Humphrey on the campaign trail. To his right is John Gilligan, former Governor of Ohio, behind him is Congressman Charles A. Vanik, and on the extreme left is Carl Stokes, former mayor of Cleveland.

(Kaselak Collection)

(Illus. 210.) Ted Kennedy leaving the park; William Stanton in the front seat.

It has been said that history repeats itself.
Would it not be grand if Euclid Beach Park in its heyday
could come again and we could all relive . . .

(Kekic Collection)

Chapter 11
The Romance

(Illus. 211.) The water *was* blue and with a sunny summer sky, a fishing pole, and a special friend, the day would be hard to beat.

214

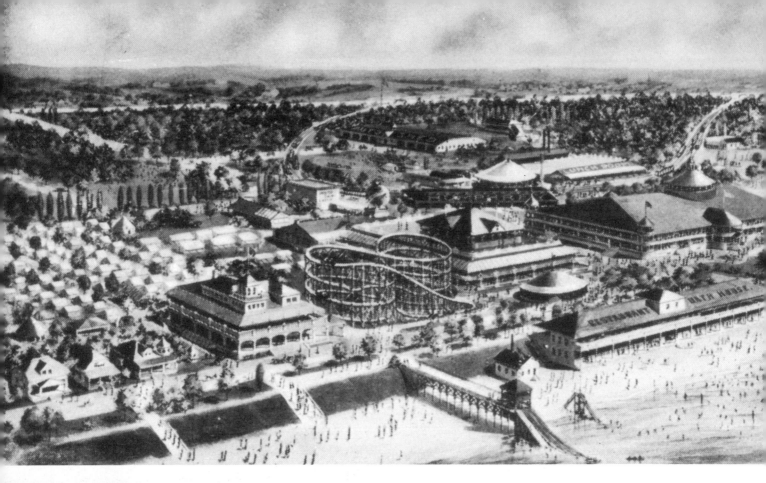

215

(Illus. 212.) An artist's aerial view represents an idealization of what amusement parks of the period looked like. Many of the structures shown were either projected or inserted for effect.

(Tom Oldham)

(Bottom Left)

(Illus. 213.) The picnic grounds near the RAVINE were thickly wooded. The soft and quiet look of the park existed from the park's earliest days. (c. 1910.)

(Western Reserve Historical Society)

(Illus. 214.) The shady RAVINE, which was later eliminated, was crossed by two bridges and provided a cool shaded walkway.

(Robert Legan)

216

(Lee O. Bush Collection)

(Illus. 215.) Faded, like so many memories, this postcard depicts the early SHOOTING GALLERY - five shots for a penny.

(Kekic Collection)

(Illus. 216.) Putting the finishing touches on the WADING POOL on the BEACH. The Humphrey cement pouring process was used to produce a place for laughing and splashing.

(Right)

(Illus. 218.) Crowds line up to see a cinema at the WORLD THEATRE.

(Illus. 217.) The early White Motor bus that was used for sight-seeing passes a line of vintage cars parked near the MERRY-GO-ROUND. They knew what "touring" meant then. The SCENIC RAILWAY station building can be seen just behind the conical roof of the MERRY-GO-ROUND. (Russell Allon Hehr Collection)

(Illus. 218A.) (inset) Another view of the WORLD THEATRE. The building stood in the area of the later DODGEM and LAFF-IN-THE-DARK.

(Kapel Collection)

(Frederick Fried Collection)

(Tom Oldham Collection)

(Illus. 219.) Maybe there is one of these old pennants or other souvenirs in your attic, packed away with a treasure of remembrances.

(Illus. 220.) A line drawing of Euclid Beach's first roller coaster, the SWITCHBACK RAILWAY.

(The Humphrey Company)

(Illus. 220A.) Another artist's rendition of the park showing the SWITCHBACK instead of the FIGURE EIGHT. The surrounding countryside differs greatly from this area of Cleveland today.

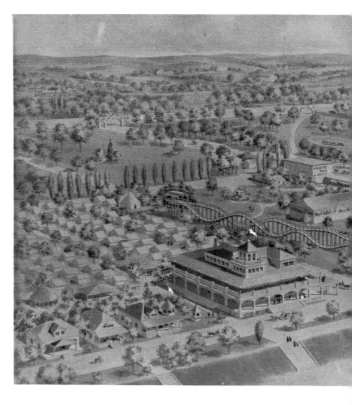

(The Humphrey Company)

(Russell Allon Hehr Collection)

Dancing in the Pavilion, Euclid Beach Park, Cleveland, Oh

(Illus. 221.) Skirts to the floor and coats with ties. Only the properly attired would sway and glide across the spacious floor of the great DANCE PAVILION. It must have been extraordinarily hot on this day since a number of coatless men are on the dance floor.

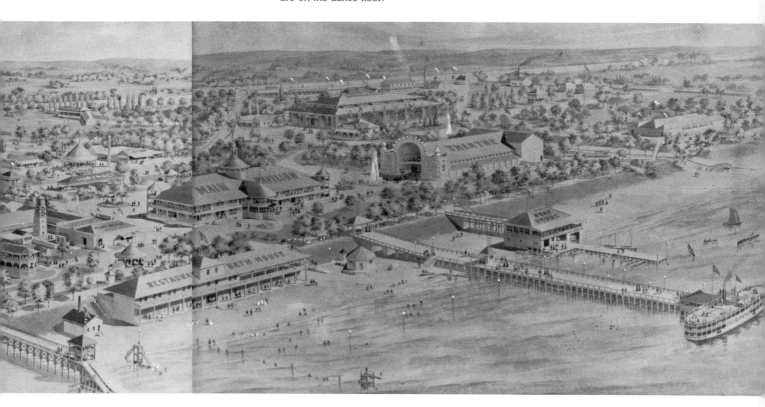

There is a young lady named Ritter
Who is always found eating a—doughnut.

EUCLID

BEACH

TEMPERANCE MORAL UPLIFTING	Originators and Sole Manufacturers of the Famous HUMPHREY POP CORN AND HUMPHREY CANDY	NO FREAKS FAKES OR FRESH PEOPLE

DANCING
BOATING
SCENIC RAILROAD
BOWLING
ÆRIAL SWING
MERRY-GO-ROUND
CAMPING
POP CORN
PHOTO STUDIO
PONY TRACK
BILLIARDS AND POOL
AUTOMATIC VAUDEVILLE
GREEN GRASS

We take this occasion to thank the pupils and alumni of East High School for the generous patronage we have received from them.

OWNERS **THE HUMPHREY CO.** OPERATORS

ROLLER SKATING
BATHING
FIGURE 8
BOX BALL
CAROUSAL
OCEAN WAVE
PICNIC GROUNDS
REFRESHMENTS
MOVING PICTURES
AUTOMOBILE GARAGE
RESTAURANT
ILLUSTRATED SONGS
LAKE BREEZES

Poet: All I need is an opening, sir.
Editor: What is the matter with the one you just came through?

(Schroyer Collection)

221

(Illus. 223.) A scene in the 1920's with eager splashers enjoying the POOL; and the PIER ready for a fireworks display as the evening progressed.

(Kekic Collection)

(Kekic Collection)

(Illus. 225.) Tin Pan Alley-ist J. Brachman combined with S.J.
Feldman to compose this "hit" (?) in 1897.

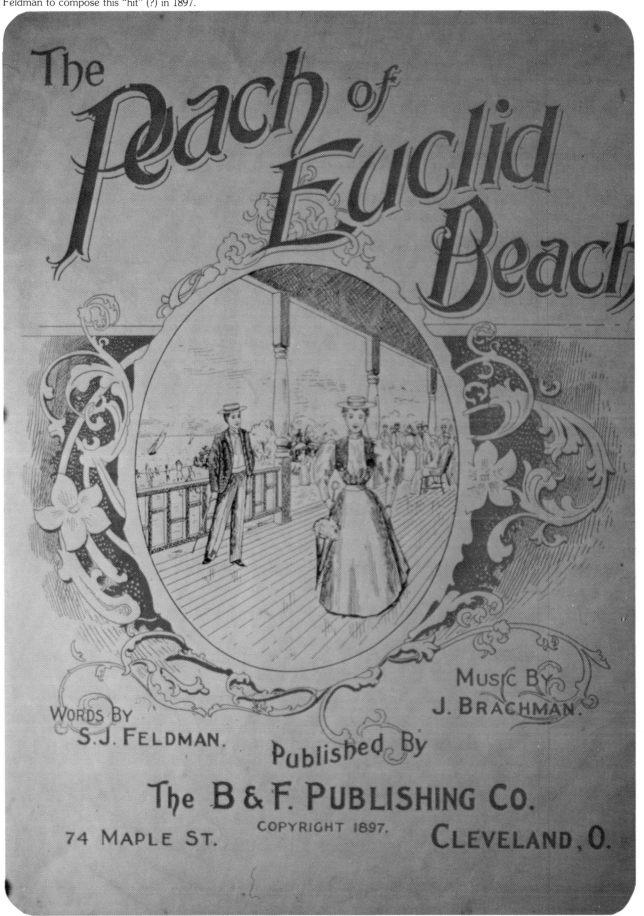

The Peach of Euclid Beach

WORDS BY
S.J. FELDMAN.

MUSIC BY
J. BRACHMAN.

Published By

The B & F. PUBLISHING Co.

74 MAPLE ST.

COPYRIGHT 1897.

CLEVELAND, O.

(Gary Lamb Collection)

(Illus. 226.) Everyone wanted to ride.

(Cleveland Press)

(Illus. 227.) Romance was inherent to the place with its soft shady walks. It was a place designed with people in mind, and people loved it.

(Kekic Collection)

(Carl L. Mower Collection)

(Illus. 228.) All aboard the SLEEPY HOLLOW.

(Illus. 229.) Nothing like a good cigar to amplify a day's enjoyment.

(Kekic Collection)

(David Humphrey Scott Collection)

(Illus. 230.) The FLYING PONIES, stripped for winter and covered with snow, await the spring gallop.

(Illus. 231.) The entrance to "paradise." (also Illus. 231A.) At the sight of the MAIN GATE, the wildest of anticipations became almost uncontrollable.

(The Cleveland Press / The Humphrey Company)

(Joe Erdalac Collection)

(Illus. 232.) The artist, Shirley Aley Campbell, describes her painting, "A Top Banana Whispers a Eulogy to a Silent Park.": "A top Banana from the Burlesque world laments the demise of burlesque amid the demise of Euclid Beach. The Racing Coaster has been dismantled and part of the Rocket Ships removed."

(Right)
(Illus. 233.) A late day, early fall pictures of the ROCKET SHIPS amid the ever present trees.

(The Cleveland Press)

229

MUSIC: Love & Marriage
LYRICS: Bob Garfield

Let's go driving on the Dodgem.
Smashing into friends as we dislodge 'em
While we all go spinning
Around the floor at Euclid Beach.

Let's go laughing in the Dark
As we and our dates have a chance to spark
When no one else is looking
As we hold hands at Euclid Beach.

When we hurtle o'er the Falls
We'll snuggle up closely
Then we'll take that spooky trip
Through those tunnels so ghostly.

After hot dogs we eat taffy
Also frozen whip till we're quite daffy
There's a place for courting
At Euclid Beach
Which we can reach
By riding out upon the trolley.

Though we're careful and even cautious
We usually eat too much and get quite nauseous
But that's a thing to be expected
When we go out to Euclid Beach.

The Whip, the Whip is supposed to scare us
And so is the wheel designed by Ferris
No matter how often we go there
We have a lark at Euclid Beach

Toot, toot goes the carousel
As we race out horses
No where else upon the earth
Are such exciting courses.

Summer nights with someone lovely
Come with us and you will see whereof we
Speak in terms so glowing
of Euclid Beach
Which we can reach
By riding out upon the trolley.

(Illus. 235.) These words were set to the song "Love and Marriage" by Bob Garfield.

(Bob Garfield)

(Illus. 234.) Balloons, as in earlier days, were popular until the last days of the park's operation. These clowns were ready and willing to fill balloons with helium.

(The Humphrey Company)

(Stephen Knapp Collection)

(Illus. 236.) A KIDDIELAND scene from a painting by Stephen
Knapp.

(Martin Linsey)

233

(Illus. 238.) For some, the FLYING TURNS was **the** ride at the Beach. It stood ominously with the details of its course hidden by the outside of the barrel.

(James P. Marcus Collection)

(Left)

(Illus. 237.) The cars are rolling, the ride has begun - "Hold onto Your Hats." The THRILLER and the FLYING TURNS are the climax of the row of high rides. The thrills and surprises of these two rides seemed to increase as the evening settled into complete darkness.

ING COASTER

(James P. Marcus Collection)   (Above)

(Illus. 239.) The majesty of the Fall clouds is a fitting backdrop to the three majestic high rides at Euclid Beach. At the left is the FLYING TURNS, next is the THRILLER, and to the right is the RACING COASTER. The picture was taken as the park entered its final days in 1969.

(James P. Marcus Collection)   (Below)

(Illus. 240.) This sight was familiar to many who watched for the winter to pass and this scene to be transformed into gleeful screams of delight, periodically drowned out by the roar and clatter of the coasters. One winter though, no spring followed.

(Richard F. Hershey Collection)

(Illus. 241.) **The** moment, the time when everything in the universe merely paused,
then . . . well, if you haven't experienced it no words can tell you what it was like.
The vista is from the top of the THRILLER'S first and highest hill, looking down on
the twin tracked RACING COASTER and southward toward Lakeshore Boulevard.
The date was the summer of 1969.

(Illus. 243.) Dusk, the lights are on and the THRILLER is ready for the plunge. The FLYING TURNS is on the left, the RACING COASTER is on the right.

(Illus. 242.) Roller Coaster structures contains an endless variety of shapes and a seemingly infinite composition of lines. This is the RACING COASTER unloading platform looking to the south out on the course. The high structure at the center is the far turn on the THRILLER course.

(Richard F. Hershey Collection)

237

(Martin Linsey)

(Martin Linsey)

(Illus. 244.) Soft summer nights lit by the lights on the rides and those strung above. The lighting never became obtrusive as at a cheap carnival. The rides, the trees, the layout of the park, and even the lighting seemed to be in harmony, designed to be enjoyed by everyone.

(James P. Marcus Collection)

(Illus. 245, 246.) Two classic views of the RACING COASTER in action on a beautiful summer day in 1969.

(Stephen Knapp Collection)

(Illus. 247.) The ROC-O-PLANE from a painting by Stephen Knapp.

(Martin Linsey Collection)

(Illus. 248.) An early evening view of the newer FERRIS WHEEL and the TILT-A-WHIRL, silhouetted by the three classic high rides. (late 1960's)

242

(Illus. 251.) Yes, that's what we're missing.

(James P. Marcus Collection)

(Illus. 251A.) Snow on the CARROUSEL.

(James P. Marcus Collection)

(Above, Left)

(Illus. 249.) The OVER THE FALLS and the boarding area of the SLEEPY HOLLOW RAILROAD during the winter of 1969-70.

(James P. Marcus Collection)

(Below, Left)

(Illus. 250.) Snow covered these roofs for many years. It would not melt into joy in the spring of 1970.

(James P. Marcus Collection)

EUCLID BEACH

**The butterflys had fallen into sleep
to dreams of dreamlessness.**

Return, down darkened paths, past questioning.
Push back, past wind, to whirl in our fantasies.
To peanut butter candy kisses, popcorn balls and littering.
The midway's life alives because we had no other need.

We must push back.
Draw pictures from strange light.
The glimmer of the rockets top the tower,
Waiting for countdown, takeoff, up the ramp, sitting, flying.
Return, the water's roar flown over.

Walking, unnoticed when we were,
So small beneath The Laughing Lady's laugh.
She laughed so hard. I know she heard us laugh and laugh.

Padlocked cold into the Thriller's frightful seat.
Oh, you were afraid, you never tried that ride?
Well, so was I. Standing in line and thrown to life.
Never to have really seen. It comes to me, tonight.
It is never known, unless tonight, inside.
Padlocked cold . . . horrors touched.
Crash, crash across the tracks, rapid.

(James P. Marcus Collection)
(Illus. 253.) Sunset on the "sunset" - Fall 1969.

(The Cleveland Press)

(Illus. 254.) It was a time to remember! Two young girls on the
GREAT AMERICAN RACING DERBY. (1938)

I know the distant cars, they pass,
Or water hits the beach with flagrant disobedience
To tortured riding, wild, thrilling, Thriller.

Come, run up the steps onto the ballroom floor.
Twirl, touch the hundred circling windows, trillion lights.

Let's walk down to the beach.
We'll talk, smoke cigarettes beneath the pier,
Tell each other about life, love.

Peter Iversen (Illus. 252.)

(Stephen Knapp Collection)

(Illus. 255.) The flying SCOOTERS from a painting by Stephen Knapp.

(Martin Linsey Collection)

(Illus. 256.) This area of the park had no end of visual interest - a lithograph by Martin Linsey of the THRILLER and the surrounding area.

Euclid Beach   Martin Linsey 1946

(Left)

(Illus. 257.) One of the two magnificent chariots onthe Philadelphia Toboggan CARROUSEL, machine no. 19.

(Eric Beheim Collection)

(Below, Left)

(Illus. 258.) Wrapped in the Stars and Stripes. The CARROUSEL was in the "white period at the time of these pictures.

(Eric Beheim)

(Right)

(Illus. 258-1.) Decorated with garlands of flowers, a magnificent member of the grand PTC CARROUSEL.

(Eric Beheim)

(Below)

(Illus. 258.2) Note the long flowing mane and tail.

(Eric Beheim)

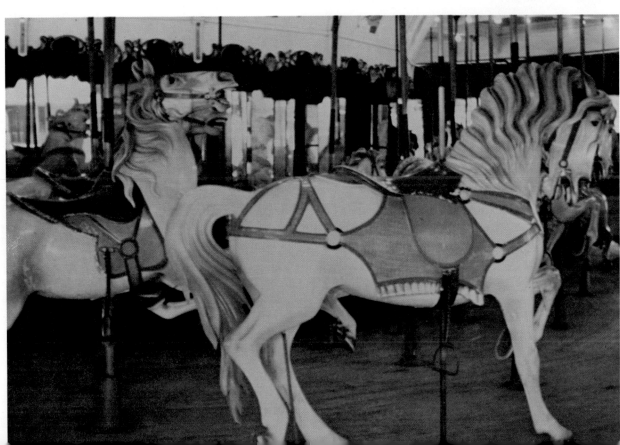

(Illus. 258-3 to 6.) The bodies of all the horses were painted white and the baroque designs on the inner panels have been replaced by Art Deco. The PTC horses of this period (1910) have exaggerated mouths and upper lips; the body/head relationship is somewhat disproportionate. None of this distracted from the fun or beauty of the machine.

(Eric Beheim Collection)

(Illus. 258-3)

(Illus. 258-4)

(Illus. 258-5)

(Illus. 258-6)

252

(Kapel Collection)

(Illus. 259.) This pre-Humphrey poster for the Beach is similar in style to the early artistic renderings, however, it pictures the park as viewed toward the southeast. The date is 1897.

253

(Illus. 260.) (Stephen Knapp)

(Kekic Collection)

(Illus. 261.) The FOUNTAIN was a place to bathe and play under the cascading water.

(Dr. Philip J. Kaplow Collection)

(Illus. 262, 263.) The FOUNTAIN was fascinating by night or day, and indeed, provided a romantic setting.

(The Cleveland Press

(The Cleveland Press)

(Illus. 264.) Where will we meet next year? The COLONNADE, September 28, 1969; the last day. The irreplaceable cannot be replaced.

(Eric Beheim Collection)

(Illus. 265.) The trees were ever present as seen in this view of the area around the DODGEM.

(James P. Marcus Collection)

(Illus. 266.) The games are over, the play silent. SKEE BALL was a popular pastime.

Chapter 12

"Wait 'til the Train Stops"

...and it did

(Kekic Collection)

(Illus. 267.) The area around the THRILLER loading platform was a popular gathering place and remained unchanged during the last few decades the park operated.

259

The ride pavilion or transfer station of the THRILLER was familiar to visitors who frequented Euclid Beach. *(Illus. 267.)* A short walk up a wooden ramp past the ticket chopper and attendant on the left; then, just a few more steps, a right turn, and the loading area of the platform was reached. At this point, the full impact of the anticipation came to bear on the stomach. After a short wait, during which there was a flashing of the signal lights and the ringing of a bell, the red-fronted THRILLER train appeared and came down the last stretch of track into the station. The "brakie" hauled back the long brake control handle, and the cars slid to a stop amid laughter, squeals, and general jubilation. After the cars emptied, the brake was released, and the empty train rumbled slowly toward the loading area. During the last years of the park's operation, Art Steele would lean forward and speak into the microphone placed near his station. The voice, made thin and tinny by the P.A. system, vigorously warned the waiting riders to "wait 'til the train stops." This warning, or a facsimile, had emanated from that platform since 1924. September, 1969, brought its last utterance.

Throughout the 1950's, Euclid Beach remained a popular summer diversion for thousands. Many outings were held at the park during this period. Numerous organizations needed no better option — there was just one place to hold the annual function — Euclid Beach Park. The Eastern Star was one such group; a group that had held their yearly picnic at the Beach over many decades.

Through the Fifties, the park offered attractions that varied little from those of the '40's. They were STILL the greatest, even though a number of the older rides, such as the SCENIC RAILWAY, the FLYING PONIES, and the outdoor WHIP, had been absent for some time. However, the excitement of the FLYING TURNS, the THRILLER, the RACING COASTER, OVER THE FALLS, the LAFF IN THE DARK, the AERO DIPS, and the two Carousels provided a significant variety of riding. *(Illus. 268, 269, 270, 271).*

(Lee O. Bush Collection)

(Illus. 267A.) The twin platforms of the RACING COASTER with it's latticework. The architecture is reminiscent of summer cottages of another era. The mood remained until the last days. The picture was taken in August of 1969.

(James P. Marcus Collection)

(Illus. 268.) "Over the top" as the two trains of the RACING COASTER begin their competition. The time is the summer of 1969.

(Lee O. Bush Collection)   (Top, Right)

(Illus. 270.) With hands held high and long hair flowing in the breeze, riders on the THRILLER approach the far turn which was located near Lake Shore Boulevard. (August, 1969).

(Illus. 271.) The gaily colored BUG with the brightly decorated FLYING SCOOTERS in the background were two familiar sights when the park was entered from the MAIN PARKING LOT. This scene was photographed during the last season.

(James P. Marcus Collection)

(Lee O. Bush Collection)   (Top, Left)

(Illus. 269.) The opening stages of the FLYING TURN'S course were a series of gentle slopes which then erupted into a semingly endless sequence of alternation turns. A person riding the FLYING TURNS for the first time might wonder what was to follow this initial deception. (August, 1969).

(Illus. 272.) The wooded vista looking toward the CARROUSEL exemplifies the atmosphere that was so much a part of Euclid Beach Park. The absence of garish decor was a hallmark of the park. (September, 1968).

(The Cleveland Press)

(Illus. 273.) The OFFICE, poured by the Humphrey cement process served as the park's headquarters until the closing in 1969.

(The Humphrey Company)

The Big Band Era had vanished, and new forms of dancing made it impossible to provide one type of entertainment suitable to all. The DANCE PAVILION was only used for private functions after 1959.

The year 1959 also marked the passing of Harvey Humphrey, son of Dudley S. Humphrey II. The park was now passed on to Dudley S. Humphrey III, and Doris (Humphrey) Mackley. The new directors of the Humphrey Compnay and Euclid Beach Park faced times that differed greatly from those before World War Two.

After 1945, the world began to see drastic changes at every level of life throughout the world. The foment of rapid and far-reaching change could be seen in politics, business, technology, and, of course, entertainment.

Yet, it was not such changes as these but, rather, the resistance to change that was notable about the Beach. Euclid Beach Park maintaining the high standards that were identified with it. It strived to keep the look of a non-contrived, peaceful, and clean park which existed until the final season. *(Illus. 272, 273).)*

The last decade the park was open witnessed the elimination of two old favorites; one was the AERO DIPS, which was removed in 1965, and the other, the GREAT AMERICAN RACING DERBY, which was sold and moved to Cedar Point Amusement Land in 1966. The cost of maintenance had become prohibitive!

There were, however, some people who remained during the last decade, among them Walter Williams and Fred Greenway. These members of the Euclid Beach "Family" could look back on many days of the park's history, millions of visitors, and countless hours of work on the many attractions that were part of Euclid Beach Park.

Conversely throughout the years that began during the second half of the Twentieth Century, many aspects of the park's operation remained unchanged. Euclid Beach enjoyed a residual popularity as many still made their journey to patronize this perennial institution. Indeed, Euclid Beach Park in the 1950's still held the distinct stature of an institution. To the younger folks of the community it had always been there, and to the older people it always would be there. The "free gate" policy was maintained; the absence of alcoholic beverages persisted; and the attempt to carry on the heritage of the Beach was sustained even though the social struggles throughout the world in the late '50's and the 1960's caused innumerable collisions. Some of these collisions came to Euclid Beach, and, on many occasions, the behavior of the crowds, in particular the larger ones, could not be predicted. Unruly persons were in more-than-ample supply.

Nonetheless, Goodyear continued to bring record numbers of guests to their picnics. And many groups enjoyed the shade of the sycamores and the "sumptuous" FROZEN WHIP. The coffee remained a monument to the coffee drinker, and the popcorn products never wavered in quality. Moreover despite the technological advances in the industry as used in the "fantastic" fantasies of Disneyland, the THRILLER's initial plunge of 71'5" *still* caused one to have second throughts as the first hill was ascended and the frights of the LAFF IN THE DARK *still* effectively persisted in giving riders a start.

Among the largest crowds were those found at the numerous political rallies, in particular the Democratic Party's "Steer Roast." These were functions of the Cuyahoga County Democrats and often featured men of high station in the party. It was at these functions that J.F. Kennedy, Hubert Humphrey (no relation to the Euclid Beach Hymphreys), and Lyndon B. Johnson spoke to crowds claimed to be nearly 100,000 persons.

As was the continued policy of the park, that which was new was brought to the Beach. Radio station-sponsored rock concerts were held, such as a ten-group show in 1966, featuring Mitch Ryder and the Detroit Wheels, Mike Scott with the Garbage Men, and others. Along with the music and personalities of the '50's and '60's, new rides like the SWINGIN' GYMS, the SCRAMBLER, and the TILT-A-WHIRL were introduced to the grounds.

The Humphrey regard for the surrounding community persisted as the "HUMPHREY FIELD" on the south side of Lake Shore Blvd. was donated for the use of Little League Baseball activities. Unfortunately, the property had to be sold in the late '60's when an amicable agreement on the taxes for that land could not be reached. The tax burden was too heavy for land that brought no return.

As usual, the summer brought summer workers from the nearby high schools and colleges. It has been verified by a number of those young people that they were fascinated by Euclid Beach and would go back to work summers if Euclid Beach Park were open today. Also, many a New York Central Railroad employee would understand such feelings since so many of them took the summers off to work at the Beach. (as guards).

It indeed was a special place which had features not found at other outdoor amusement parks. A small detailed example was a series of covered walks constructed to connect the COLONNADE, MAIN POPCORN STAND, CARROUSEL, DANCE PAVILION, PENNY ARCADE, GREAT AMERICAN RACING DERBY, and DODGEM. These were locations that could function when it was raining. Not only did the covered walks and sheltered rides help salvage a day's outing that proved to be too moist, but they helped salvage income for the park if the weatherman's work was unsatisfactory.

As the 1960's progressed, the face of Euclid Beach Park *did* change. Besides the removal of the GREAT AMERICAN RACING DERBY and the AERO DIPS roller coaster, the great GAVIOLI ORGAN of the ROLLER RINK was sold, and "ANTIQUE CARS" roamed the former solid maple skating surface. So well laid was the ROLLER RINK floor that removing it after the park's closing was one of the most difficult of wrecking tasks.

And yet, in many ways, the darkened DANCE PAVILION, the empty lot north of the ROLLER RINK, and the open area on the BEACH BLUFF where the BATH HOUSE had once stood were acceptable. Time had moved on. The vacant, darkened spaces on the countenance of Euclid each Park were like teeth absent from an aging face. Nevertheless, when it was announced in 1968 that the next summer would be Euclid Beach's LAST season, *it seemed unbelievable.* For a number of years the park's closing had been rumored, but when it finally occurred, it was UNREAL. *(Illus. 274.)* Articles of differing viewpoints about this tragic event flew at readers via the Cleveland and suburban newspapers, but no suitable answer or solution was *ever* produced. The "tumult and the shooting died." In fact, the park had operated at a loss for a number of years preceding 1968. Anyone with the slightest business knowledge understands that businesses are not charitable affairs and do cease to exist when the expense of operation exceeds income. To understand the multitude of reasons why Euclid Beach closed for its final season on September 28, 1969, would take a team of sociologists, economists, psychologists, historians, business analysts, and, most of all, the passage of time to put all the events of the post World War II decades in perspective. Above and beyond that, it has not been the concern of these pages to attempt to capsulize in some very accessible manner an answer to this frequently uttered question. The "season" represented in this volume is a brief yet hopefully significant look at but a single example of one of the great American institutions — this country's unique interpretation of outdoor amusement. Of the many very special parks the nation has known, Euclid Beach Park in Cleveland, Ohio, represented an example of what was and is possible; what is and was particularly American; and what was and is, like so many valuable attributes of the United States, threatened with extinction.

(James P. Marcus Collection)

(Illus. 274.) For the last time.

The last year of the 1960's and the first years of the 1970's witnessed the loss of a number of classic amusement parks. Chicago's renowned Riverview Park closed, as did the beautiful Coney Island on the Ohio River near Cincinnati. Like the carousel, a product of human hands and human care, the so called "traditional" park, also a product of human hands and human care, began to disappear.

The discovery of the suburbs and the migration out of urban centers may have left parks like Euclid Beach and Riverview behind. Or, perhaps, in the deluge of "things" that have cluttered up our lives for the last twenty-five years, these invaluable places were simply buried.

New and beautiful parks have sprung up around the country, and their attendance has been incredible. Still, they lack one thing — age! If the spirit of the Beach will forgive us this example: new parks prove that character takes time, just as a bottle of fine wine does not mature in a month.

The day was clear and cool that Sunday, the 28th of September, 1969. Clouds hung in a classic early Fall manner as the MAIN GATE arch was pierced for the last time by anxious riders. Most who came (and there were not as many as should have been there) were there to visit an old friend for a final time. Some who came could not stay until the very end — they left with their last vision being that of the park in operation. Nevertheless, the park closed early that day; only a few ears heard Mr. Steele say the the last time, "Wait 'til the Train Stops." He said it, and the train did stop . . . *forever (Illus. 275, 276, 277, 278, 279.)*

(Illus. 275.) All the trains stopped. Here is the approach to the THRILLER platform. (Fall, 1969).

(Joel C. Warren Collection)

(Illus. 276.) Brake handles that were never to be tugged again. The THRILLER'S station. (Fall, 1969).

(Joel C. Warren)

(Joel C. Warren)

(Illus. 277.) The cars stood covered never to "fly" the "Turns" again. (Fall, 1969).

(Joel C. Warren)

(Joel C. Warren)

(Illus. 278.) A few scattered leaves and the wind replaced the shuffle of eager feet and the rumble of the approaching train. The THRILLER (Fall, 1969).

(Illus. 279.) The last race is over but we all have lost. The RACING COASTER platform, after the close, September, 1969.

EPILOGUE

Shortly after the park closed in September of 1969 the acreage on which the amusement area existed was sold by the Humphrey Company. Hi-rise apartment buildings were later erected on the site.

(The Cleveland Press)

(Illus. 280.) A ravaged scene looking toward the AVENUE THEATRE and the OFFICE.

(James P. Marcus Collection)

(Illus. 281.) Bringing down a house full of echoes.

(James P. Marcus Collection)

(Illus. 282.) And the "Great" DANCE PAVILION was no more, February 23, 1972.

(James P. Marcus Collection)

(Illus. 283.) Only the skunks picnicked here until the final demise.

(James P. Marcus Collection)

(Illus. 284.) And the horses ran away as only the memory was left to ride the
noble mounts carved of wood. The Sycamores remained to stand hollow guard.

(James P. Marcus Collection)

(Illus. 285.) This scene would not become a postcard. The last of the great high rides waits to be felled. Scattered THRILLER cars stand in front of the FLYING TURNS structure.

(James P. Marcus Collection)

(Illus. 286.) Like fossils of some extinct species, the remains of the high rides stood, waiting for the inevitable. The sounds of another time could almost be heard.

(James P. Marcus Collection)

(Illus. 288.) A facade, a hill, and an idle PADDLE WHEEL.

(James P. Marcus Collection)

(Illus. 289.) Weeds grow where throngs had parked their cars. The LOG CABIN, too, met the vandals' ignorant matches as "de-creation" set in.

(James P. Marcus Collection)

(Illus. 290.) A bridge from nowhere to nowhere. The MINIATURE GOLF COURSE (PEE WEE).

(James P. Marcus Collection)

(Illus. 291.) A permanent drought, no more stream, no more plunges . . . no more.

(James P. Marcus Collection)

(Illus. 287.) The end was imminent.

(James P. Marcus Collection)

(Illus. 287A) Going!

275

(James P. Marcus Collection)

(Illus. 287B.) Going!

(James P. Marcus)

(Illus. 287C.) Gone! - the first hill is felled while the rest of the structure hangs on in defiance.

(Russell Allon Hehr Collection)   (Illus. 292.) Lake Erie persists in erasing the traces of the past and the PIER.

(Illus. 293.) Leaves gather on the ascending slope of the FLYING TURNS in the fall of 1969.

(Joel C. Warren)

(Illus. 295.) No tickets on sale! Euclid Beach Park is Closed for the Season . . . all the seasons except those that live in the memory.

(Illus. 294.) The THRILLER is gone.

(The Scoop)

(Joel C. Warren)

279

(Illus. 296.)   (James P. Marcus Collection)

APPENDIX A

THE HUMPHREY LINEAGE

Norsemen came with William the Conqueror to England in 1066. Among them was a Humphrey who began the English branch of the family.

Michael Humphrey of Byne Regis, England came to America in 1640 to establish the American Branch. He first settled in Dorchester, Mass., and later in Windsor, Conn. He manufactured tar and turpentine and engaged in various enterprises.

He married **Priscilla Grant** whose lineage was the same as that of General U.S. Grant.

Their son, **Samuel Humphrey,** was born in Windsor, Conn. Oct. 24, 1653. He became a lieutenant.

His son, also called **Samuel Humphrey,** was born at Sunbury, Conn. on May 17, 1686. He became an ensign.

His son, **David Humphrey,** was born at Simsbury, Conn. June 5, 1726.

His son, **Dudley Humphrey,** was born at Goshen, Conn. on October 20, 1770. He came to Ohio in 1837 and began the Ohio branch of the family. He settled in Parma, Ohio.

He married **Polly M. Sherman** in 1795. Her lineage is traced with that of General William Tecumseh Sherman.

They had 10 children.

Their son, **Dudley Sherman Humphrey I,** was born at Goshen, Conn. on Nov. 21, 1814. He grew up in Connecticut but moved to Parma, Ohio with his parents in 1837. He was well educated. He later moved to Townsend, Ohio (Huron County) where he was associated with his brother William in lumber and clock businesses. They bought large tracts of land for timber and operated sawmills on an extensive scale (more than 40 in various Western States).

He married **Mabel T. Fay** of Parma, Ohio on March 10, 1847. She was the second white child born in Parma, Ohio.

They had 5 children:
1. **Dudley Sherman Humphrey II**   2. **Mina Sherman**   3. **Harlow**
4. **David H.**   5. **Mary Malinda.**

Their son, **Dudley Sherman Humphrey II** was born on the family farm in Huron County near Wakeman, Ohio on May 19, 1852. He was educated in schools of the district, then attended Buchtel University, Akron. He was in business with his brothers David H. and Harlow. After the death of their father they took on his business in 1876.

He married **Effie D. Shannon** of Buffalo, New York.

They moved to Cleveland in 1891.

They had 3 children:
1. **Harvey John**   2. **Mabel Elizabeth (Killaly)**   3. **H. Louise.**

Their son **Harvey John,** was born on the family farm in Huron County near Wakeman, Ohio in 1884.

He married **Catherine Fuldauer** of Cleveland on Aug. 8, 1906.

They had 2 children:
1. **Dudley Sherman Humphrey III**   2. **Doris (Mackley).**

Their son was Dudley Sherman Humphrey III.

In 1893 the 7 founders of the Humphrey Company were:

David Humphrey (brother of Dudley Sherman Humphrey II)
Dudley Sherman Humphrey II
Mrs. Dudley Sherman Humphrey II
Harlow Humphrey (brother of Dudley Sherman II)
Harvey Humphrey (son of Dudley Sherman Humphrey II)
Linnie Humphrey (sister of Dudley Sherman Humphrey I)
Mabel Humphrey (daughter of Dudley Sherman Humphrey II)

APPENDIX B

ACREAGE and ACQUISITION PLAT
OF EUCLID BEACH PARK

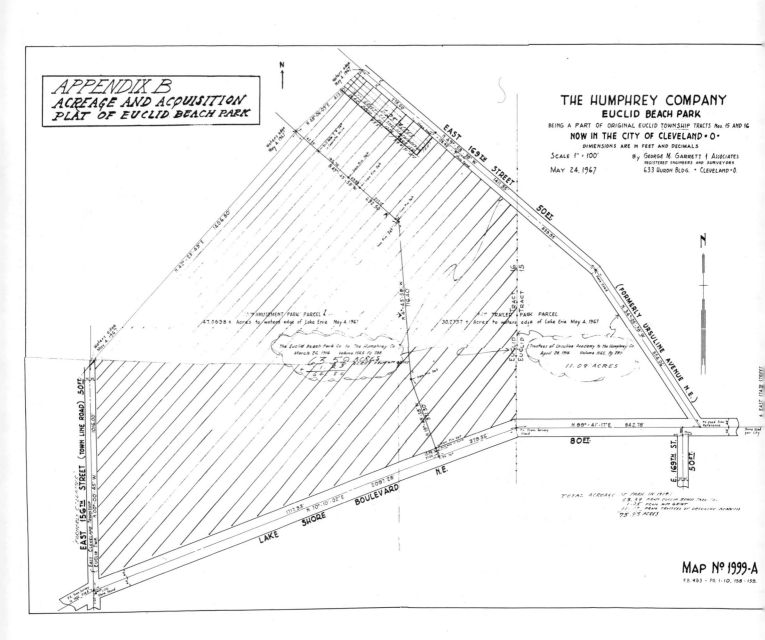

APPENDIX C

TRANSPORTATION TO and FROM
THE PARK by LOCAL STREETCAR
and INTERURBAN LINES

During the last days of the trolleys, there was through service to the BEACH on all three lines. After 1948, E. 140 St. was bussed and the big articulated Euclid streetcars never again went to Euclid Beach, turning around at Coit Rd. Loop.

A. To and from Square via St. Clair Avenue
B. To and from Square via Superior Avenue
C. To and from Square via Euclid Avenue
D. To Willoughby, Painesville, Ashtabula, & connections East.

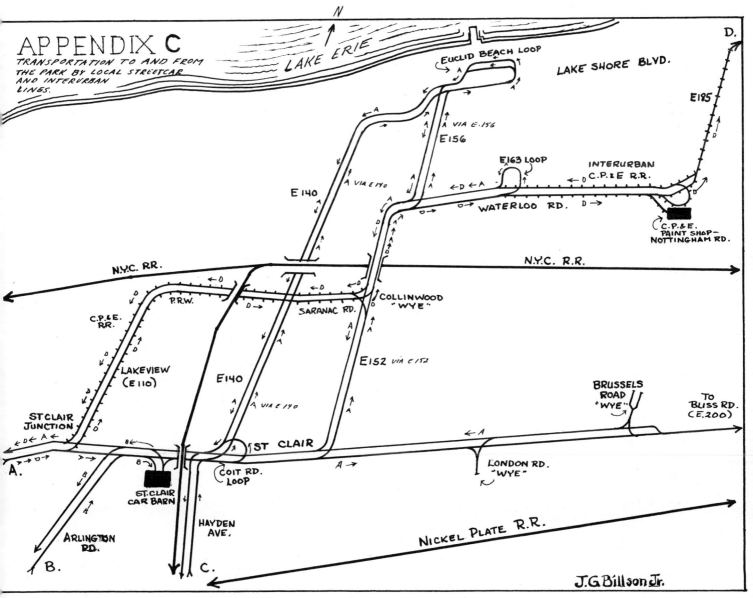

APPENDIX C
TRANSPORTATION TO AND FROM THE PARK BY LOCAL STREETCAR AND INTERURBAN LINES.

LAKE ERIE

EUCLID BEACH LOOP
LAKE SHORE BLVD.
E 185
E 156
A VIA E 156
E 163 LOOP
INTERURBAN C.P.&E R.R.
E 140
A VIA E 140
WATERLOO RD.
C.P.&E. PAINT SHOP— NOTTINGHAM RD.
N.Y.C. R.R.
N.Y.C. R.R.
P.R.W.
C.P.&E. RR.
SARANAC RD.
COLLINWOOD "WYE"
E 152 VIA E 152
LAKEVIEW (E 110)
E 140
A VIA E 140
BRUSSELS ROAD "WYE"
TO BLISS RD. (E.200)
ST CLAIR JUNCTION
ST CLAIR
LONDON RD. "WYE"
COIT RD. LOOP
ST. CLAIR CAR BARN
HAYDEN AVE.
ARLINGTON RD.
NICKEL PLATE R.R.
J.G. Billson Jr.

284

APPENDIX D

ANNUALS, PICNICS, SHOWS, EVENTS, OUTINGS, AT EUCLID BEACH PARK
A representative list, not complete.

ANNUAL PICNICS and OUTINGS

A & P Company
AFL - CIO
Addressograph - Multigraph Corp.
Al Koran
Al Sirat Grotto
Amalgamated Clothing Workers
American Institute of Banking
American Legion
American Steel & Wire
Arene Order of Eastern Star
Army - Navy Relief
Association of Polish Women
B.F. Goodrich Tire & Rubber Co.
Bailey Company
Bedford Merchants
Belle Vernon Day
Biglow F&AM
Bloomfield Company
Bowlers Day
Boys Town of Cleveland
Brenton D. Babcock F&AM
British Associations
Brooklyn Merchants
Burton Schools
Butchers
C.A. Grasselli Club of the Blind
Cathedral Latin Alumni
Catholic Elementary Schools
Catholic High Schools
Catholic Ladies of Columbia
Catholic P.T.A. League
Catholic Youth Organization
Chagrin Falls Community Day
Cleveland Athletic Club
Cleveland Cap Screw Company
Cleveland Diesel
Cleveland Electric Illuminating Co.
Cleveland F&AM
Cleveland Federation of Labor
Cleveland Federation of Musicians
Cleveland Heights Community
Cleveland Order of Eastern Star
Cleveland Plain Dealer
Cleveland Play Grounds
Cleveland Pneumatic Tool
Cleveland Press
Cleveland Press Kiddies Day
Cleveland Railway
Cleveland Roller Club
Cleveland Trust Club

Cleveland Twist Drill Company
Coca Cola Day
Collinwood Day
Community Temple
Cooperative Stove
Customers & Druggists Day
Cuyahoga Pythian Association
Cuyahoga Works
Dames of Malta
Dancing Masters Association
Daughters of American Revolution
Davis Laundry
Democratic Steer Roast
DeMolay - Rainbow Girls
Dyke School of Commerce
Eagle Hardware
East Cleveland Community Day
East Side Bakers Association
East Side Pioneers
Elbrook Order of Eastern Star
Elwell - Parker Electric Company
Elysium Figure Skating Club
Euclid Temple
Euclid Community Day
Euclid F&AM
Euclid Schools
Fairport Community Day
Federal Reserve Employees
Federation of Telephone Workers
Firestone Tire & Rubber Company
Fisher Foods
Forest City F&AM
Fraternal Order of Eagles
Friendship Order of Eastern Star
Garfield Heights Community Day
Gaston G. Allen F&AM
General Electric Company
Geneva Community Day
German Ladies
Glenville F&AM
Glenville Field Day
Glenville Order of Eastern Star
Goodyear Tire & Rubber Company
Gottfried Employees
Gracemont School
Graphite Bronze Company
Green Thumb Day (Gardeners outing)
Grocers
Grotto Picnic (see Al Sirat Grotto)
Harris - Seybold Company

Harris - Seybold - Potter
Hartford Cleveland Club
Harvey Rice School
Heights High Day
Heights Temple
Higbee Company
Hough Community Day
Hydraulic Equipment Company
Interior Steel Equipment Company
Iris F&AM
Irish American Democratic
Irish Civic Association
     (host of Parmadale Children's Home)
Irish Republicans
Italian Day
Jewel Tea Company
Jewish Bakers
Jewish Community Center
Jewish War Veterans
Junior Aviators
K.P. & Chicago Pneumatic Tool
Kiwanis Clubs
Knights of Maccabees
Knights of Pythias
Kroger Company
Lakewood Schools
Leece - Neville Company
Letter Carriers
Liberty Order of Eastern Star
Lynite Club of Aluminum Co. of Amer.
MANX Society
Marbles Champions of Northern Ohio
Marquette Metal Products
Masonic Lodge (various Lodges)
Master Bakers Association
May Company
Mayfield Schools Day
Mayflower School
Mentor Community Day
Metal Trades
Milk Dealers
Milkmen
Model Aviators
Monarch Aluminum Manufacturing Co.
Mound School
National Aeronautic Association
National Rubber Machinery Company
Newburgh F&AM
Newburgh Wire Works
Nickle Plate Association

Northeast Community Day (Collinwood)
Northeast YMCA
Nottingham School
O.N. Steele F&AM
Odd Fellows
Oheb Zebek Congregation
Ohio British Association
Ohio Malta Field Day
Old Classmates Day
Orange Schools
Orangemen
Order of Eastern Star (various Lodges)
Orphan's Day (sponsored by Cleveland AAA)
Osborn Manufacturing Company
P.A. Geier Company
Painesville Community Day
Painesville Telegraph "Thanks Day"
Parker Appliance Company
Parma Schaaf High
Parmadale Children's Home
Peerless Motor Car Company
Pesco Products Company
Petroleum Dealers
Pipe Machinery Company
Police & Firemen's Athletic Club
Polish Day
Presbyterian Union
Press Comic Page Picnic
Press Family Day
Printz - Biederman Company
Protected Home Circle
Pythian Day (see Knights of Pythias)

Rainbow Girls
   (see DeMolay - Rainbow Girls)
Rameses F&AM
Reliance Electric Company
Republican Rally (GOP Rally)
Richman Brothers Company
Roller Skaters Picnic
S.K. Wellman Company
St. Aloysius Mother's Union
St. Stanislaus
Scotch Day
Second Shift Night
Senior Citizens
Shaker Heights Schools
Shaw High Day
Shaw - Kirk Day
Shriners
Slovenian M.B.A.
Slovenian Woman's Union
Sohio
South Euclid Community
South Euclid Schools
Speck Baking Company
Suburban Schools Day
Suburb's Day
   (sponsored by Sun Newspapers)
Sun Papers
Tacoma Synagogue
Tall Cedars
Taylors T.M.B.A.
Telephone Company
Telling - Belle Vernon

The Temple
Temple on the Heights
   (see Heights Temple)
Thompson Products Company
Timken Roller Bearing Company
Townsend Clubs
UAW
Union Buyers Club
Union Trust
United British Society
United Order of Eastern Star
Veterans of Foreign Wars
Villa Angela
W.S. Tyler Company
Wakeman Community Day
Walnut School
Welsh Society of Cleveland
West Side Ladies Club
West Side Pioneers
Westgate (Shopping Center) Day
Wheaties Day
White Motor Company
White Sewing Machine Company
Willard Battery
Willoughby Community Day
Willoughby Schools
Woman's Benefit Association
Women's Democratic Club
Woodland Hills Community Day
Woodman Circle
Woodmens Day
Woodward F&AM
Woolworth Stores
Y.M.C.A.

EVENTS

Camper's Night
Glenn Curtiss Flight
Harry Atwood Flight
      Cedar Point to Euclid Beach, 1911
Irish Day Marathon (Annual)
      26 mile run to Euclid Beach
Jack Graney (announcer) and Cleveland Indians team
      members visit (1942)
Jackie Coogan visit (1924)
Miss Lily Irvine Flight (23 July 1914)
      Cedar Point to Euclid Beach in 60 minutes
NAAP convention (1930)
      National Association of Amusement Parks
Ping Pong Tournament (Annual)
Press National Marbles Tournament (Annual)

SHOWS

Auto Show
Boat Sale-A-Thon (1963)
Doll Show (27 August 1911)
Fall Fair & Exposition (Aug. 23 - Sept. 7, 1930)
      pertaining to various phases of industry and
      home economics
Goulardi (26 July 1963)
      Host of WJW "Shock Theatre"
Gus Augspurg's "Jungle Wonders" Animal Act (26 July 1963)
High Diving Champions (1961)
Punch & Judy Marionettes (4 August 1937)
Trapeze Act (24 June 1964)
Underwater Games (27 Sept. 1959)
      sponsored by Cleveland Skin Divers Club
Water Ski Show (1963)

APPENDIX E

EUCLID BEACH BALLROOM

SEASON	EUCLID BEACH ORCHESTRA	GUEST BANDS*		
Pre 1907	John Kirk			
1907-1924 (18 yrs.)	Louie J. Currier			
1925-1926 (2 yrs.)	Frank Wilson			
1927-1931 (5 yrs.)	Joe Smith			
1932-1934 (3 yrs.)	Larry Revell	SUNDAYS ONLY: (1932-35)		
1935 (1 yr.)	Austin Wyle	Don Bestor Archie Bleyer Eddie Duchin Larry Funk Isham Jones Al Katz	Vincent Lopez Ozzie Nelson Red Nichols George Olsen-Ethel Shutta Harry Reser Paul Sprecht	
1936-1942	— — — — — — —	1-3 WEEK ENGAGEMENTS: (1936-44)		
		Charlie Agnew Gus Arnheim Lee Allen Ralph Barlow Blue Baron Gene Beecher Jimmy Bennet Tommy Blue Ace Brigode Paul Burton Jack Crawford Lee Dixon Cal Dalton	Larry Funk Tom Gentry Emerson Gill Cecil Golly Little Joe Hart Jess Hawkins Ray Herbeck Tiny Hill Jimmy Joy Aud King Avars LaMarr Jimmy Livingston Carl Lorch	Red Nichols Clint Noble Orrin Tucker Bob Pettay Manny Prager Chic Scoggin Gene Sullivan Vic Stuart Lang Thompson Ralph Webster Anson Weeks Lawrence Welk Austin Wylie
1943-1944 (2 yrs.)	George Duffy	George Duffy Gene Erwin Art Farrar	Hal Lynn Russ Lyons Earl Mellen	
1945-1959 (15 yrs.)	Vic Stuart	POLKA NIGHT ON WEDNESDAYS, EARLY 1950's		
		Chester Budny Johnny Pecon Johnny Vadnal Frank Yankovic		

*A representative list only and certainly not all-inclusive.

APPENDIX F

DIMENSIONS OF THE RIDES

A Representative List, Not Complete.

AERO DIPS

Irregular area roughly 375' x 100'
(Plans lost, no details available.)

BUG

100' diameter

CARROUSEL

90' diameter of housing
4 abreast
2 chariots
Philadelphia Toboggan Co.

CIRCLE SWING

Area for loading on **ground** 110'5".
(Platform above ground was added later.)

DODGEM

143' x 90'
(Largest in U.S.)
Capacity per rid 100

FIGURE EIGHT

Occupied an area roughly 225' x 80'

FLYING PONIES

57'6" diameter
10° pitch of ride and platform

FLYING SCOOTERS

Planes could be maneuvered to a height of 21'.
49' diameter of device
Center pier 17'2"
89' diameter to fence
Scooters were 4' x 2' 8"
Scooters were 15' apart cc
From arm to ground 25'

FLYING TURNS

Irregular. Contained within an area 261'6"
x 61'10".
Turn at top of first hill 17' radius
Complete circle curves 32' 10-1/2" diameter (6)
Ascent to top of first turn 214'1"
4 quarter turns
1 half turn at top of first hill
Route 1, 320' on plan (does not account
for undulation.)

GREAT AMERICAN RACING DERBY

114' diameter of housing
24 support columns on outside, 15' cc.
Capacity 128 passengers per trip

LAFF-IN-THE-DARK

Overall 192'8" x 56'8"
Semicircular ends 28'4" radius
17'8" to ridge of roof
13'8" outside wall height
Capacity 360 passengers per hour

MILL CHUTE

(1920) Philadelphia Toboggan Co.
Channel 1190' long
Water 22" deep
Elevation of channel varies each 100' from 2'2" at
    station 0 (where people got on) to 3'6" at Station 10
    (beginning of hill). Top of channel will to bottom of
    concrete is generally 6'6". Running water level varies
    with elevation of channel. Floor of channel
    (bottom of water) vaires.
Hill (1920) 30' high
Descent (1020) of hill 20'
Ascent (1920) of hill 20'
Wind on hill at 30 lbs./sq. ft.
Windward frame at 50% load
Boat loading on 1 stringer
    Max 14,700 lbs.
    Max. shear 1,160 lbs.

OVER THE FALLS

(1937) Old channel of Mill Chute used
Channel route 1, 184' including ascent & descent
    of hill
Channel 4' wide
Lagoon 90' x 20' on the north and 24' on the south
Hill 37' high
Hill descent 50° (steepest in park)
Hill ascent 4.07 grade

RACING COASTER

Miller design for Ingersoll Engineering & Const. Co.,
    Pittsburgh, Pa.
Double track incline 162' to first hill crest
First hill 59' high
72 passengers per trip
2,814' track route up and down (2 trains & tracks)
1,828' on ground plan route
Descent angle of hill 30°

ROCKET SHIPS

101'5" tower
Platform 43' diameter

SCENIC RAILWAY

Overall
   86' at station end (north)
   72'8" at south turnaround
Track 560' **on plan**
   (this does not account for up and down footage).

"SWITCHBACK"

450' tower to tower
350' length of track (double), therefore ride was 700'
   (this does not account for the up and down footage)
Towers were roughly 50' wide but were irregular shaped
Starting hill (each end) 35' high

THRILLER

Station curve to first hill 60'
First turn to west 50' radius
Second turn to east 45' radius
First hill 71'5"
Second hill 60'6" (later towered)
Philadelphia Toboggan Co.
2,927' (actual up & down track length)
Descent angle of hill #1 was 40°
Ascent angle to top of hill #1 was 20°
Capacity 800 people per hour

WITCHING WAVES

Overall
192'8" x 56'8"
Semicircular ends 28'4" radius
Center island 14'8" x 56'8"
   4' high above undulating track
Track 21' wide
17'8" to ridge of roof
13'8" height of outside posts

ZOOMER

Length of Monorail c. 950'

APPENDIX G

DIMENSIONS OF BUILDINGS
A Representative List, Not Complete

BATHHOUSE

Irregular
213' north facade
 56' west facade
150' south facade with 25' setback

BOWLING ALLEY

160' south facade
 93'4" west facade
 60' east facade
110' north facade with 35' setback

CARROUSEL HOUSING

90' Diameter

CIGAR STAND

7'6" square

CIRCLE SWING PLATFORM

43' Diameter

COLONNADE

240' X 180'
Divided into 3 bays. Each bay of 60' was recessed by
   20' to the west on the north facade.
North facade was irregular.
120 columns 20'0" CC.
17'0" to roof slab from floor.
Column steel extended 3'0" above roof for planned
   2nd floor.
Capital of columns 4'6" diameter below 7' square slab.

DANCE PAVILION

204'6" X 120' west end
105' east end
Concrete promenade around Dance Pavilion (1916)
228'6" X 171'6" overall
slab 5' thick supported on 8" diameter columns
8' apart
southeast end irregular

DODGEM HOUSING

143' X 90'
(Largest in U.S.)

FLYING PONIES HOUSING

57'6" Diameter
10° angle of tilt

GARAGE

Irregular
110'4" north facade
121'6" east facade
82' west facade
87'10" south facade

GREAT AMERICAN RACING DERBY HOUSING

114' Diameter
24 supporting columns on outside 15' CC.

GROVE LUNCH Serving Area

Concrete slab 45'6" X 60'

KISS STAND

Irregular
30' X 18'

LAFF IN THE DARK HOUSING

192'8" X 56'8" overall
Semicircular ends 28'4" radius.
17'8" to ridge of roof
13'8" outside wall height

LOG CABIN

Walls were zig zag
Overall dimensions were 82' X 134'.
Central bay to ridge 34' high
Central bay sizes 23' high
Aisles 19' at peak
Aisles 15' at gutter

LOGANBERRY & GINGER ALE STAND - BASEMENT WALL

Irregular
50'9" X 37' X 47' X 36'

OFFICE :SECOND: (CEMENT)

36'4" X 35'2"
Outside walls 8" thick of poured, reinforced concrete.

PIER

Plats give various dimensions
1914 - 648'
later plats show 550'

POST OFFICE

22' square

ROCKET SHIPS PLATFORM FOR LOADING

43' Diameter

ROLLER RINK

261' X 100'3"
(was enlarged in 1909)
Ends radius 50'
Outside walls 10'3" high.
Skating track 35' wide.
Central ovoid skating area (containing organ) 34' wide.
Central bay 19' to ridge.
Clerestory 4'10' high.

SKEE BALL

100' X 56'
Side porch on west 15' X 35'

SURPRISE HOUSE

Front facade 62'1" wide
Center bay (entrance) was 28'9" wide.
2 side bays with laughing figures in niches were each
16'8" wide by 25'4" high.
98' overall length, irregular, 108'

THEATRE (AVENUE THEATRE)

73'5" X 122'9"

WITCHING WAVES HOUSING

56'8" X 192'8" overall semicircular ends 28'4" radius
17'8" to ridge of roof
13'8" outside walls
Center island 14'8" X 56'8" semicircular ends, 4' high
Track (undulatory) 21' wide.

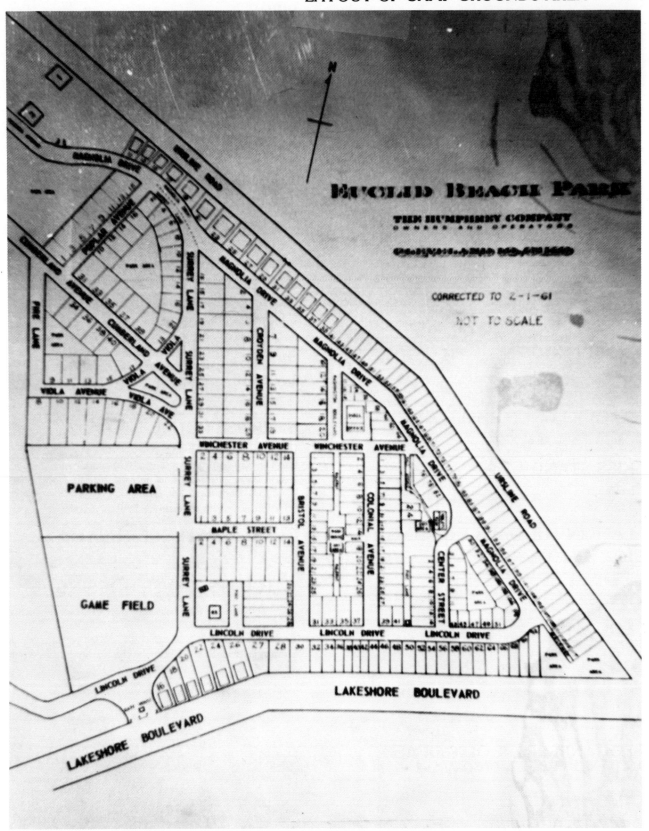

APPENDIX I

NOTES FROM THE FRANK KILBY DIARIES

1921 - 12 accidents recorded (total)
1925 - 6/14 "opened bathhouse"
      9/25 "lightning hit rink and Derby Racer"
1927 - 6/25 "opened Red Bug Blvd." / "opened Outdoor Dance Floor"
      6/6 "garages burned"
1929 - 9/13 "McDonald got smashed up today"
      9/9 "D.S.'s 50th Anniversary"
1932 - 6/2 "finished new Skee-Ball Alleys"
      6/13 "cut admission to 40¢ at Rink"
      6/19 "started to coat rink roof"
1933 - 9/7 "D.S. died 4:00 A.M."
      9/19 "buried D.S. today"
1937 - 10/13 "Schultz completely rebuilt Carousel & Swing Organs, $286.90 - 161 hrs."
1938 - 12/11 "Luna Park Rink burned today"
1939 - 10/26 "Elysium opened today - big crowd, 1,114"
1943 - 10/9 "Schultz finished Carousel organ today"

TICKETS SOLD
July 4, 1933

Main Lunch	8,000
New Lunch	9,580
Lake Lunch	8,150
No. 1 Weiner	6,730
No. 2 Weiner	5,400
Frozen Whip	19,240
Pop Corn	27,790
Thriller	14,950
Laff-in-Dark	14,240
Flying Turns	12,200
Dodgem	10,390
Racing Coaster	8,800
Amer. Derby	10,260
Dance Hall	16,840
Miniature R.R.	4,050
Rink	3,610

SEASON - 1933

Popcorn	$32,817.00
Dance Hall	32,278.60
Frozen Whip	20,624.50
Main Lunch	9,787.60
New Lunch	11,339.50
Lake Lunch	8,415.25

ATTENDANCE AND EARNINGS
AT RINK AND HOT DOG STANDS

	RINK			HOT DOG STANDS		
Year	Attendance	Rink $	Skate Check $	No. 1	No. 2	
1921*	86,497	$39,009.40	$3258.90			
1925*	90,549	40,738.85	3483.60			
1926				sold 10,055	sold 5,795	
1927	80,329			sold 10,956	sold 6,045	
1928				sold 7,800	sold 4,680	
1929				sold 20,270 [doz.]	sold 7,235 [doz.]	348 gals. horseradish
1930				sold 7,380	sold 4,800	
1931				sold 4,980 $12,652.30	sold 3,480 $ 4,957.60	
1932		12,809.70	1,007.10	sold 3,240 $ 7,677.60	sold 2,280 $ 3,403.30	
1933		10,827.65	778.80	sold 3,348 $ 6,603.50	sold 2,760 $ 3,013.50	
1934						
1935	38,627	14,274.50	963.00	$ 9,420.30	$ 3,667.00	
1936	50,039	14,092.20	1267.30	$15,543.30	$ 5,294.50	
1937	60,378	22,812.10	1799.00	$16,797.50	$ 6,474.00	
1938	55,783	20,107.60	1661.25	$13,884.75	$ 6,037.50	
1939	52,774	19,411.30	1562.75	$15,227.00	$ 7,767.75	
1940	49,527	19,062.45	1529.50	$16,635.50	$ 8,073.75	
1941	53,481	22,837.00	1756.75	$28,568.00	$13,181.75	50,722 lbs. weiners
1942	61,531	27,088.80	2445.00	$41,549.10	$17,916.00	
1943	57,035	29,382.90	2213.40	$62,868.90		43,237 doz. rolls
1946	48,134					
1947	29,232					

*14,391,874 tickets

APPENDIX J

LOCATIONS ON THE MAPS ON PP. 189 and 190

APPENDIX J

LOCATIONS ON THE MAPS LISTED BY NUMBER
on pp. 189 and 190

1. East 156th Street
1. Collamer
2. Lake Shore Blvd.
3. Auto Exit Gate
3. Exit Gate for Autos
4. Cottage
5. House
6. House
7. West Gate (1895)
8. Stables (1895)
9. Cobb Farmhouse
9. Office: first:
9. Dudley S. Humphrey, III House
10. Bowling Alley
10. Lake Lunch
11. Ravine (later covered over)
12. Bridge across Ravine
13. Beach of Euclid Beach Park
14. Turnpike (ride)
15. Parking lot - main
15. Main Parking Lot
16. Outdoor Theatre
17. Log Cabin
18. Office: second: of concrete
18. Concrete Office
18. Cement Office
19. Annex
19. Stage Housing of Avenue Theatre
20. Mural of a "Ballerina Riding a Runaway Horse"
20. "Ballerina Riding a Runaway Horse" on the covered-over stage opening of Theatre
21. Dippy Whip (ride)
22. Coffee Break (ride)
23. Theatre (Avenue Theatre)
23. Avenue Theatre
24. Pee Wee Miniature Golf
25. Bug (ride)
26. Caterpillar (ride)
27. Aerial Swing (ride)
27. Aeroplanes (ride)
27. Circle Swing (ride)
27. Rocket Ships (ride)
28. German Village
28. German Garden
29. Pier
30. Main Gate
30. Gate (main)
31. Bicycle Track
32. MacLevie Cottage
33. Shop
34. Garage
35. Skee Ball

36. Flying Scooters (ride)
37. Ballroom (inside of Dance Pavilion
37. Dance Floor
38. Dance Pavilion
38. Dance Hall
39. Promenade (concrete) around Dance Pavilion
39. Platform of concrete around Dance Pavilion
40. Men's Washroom (under northwest section of Dance Pavilion)
41. Women's Washroom (southeast section of Dance Pavilion)
42. Outdoor Dance Floor
43. Shuffleboard Courts
44. Ping Pong Tables
45. Table Tennis
46. Fountain
47. Circular Pool (near Pier)
48. Sea Swing (ride)
49. Cafeteria (Bluff level)
49. Crosby's-on-the-Lake
50. Bath House (Beach level)
51. Ocean Wave (ride)
52. Swingin' Gyms (ride)
53. Post Office
53A. Link Trainer (ride)
54. House
55. House
56. Cottage
57. Miniature Railroad (ride): #1:
58. Ostrich Farm
59. Pony Track (ride) (live)
59A. Kiddie Cars (ride)
60. Street Car Station: #2: (near **later** Kiddie Land)
60. Trolley Station: #2: (near **later** Kiddie Land)
61. Grove Lunch
62. Colonnade
63. Merry-Go-Round (ride)
64. Street Car Station: #1: (near Dance Pavilion)
64. Trolley Station: #1: (near Dance Pavilion)
65. Drink Stand
66. Candy Stand
66. Popcorn Stand
67. Hot Dog Stand
68. Sun Tan Links
69. Fun House
69. Surprise House
69. Funscience Hall
70. Photo Gallery
71. Flying Ponies (ride)
71. Japanese Flying Ponies (ride)

72. Carrousel (ride) (1910 - 1969), #19
73. Cigar Stand
74. Giant Slide (ride)
75. Crystal Maze: #2: (1926)
76. Penny Arcade
77. Edison
78. Main Lunch (near Roller Rink)
79. Soda Grill
80. Crystal Maze: #1: (1896)
81. Penny Arcade (early)
82. Figure Eight (ride)
83. Aero Dips (ride)
83. Velvet Coaster (ride)
83. New Velvet Coaster (ride)
83. New Velvet Ride (ride)
84. Switchback Railroad (ride)
84. "Switchback" (ride)
84A. Remo Escalator to the
     Switchback Railway)
84A. "Escalator" (to the
     Switchback Railway)
85. Skating Rink
85. Roller Rink
86. Antique Autos (ride)
86. Antique Cars (ride)
87. Pool (rectangular)
    (on Beach near Bath House)
87. Wading Pool
88. Chute (ride)
    (on Lake Erie Beach)
89. "Ferris" Wheel: first: (1896) (ride)
90. Refreshment Stand at
    Trolley Entrance
91. Trolley Station: #3:
    (fronting on Lake Shore Blvd.)
92. Covered Walk from Trolley Station
93. Minature R.R. (ride): #2:
    (Sleepy Hollow R.R.)
94. Whip (ride)
95. Rotor (ride)
96. Bubble Bounce (ride)
97. Over The Falls (ride)
97. Mill Chute (ride)
97. Old Mill (ride)
98. Scenic Railway (ride)
98. "Old Scenic" (ride)
99. Haunted Swing (ride)
100. Great American Racing Derby
     (ride)
101. "Ferris" Wheel (ride)
102. Tilt-A-Whirl (ride)
103. Around the World (theatre)
104. Photos Stand
105. Dodgem (ride)
106. Red Bug Blvd. (ride)
107. Derby Racer (ride)
107. Racing Coaster (ride)
107. Derby (ride)
108. Thriller (ride)
109. Flying Turns (ride)
110. Zoomer (ride)
111. Barber Shop
112. Witching Waves (ride)
113. Laff in the Dark (ride)

114. Scrambler (ride)
115. Rock-O-Plane (ride)
116. Hurricane (ride)
117. Octopus (ride)
118. Bleachers of Baseball Field
119. Baseball Diamond
120. Cottages
121. Kinetoscope
122. Dudley Sherman Humphrey,
     II residence
122. Castle Inn
122. Residence of Dudley Sherman
     Humphrey, II
123. Doris (Humphrey) Mackley
     residence
124. Bluff
125. Boat Livery
126. Camp Grounds
127. Ursuline Avenue, N.E.
128. Beulah Park
129. Lakewood Inn
130. Tabernacle
131. Beach Hotel
132. Green Brook (covered over)
133. Ursuline Academy
134. Parking Lot: 2:
135. Hook & Ladder, K.F.D. #1 (ride)
135. Kiddieland Hook & Ladder (ride)
136. Kiddie Mill (ride)
136. Kiddie Over the Falls (ride)
137. Kiddie Boats (ride)
138. Kiddie Pony Track (ride)
     (artificial)
139. Lunch Stand in Colonnade
139. Colonnade Lunch Stand
140. Picnic Tables in Colonnade
140. Colonnade Picnic Tables
141. Kiddie Autos (ride)
142. Kiddie Carousel (ride)
143. Kiddie Whip (ride)
143. Fairy Whip (ride)
144. Kiddie Pigs (ride)
145. Kiddie Ferris Wheel (ride)
     (moved several times)
146. Kiddie Bug (ride)
147. Kiddie Aeroplanes (ride)
147. Kiddie Rocket Ships (ride)
147. Kiddie Circle Swing (ride)
147A. Kiddie Swans (ride)
148. Cement Fancy Work in
     Colonnade open area
149. Balloon & Souvenir Stand
149. Souvenir Stand in Colonnade
150. Glass Blower in Colonnade
     (moved several times)
151. Shooting Gallery (bullets) in
     Colonade (moved several times)
152. Frozen Custard Stand
153. Sugar Cone Production
154. Par Three, Chip and Putt Golf
     Course (across Lake Shore Blvd.)
155. Driving Range
     (across Lake Shore Blvd.)
156. Parking Overflow
157. Humphrey Field

APPENDIX K

MISCELLANEOUS

Announcer for Park Broadcasts
   on WTAM Radio (from Dance Floor): Gene Hamilton.

Ball Diamond near Thriller
   Regulation size for either hard or soft ball.
   Bleacher seats along low hills of Thriller.

"Ballerina . . . " Mural
   Painted by Joe Davis in 1930.

Boats for EBP (Euclid Beach "Tubs")
   Left the foot of Superior St. for EBP every 1½ hours, daily,
      commencing at 8:30 A.M.
   "For picnics, excursions, etc., call City office 2222,
      or Park 3841."

Broadcast Theme Song on WTAM from Dance Hall
   "By the sea, by the sea,
   by the beautiful sea."

Bubble Bounce
   Operated by two pistons, 100 lbs. air pressure. (1938)

Bug (ride)
   Earned its cost by July 4th of its first season.

Burned Buildings after Park Closing (1969)
   see Fires at EBP after Park Closed (Sept. 1969)

"Burner-with-a-Brain" Stoves
   Used to cook Hot Dogs (frankfurters) (1961).

Cafeteria
   Accommodates 800. "Enlarged" 1926 season.

Camp Ground Tend & Cottage Rental Fees.
   1933 - 4 rm. tent: $4 per day
         $25 per wk.
         $220 per season
         (2 double beds, camp chairs, clothes tree, etc.)

      Cement cottages:
      $300 - 325 per month (depending on size)

      Trailer space:
      $7.50 per wk.

Circle Swing
   Cost of ride c. $10,000.00
   Earnings 1902 - 1903; $400,000.00
   Revised plans were purchased by Sea Breeze Park,
      Rochester, N.Y.

Colonnade Column Forms
   by Con-Service Erection Co.
   (20' apart cc. 17' high)

Cone Machines for making Frozen Whip
   Owned and operated by Purity Cone Co. (1933).

Cost of Rides:
   Circle Swing, c. $10,000 (1902)
   Scenic Railway, $50,000 (1907)
   Antique Car Ride & Turnpike @ car, $18,000 (1964)
   Racing Coaster $45,000 (1913)
   Thriller $90,000 (1924)

Designers & Manufacturers of Rides — a partial list,
not complete

Aero Dips (1909 - 1965)
   John A. Miller
Antique Auto Ride (1963 - 1969)
   By Gillmore & Olson Co. plan dated 1/10/63.
Auto Train
   Fadgl Bus Co. of San Francisco, Calif.
   (brought to EBP from Panama Pacific Expo.)
Bubble Bounce (1939)
   Custer Specialty Co.
Bug (late '20s)
   Traver Engineering Co.
Carousel #9 (1905 - 1909)
   Philadelphia Toboggan Co.
Circle Swing (1902 - 1969)
   Traver Engineering Co., Beaver Falls, Pa. 1902.
   Gondolas; (1902 - 1926)
   Aeroplanes (Biplanes) (1927 -   )
   Rocket Ships
"Cupid's Post Office" in Penny Arcade
   Mills Novelty Co., Chicago, Ill.
"Digger" in Penny Arcade (Iron Claw)
   Exhibit & Supply Co.
Dodgem (1921 - 1969)
   W.F. Mangels
   earlier cars 1921 - 1929
   later cars 1930 - 1969 by Dodgem Corp. of
      Lawrence, Mass.
   60 cars
"Ferris" Wheel (1896 - 1901)
   Buckeye Observation Wheel Co.
"Ferris" Wheel: second: (1963 - 1969)
   Plans dated 11 Jan. 1963, by Eli Bridge Co.,
      Jacksonville, Ill.
   (Plan for #5 Wheel & #10 Wheel
      with electric motor drive.)
Figure Eight (1904 - 1908)
   Philadelphia Toboggan Co.
Flying Ponies (1903, remodeled 1909)
   Herschell-Spillman
Flying Scooters (1938 - 1969)
   Bisch - Rocco, Chicago, Ill.
Flying Turns (1929 - 1969)
   Designed by Bartlett and Miller
"Grandmother" in Penny Arcade
   Wm. Gent Vending Machine Co.
Great American Racing Derby (1921 - 1965 at EBP)
   Prior & Church
"Iron Horse" in Penny Arcade
   International Motoscope Reel Co., Inc., NY, NY
"Love Tester" in Penny Arcade
   Exhibit & Supply Co.
Main Gate
   Permastone finish of Chas. S. Bonnell

Merry-Go-Round (1896) Old #9
    Philadelphia Toboggan Co.
Mill Chute (1921, revised 1937)
    Philadelphia Toboggan Co.
Miniature Train (1900s) (steam)
    Herschell-Spillman
Ocean Wave (c. 1911)
    Herschell-Spillman Co.
Over The Falls (1937 - 1969)
    Revised from Philadelphia Toboggan Co.
        by Park crew
    Revised plans were purchased by Sea Breeze Park,
        Rochester, N.Y.
Racing Coaster (1913 - 1969)
    John A. Miller
    constructed for Ingersoll Eng. Co. of Pittsburgh, Pa.
Red Bug Blvd. (1927 - 1930s)
    Custer Specialty
Scenic Railway (1907 - 1937)
    La Marcus Adna Thompson
Sleepy Hollow R.R. (1926)
    Dudley Humphrey Scott & Bill Parker
Swings (1896)
    Herschell-Spillman
Switchback Railway (1896 - 1904)
    La Marcus Adna Thompson
Thriller (1924 - 1969)
    Philadelphia Toboggan Co.
Tilt-A-Whirl
    plans dated 2/6/64 by
        Sellner Mfg. Co., Fairbault, Minn.
Turnpike (1962 - 1969)
    Arrow Development Corp.
Uncle Sam's Grip Machine in Penny Arcade
    Caille Bros.
Whip
    W.F. Mangels (12 cars)
Zoomer (late '20s)
    Custer Specialty Co.

Dodgem
    Rubber tires made by Goodrich Rubber Co.

Euclid Beach Park Co. Office (1895)
    222 Society for Savings Bldg.
    John Flynn, Sec. & Treas.

Euclid Beach Park Co. Office (1896)
    409 The Century, 197 Superior
    W.R. Ryan, pres.
    B.G. Tremain, sec.
    Chas. O. Evarts, treas.

Euclid Beach Part Co. Office (1897)
    105 The Beekman,
    204 Superior Ave.
    W.R. Ryan, pres.
    B.G. Tremaine, sec.
    Chas. O. Evarts, treas.

Euclid Beach Park Co. Office (1899)
    Downtown office, 225 Superior St.
    Lee Holtzman, gen. mgr.
    J.A. Smith, pres.
    Geo. W. Barnes, vice pres.
    R.S. Tremaine, sec.
    Chas. O. Evarts, treas.

Fires at EBP after Park Closed (Sept. 1969)
    Dance Pavillion burned Wed. eve.,
        23 Feb. 1972.
    Log Cabin burned Fri., 28 May 1971.
    Surprise House burned Mon., 27 Dec. 1971.
    Theatre (Avenue Theatre) burned
        26 Nov. 1971.

Flying Turns
    Lumber supplied for by Harvard Lumber
        Co., Cleveland, Ohio

Flying Turns, Cars of
    "Takes 6 weeks to take apart,
        inspect and repair them."

Fuel to Cook Hot Dogs (Frankfurters) (1961)
    Gas through "Burner-With-A-Brain" stoves.

Fun House (Surprise House)
    Capacity of over 300 per hour.

Hot Dogs (wieners, frankfurters), Brand of
    "Sylvana Brand" used exclusively by EBP.

Hot Dog (weiner) & Hamburg Machines
    Supplied by Wm. B. Berry Co.,
        Boston, Mass.

Lumber for Thriller & Flying Turns
    Supplied by Harvard Lumber Co.,
        Cleveland, Ohio (1930)

Mural "Ballerina . . . "
    Painted by Joe Davis in 1930.

Organ at Carrousel (1910)
    Purchased by Frank Kapel, Kirtland, Ohio
    Style #188, built by
        North Tonowanda Musical Inst. Works.
    Five registers: trumpets, trombones,
        clarionettes, open & stopped base.
    White enamel front.
    52 keys.

Organ at Merry-Go-round (1896)
    Cost $2,000 (1896)
    Band Organ.

Organ at Rocket Ships
    Purchased by Frank Kapel, Kirtland, Ohio.
    Style A, Artizan Band
    46 keys.

Organ at Roller Rink (1910 - 1962)
Gavioli
$15,000 (sold for originally).
110 keys.
First used in Elysium.

Organ Maintenance
by Wm. Schultz

Paint for Park — Green
Supplied by Durable Products Co.,
Cleveland, Ohio (1930)

Park Plan Dance Format
12 dance sets per hour
@ 5 minutes long.
2 dances per set @ 2½ minutes long.

Parking Lots
12,000 car capacity

Picnic Tables — Number of Settings
Lake Lunch — Outside tables, c. 1500.
Colonnade, Main & Lake Lunch —
under cover, 2500.

Rides Moved **from** EBP

Carrousel
Shipped to Leisure Systems Development
Ltd., Toronto, Canada
(3/21/70 Cleveland Press Article)
1974 — Old Orchard Beach,
Maine (NCA)

Flying Ponies
Moved to Rye Beach
Great American Racing Derby
1921 - 1965 at EBP
Moved to Cedar Point,
Sandusky, Ohio (1965)
Merry-Go-Round (1896)
Old #9
Moved to Laurel Springs,
Hartford, Conn; then to shop 1925,
then became #74R (1926).
Mt. Gretna, Penna.

Roller Rink (1902 - 1962)
used for Antique Cars 1963 - 1969

Statistics for 1948 Season
Gross revenue approx. 1¼ million
for 1948.
400 workers employed during season
at full operation.
60 workers full time.
70 families in trailer camp.
160 tent dwellings
Summertime population 1,500.

Steepest Hill of the Rides
was that of Over the Falls, 50′ descent.

Sun Tan Links (1930)
Run by Florida Landscape Co.

Thriller
Lumber supplied for by
Harvard Lumber Co., Cleveland, Ohio

FOOTNOTES

CHAPTER I

1. Elroy McKendree Avery, A HISTORY OF CLEVELAND AND ITS ENVIRONS (New York: Lewis Pub. Co., 1918), p. 167.

2. Advertisement about Euclid Beach Park in the CLEVELAND PLAIN DEALER, 22 June 1895, p. 5.

3. Advertisement about Euclid Beach Park in the CLEVELAND LEADER, 29 June 1895, p. 7.

4. CLEVELAND PLAIN DEALER, 7 July 1895, p. 9.

5. Theatre Section, CLEVELAND PLAIN DEALER, 14 July 1895.

6. CLEVELAND PRESS, 7 June 1897, p. 2.

7. CLEVELAND PLAIN DEALER, 21 July 1898, p. 5.

8. Advertisement about Euclid Beach Park in the CLEVELAND PLAIN DEALER, 3 June 1899, p. 5.

9. EUCLID BEACH PARK, SEASON 1899, booklet, (Ward and Shaw, 1899), p. 5.

CHAPTER II

10. Sherman Gwinn, "What He Learned at 14 Helped Him 'Come Back' at 40", THE AMERICAN MAGAZINE, April 1927, p. 61.

11. THE HUMPHREY COMPANY SCRAPBOOK: 1893 - 1969, (containing notes, clippings, photos, mementos, memorabilia, plans, plats, personal accounts), 2 jumbo volumes. It must be noted that often dates or sources of the material in it were not included by the compiler/s. Wherever the authors have found the missing data they have added it to these footnotes. Also, because the scrapbook is not paginated and because the authors would not arbitrarily assign pages to it because of its fragile condition, no page citations are given.

12. Gwinn, 193.

13. Gwinn, 194.

14. Gwinn, 194.

15. Gwinn, 194.

16. Gwinn, 195.

17. Gwinn, 196.

18. Gwinn, 196.

19. Gwinn, 196.

20. Gwinn, 197.

21. Gwinn, 197.

22. Gwinn, 197.

23. Gwinn, 197.

24. HUMPHREY SCRAPBOOK.

25. HUMPHREY SCRAPBOOK.

26. HUMPHREY SCRAPBOOK.

27. NEW YORK HERALD, 10 August 1902.

28. HUMPHREY SCRAPBOOK.

29. HUMPHREY SCRAPBOOK.

30. HUMPHREY SCRAPBOOK.

31. Advertisement about Euclid Beach Park run in the CLEVELAND PLAIN DEALER, 1907.

32. HUMPHREY SCRAPBOOK.

CHAPTER III

33. HUMPHREY SCRAPBOOK.

34. Separate typed list inserted in the HUMPHREY SCRAP-BOOK.

CHAPTER IV

35. Interview with George Reinhard, 24 June 1976.

36. PHILADELPHIA TOBOGGAN CO. CATALOG, n.d.

37. HUMPHREY SCRAPBOOK.

38. HUMPHREY SCRAPBOOK.

39. HUMPHREY SCRAPBOOK.

40. EUCLID BEACH PARK, SEASON 1899, p. 39.

41. EUCLID BEACH PARK, SEASON 1899, p. 39.

41a. Frederick Fried, A PICTORIAL HISTORY OF THE CAROUSEL (New York: A.S. Barnes, 1964), p. 217.

42. Authors' estimate.

43. HERSCHELL - SPILLMAN CATALOG, 1911, p. 30.

44. AMUSEMENT PARK MANAGEMENT MAGAZINE, August 1930, p. 33.

45. Glenn C. Pullen article, CLEVELAND PLAIN DEALER, 16 May 1935, p. 12.

46. Interview with William Parker, 21 June 1976.

47. Parker interview.

48. Parker interview.

49. HUMPHREY SCRAPBOOK.

50. Interview with Bob Legan, 31 August 1976.

CHAPTER VI

51. EUCLID BEACH PARK, SEASON 1899, p. 33.

52. EUCLID BEACH PARK, SEASON 1899, p. 33.

53. Authors' account.

54. Charles J. Avellone interview (telephone), 23 February 1976.

55. Avellone interview.

55a. Bob Seltzer article, CLEVELAND PRESS, 25 July 1962.

56. John Tierney interview (telephone), 18 February

57. Tierney interview.

58. FRANK KILBY DIARY, 1957.

CHAPTER VII

59. HUMPHREY SCRAPBOOK.

60. EUCLID BEACH PARK, SEASON 1899, p. 19.

61. HUMPHREY SCRAPBOOK.

62. FRANK KILBY DIARIES, 1929, 1943.

63. Walt Williams interview, 29 July 1976.

64. Typed notes by Doris Mackley about Euclid Beach Park, dated 28 June 1955, in the Cleveland Public Library History Department clipping file under Cleveland - Euclid Beach.

65. EUCLID BEACH PARK, SEASON 1899, p. 13.

66. EUCLID BEACH PARK, SEASON 1899, p. 13.

67. EUCLID BEACH PARK, SEASON 1899, p. 72.

68. HUMPHREY SCRAPBOOK.

69. John Cleary, "Strictly Business", newspaper article (no name of source), May 1948.

70. EUCLID BEACH PARK, SEASON 1899, p. 13.

CHAPTER IX

71. AMUSEMENT PARK MANAGEMENT MAGAZINE, August 1930, p. 42.

72. Local newspaper article, 29 May, 1931.

73. Local newspaper article, 1969.

74. Commemorative folder about the ballroom plaque, passed out 7 July 1955.

CHAPTER X

75. "Atwood Reaches Cleveland in Record Flight," p. 1, CLEVELAND PLAIN DEALER, 18 August 1911.

76. Norman Siegel, "Here's One Boyhood Story Bob Hope Won't Recall On His Show Tonight," CLEVELAND PRESS, July 1939, p.

77. Kaye Ballard interview.

BIBLIOGRAPHY

Allan Herschell Co. *Carousels (Merry-Go-Rounds)* [*Catalogue Four*]. North Tonowanda, N.Y.:
    Allan Herschell Co., n.d. (Also republished by Vestal Press, Vestal, N.Y.).

Artale, Jane. "Goodbye, Euclid Beach." *Cleveland Plain Dealer,* 2 Sept. 1969, Sunday Magazine, pp. 22-25.

"As a Distinguished Citizen . . . " *Cleveland Plain Dealer,* 18 Sept. 1932.

"The Ashes Hold Memories After Old Dance Hall Burns." *Cleveland Press,* 25 Feb. 1972.

Avery, Elroy McKendree. *A History of Cleveland and Its Environs; The Heart of New Connecticut.*
    Chicago: Lewis Publishing Co., 1918.

Battle, John, III. "Collinwood Folks Bid Fond Farewell to Euclid Beach Park." *The Scoop,* 2 March 1972, p. 1.

Bowers, Q. David. *Encyclopedia of Automatic Musical Instruments.* Vestal, N.Y.: Vestal Press, 1972.

Boyer, Dwight. "The Best Job in the World?" *Cleveland Plain Dealer,* Sunday Magazine, pp. 32-33.

Braithwaite, David. *Fairground Architecture.* New York: Praeger, 1968.

Cartmel, Robert. *The Great American Scream Machine.* (unpublished book)

Christiansen, Harry. *Trolley Trails Through Greater Cleveland and Northern Ohio,* Vol 2. Cleveland, Ohio:
    The Western Reserve Historical Society, 1975.

Cleveland City Directories. Cleveland, Cleveland Directory Publishing Co. 1893 - 1970-71.
    (title varies to *Cleveland Directory*)

Cleveland - The City of Progress and Health. pamphlet, n.s. [1923], p. 29.

Cleveland Topics (later called *Cleveland Town Topics*). Cleveland, Ohio: Cleveland Topics Co. Weekly.
    1887 - 1915
    1916 - 1921 Cleveland Topics (absorbed by bystander)

Cockayne, Eric V. *The Fairground Organ.* [Plymouth, England]: David and Charles: Newton Abbot, n.d.

Collier, Joe. "Museum Tunes In on Famed Organ." *Cleveland Plain Dealer,* 17 July 1965.

Condon, George E. *Cleveland; The Best Kept Secret.* Garden City, N.Y. Doubleday & Co., 1967.

Curtiss, Cornelia. "Doris Humphrey of Euclid Beach." *Cleveland News,* 14 Aug. 1946.

Curtiss, Glenn H. "Curtiss Says 'Twas Hardest Trip I've Had." *Cleveland Press,* 2 July 1910, p. 1.

"D.S. Humphrey." *Cleveland News,* 7 Sept. 1933.

"D.S. Humphrey, Good Citizen." *Cleveland Plain Dealer,* 8 Sept. 1933.

"D.S. Humphrey, 'Popcorn King,' is Dead at 81." *Cleveland News,* 7 Sept. 1933.

"D.S. Humphrey Rites are Set." *Cleveland News,* 8 Sept. 1933.

"D.S. Humphrey Rites Tomorrow." *Cleveland Plain Dealer,* 8 Sept. 1933.

"Dance Club to Get Euclid Beach Permit." *Cleveland Press,* 23 May 1947.

"Daughter of Euclid Beach Founder Dies." *Cleveland Plain Dealer,* 26 Sept. 1958.

Dudas, Jim. "Euclid Beach: Forgotten - But Not Gone." *Cleveland Press,* 7 May 1971, pp. 3-4.

"Euclid Beach A Pleasant Memory." *Cleveland Plain Dealer,* 29 Sept. 1969.

"Euclid Beach Bus to Start Sunday." *Cleveland News,* 22 May 1946.

"Euclid Beach Carousel is Classic to New Owner." *Cleveland Plain Dealer,* 28 Aug. 1969.

"Euclid Beach Leases Rink to Private Club." *Cleveland News,* 12 April 1947.

"Euclid Beach Log Cabin Destroyed." *Plain Dealer,* 29 May 1971.

"Euclid Beach Opening Skips Dancing, Bathing." *Cleveland Press,* 14 April 1947.

"Euclid Beach Pilosophy for Success Was Right Blend of Wholesome Fun." *Cleveland Press,* 5 Oct. 1968.

Euclid Beach Park [Co.]. *Euclid Beach Park, Season 1899* [booklet]. Cleveland, Ohio, Ward and Shaw, 1899.

"Euclid Beach Park to Close in 1969." *Cleveland Press,* 7 June 1968.

"Euclid Beach Park Today." *Cleveland Press,* 20 Sept. 1972, p. B-4.

"Euclid Beach Philosophy for Success . . ." *Cleveland Press,* 5 Oct. 1968.

French, Winsor. "Winsor French." *Cleveland Press,* 10 Jan. 1953, 24 Jan. 1953, 31 Jan. 1953, 7 Feb. 1953, 21 Feb. 1953, 28 Feb. 1953, 7 Mar. 1953, 14 Mar. 1953, 30 May 1961, 12 June 1961, 3 Feb. 1962.

Fried, Frederick. *A Pictorial History of the Carousel* N.Y.: A.S. Barnes, 1964.

Frohman, Charles E. *Cedar Point Yesterdays.* Columbus, Ohio: The Ohio Historical Society, 1969.

"Fun in the Good Old Days." *Cleveland Plain Dealer,* 1 Jan. 1950. pp. 4, 5. Pictorial Magazine.

Garling, Pat. "Ride About to End for Euclid Beach." *Cleveland Plain Dealer,* 1 Sept. 1969.

Gavioli & Co. *Societe Des Anciens Etablissements,* Gavioli & Co. New York, N.Y.: Gavioli & Co. New York Branch, n.d. (also republished by Vestal Press, Vestal, N.Y.)

"Ghost of Summer Haunts Euclid Beach." *Cleveland Press,* 8 Oct. 1964, p. C-12.

Griffin, Al. *Step Right Up, Folks.* Chicago: Henry Regnery Co., 1974.

"H. [arvey] J. Humphrey, Head of Euclid Beach, Dies." *Plain Dealer,* 14 June 1959.

"Harlow Humphrey Expires Suddenly." *Cleveland Plain Dealer,* 25 Nov. 1918.

Hatcher, Harlan. *The Western Reserve; The Story of New Connecticut in Ohio.* Indianapolis: Bobbs-Merrill, 1949. Cleveland: World Publishing Co., 1966, (Rev. Ed.).

Hirschfeld, Mary. "Euclid Beach Park A Family Project." *Christian Science Monitor,* 26 Aug. 1954.

"Hold Humphrey Rites at Home." *Cleveland Press,* 8 Sept. 1933.

Hume, Jack. "50 This Summer." *Cleveland Plain Dealer,* 25 May 1950.

Humphrey, Dudley S. [III]. "Euclid Park: A Community Asset." *Plain Dealer,* 10 Sept. 1965.

Humphrey Company, The. *Scrapbook: 1893 - 1969,* 2 Vols. Cleveland, Ohio, Euclid Beach Park: The Humphrey Company, 1893 - 1969.

"Humphreys Mark Golden Wedding." *Cleveland Plain Dealer,* 4 Sept. 1923.

Interview with Dearv *Barton,* Cleveland, Ohio, 13 Jan. 1976.

Interview with Ronald *Dietz,* Painesville, Ohio, 11 Aug. 1976.

Interview with John *Harvey,* and Eugene *Stuart,* Euclid, Ohio, 23 June 1976.

Interview with Emma *Karnatz,* Cleveland, Ohio, 24 June 1976.

Interview with Jane *Kramer,* Charles *Smith,* Robert *Ward,* Euclid Beach Park, 22 June 1976.

Interview with Bob *Legan,* Euclid, Ohio, 31 Aug. 1976.

Interview with Roy *Mizner,* Mentor, Ohio, 10 Nov. 1975.

Interview with J.O. *Murray,* Cleveland, Ohio, 30 June 1975.

Interview with Martin *Opalk,* Euclid, Ohio, 22 June 1976.

Interview with William *Parker,* Cleveland, Ohio, 21 June 1976.

Interview with Henry *Prekel,* Euclid, Ohio, 31 Aug. 1976.

Interview with George A. *Reinhard,* Euclid, Ohio, 24 June 1976.

Interview with David H. *Scott,* Cleveland, Ohio, 27 Sept. 1976.

Interview with John W. *Stoneback,* Euclid, Ohio 21 June 1976.

Interview with Walter *Williams,* Euclid Beach Park, Ohio, 29 July 1976.

"Kathryn Humphrey, Park Operator Dies," *Cleveland Plain Dealer,* 19 Sept. 1974.

Kelly, Michael. "1966 Last Year for Euclid Beach?" *Plain Dealer,* 27 Aug. 1965.

Kilby, Frank *Diaries* (Various dates) Cleveland, Ohio: Frank Kilby, various dates.

Klaric, Betty. "Euclid Beach Future is Up for Ideas." *Cleveland Press,* 12 Sept. 1968.

Kurlander, Regine V. "Buys Back Bean Land, Plants Lucky Pop Corn." *Cleveland Plain Dealer,* 28 May 1930.

Kyriaze, Gary. *The Great American Amusement Parks.* Secaucus, N.J.: Citadel Press, 1976.

Lake, O.J. *Atlas of Cuyahoga County, Ohio.* Philadelphia: Titus, Simmons & Titus, 1874.

Land Title Guarantee and Trust Co. Calendars. "Cleveland Old and New." 1942, 1946.

"A Landmark Falls." [Racing Coaster] *Plain Dealer,* 26 Feb. 1972.

"Left $68,205 Estate." *Cleveland Plain Dealer,* 30 Mar. 1934.

Liederbach, Robert J. *Cleveland Past.* Cleveland, Ohio: Dillon/Liederbach, 1975.

McCullough, Edo. *Good Old Coney Island.* N.Y.: Charles Scribner's Sons, 1957.

Mackley, Doris (Humphrey) *Euclid Beach Park,* a typed article in the Cleveland Public Library History Dept. clipping file Cleveland, Ohio: 28 June 1955.

Mackley, Doris Humphrey. "Popcorn Mistake Not French's." *Cleveland Press,* 13 March 1953.

Mangels, William F. *The Outdoor Amusement Industry.* New York: Vantage Press, 1952.

Manuscript information by Cecil *Golly,* Minn., Minn., 18 Aug. 1976

Manuscript information by Harry H. *Hershey,* Nokomis, Fla., 20 Aug. 1976.

Manuscript information by Dave *Hyman,* South Euclid, Ohio, 26 July 1976.

Manuscript information by Everett *Jones,* Shaker Hts., Ohio, 10 Jan. 1976.

Manuscript information by Bob *Pettay,* Bradenton, Fla., 27 Aug. 1976.

Manuscript information by Eddie *Robinson,* Cleveland, Ohio, 25 June 1976.

Manuscript information by Henry (Hank) *Schneider,* Cleveland, Ohio, 10 May 1976.

Manuscript information by Emil *Sholle,* University Hts., Ohio, 19 Dec. 1975.

Manuscript information by John *Tierney,* Cleveland, Ohio, 18 Feb. 1976.

Manuscript information by Erwin R. *Wahl,* Avon Lake, Ohio, 25 Sept. 1976.

Manuscript information by Frank *Yankovic,* Cleveland Hts., Ohio, 6 Sept. 1976.

"Memories Up in Smoke," *Cleveland Press,* 28 May 1971.

Moats, Alan. "Fun House Fire at Euclid Beach Draws Protests." *Cleveland Press,* 28 Dec. 1971.

"Mrs. D.S. Humphrey is Dead at 86." *Cleveland Press,* 17 Apr. 1945.

"Mrs. Dudley Humphrey . . ." *New York Times,* 18 Apr. 1945.

"Mrs. Kathryn Humphrey." *Cleveland Press,* 19 Sept. 1974.

"New Towers Over the Old." *Cleveland Press,* 4 Apr. 1973. p. 1.

Niagara Musical Instrument Mgf. Co. *Military Band Organs.* North Tonowanda, N.Y.: Niagara Muscial Instrument Mfg. Co. n.d. [title page different from cover] (Also reprinted by Vestal Press, Vestal, N.Y.)

North Tonowanda Musical Instrument Works *Automatic Military Bands* North Tonowanda, N.Y.: North Tonowanda Musical Instrument Works, n.d. (also republished by Vestal Press, Vestal, N.Y.)

"Park Opens with Rink on Schedule." *Plain Dealer,* 25 Apr. 1947.

Philadelphia Toboggan Co. *Cashing In on the Play Instinct.* Germantown, Phila., Penna.: Philadelphia Toboggan Co. n.d. (also reprinted by Vestal Press, Vestal, N.Y.)

Pilat, Oliver and Jo Ransom *Sodom by the Sea.* Garden City, N.Y.: Doubleday Doran & Co., 1941.

"Pioneer Businesswomen." *Cleveland Press,* 18 Apr. 1945.

"Plunge from Roller Coaster Kills Youth, 19." *Plain Dealer,* 3 July 1949.

"Popcorn Balls in Moratorium." *Cleveland Plain Dealer,* 29 Sept. 1969, p. 2-D.

"Popcorn by the Lake." *Cleveland Plain Dealer,* 23 Aug. 1959, p. 2, Pictorial Magazine.

"Popcorn, Peanuts, Fun Ready at Euclid Beach." *Cleveland Press,* 19 Apr. 1958.

Prospectus of the Euclid Beach Park Co. [1894] (typed)

Rose, William Ganson. *Cleveland; The Making of a City.* Cleveland and N.Y.: The World Publishing Co., 1950.

Rudolph Wurlitzer Mfg. Co. *Wurlitzer Military Band Organs.* North Tonowanda, N.Y.: Ruldolph Wurlitzer Mfg. Co., n.d. (also republished by Vestal Press, Vestal, N.Y.)

Sanborn Map Co. *Sanborn Insurance Maps.* [Cleveland] New York: Sanborn Map & Publishing Co. 1886-7 corrected to 1894, 1903 - 1929 corrected to 1943.

"Save the Beach." *Cleveland Press,* 15 Dec. 1969.

Spillman Engineering Corporation. [Catalogue] *Spillman Engineering Corporation Amusement Outfitters.* North Tonowanda, N.Y.: Spillman Engineering Corp., n.d. (also republished by Vestal Press, Vestal, N.Y. 13850).

"Spring Cleaning." *Cleveland Plain Dealer,* 20 Apr. 1950.

Swindell, Mary. "The Sound of Silence Haunts Euclid Beach Park." *Cleveland Press,* 22 Sept. 1969, p. A-12.

Tape of one hour broadcast on Euclid Beach Park of Reagan C. *Smith,* Cleveland, Ohio, 23 Aug. 1976.

Telephone conversation with Alden *Armstrong,* Cleveland, Ohio, 19 Feb. 1975.

Telephone conversation with Charles *Avellone,* Parma, Ohio, 26 Jan. 1976.

Telephone conversation with Kaye *Ballard,* (in Cleveland, Ohio), 15 Feb. 1975.

Telephone conversation with Jerry *Borden,* Cleveland Hts., Ohio, 28 Jan. 1976.

Telephone conversation with Art *Broze,* Cleveland, Ohio, 20 June 1976.

Telephone conversation with Mrs. Arthur *Kozlik,* Cleveland, Ohio, 13 Mar. 1976.

Telephone conversation with Eddie *Robinson,* Cleveland, Ohio, 25 June 1976.

Telephone conversation with Henry "Hank" *Schneider,* 10 May 1976.

Telephone conversation with Emil *Sholle,* University Hts., Ohio, 19 Dec. 1975.

Telephone conversation with John *Tierney,* Cleveland, Ohio, 18 Feb. 1976.

Thomas, Jason. "Euclid Beach Park Died Along with Once-Clear Lake." *Cleveland Plain Dealer,* 11 Oct. 1970, p. 5-Z.

"Today's Bio . . . She Likes Long Skirts, Wears Short Ones." *Cleveland Press,* 7 Dec. 1929. [Louise Humphrey]

Vestal Press. *Selected Spillman & Herschell Merry-Go-Round Material.* Vestal, N.Y.: The Vestal Press, c. 197

Vormelker, David. "Popping Noises at Euclid Beach All Started Near Wakeman." *Cleveland Plain Dealer,* 6 Aug. 1965.

W.F. Mangels Carousel Works *Catalogue No. 3.* Coney Island, N.Y.: W.F. Mangels Carousel Works, n.d. (also reprinted by Vestal Press, Vestal, N.Y.)

W.F. Mangels Co. *"The Whip" Latest Sensational Amusement Ride.* [Catalogue] Coney Island, N.Y.: W.F. Mangels Co., [1920-1921] (also republished by Vestal Press, Vestal, N.Y.)

"The Wonderful Flying Machine." *Cleveland Plain Dealer,* 1 Jan. 1950, p. 19, Pictorial Magazine.

Widder, Milt. "Euclid Beach Section Sold." *Cleveland Press,* 21 Oct. 1970.

Widder, Milt. "Euclid Beach Sells an Old Timer." *Cleveland Press,* 11 Nov. 1966, p. D-6.

"Win East Cleveland Wedding Prizes." [wedding at Euclid Beach Park] *Plain Dealer,* 13 July 1950.

Advertisements about Euclid Beach in the Cleveland Plain Dealer.
15 May 1910, p. 2A - "One Fare."
26 May 1912, p. Ed. 2. - "Dining Hall . . ."
2 June 1912, p. Ed. 6. - "Now Open . . ."
30 June 1912, p. Ed. 6. - [Ad]
30 May 1913, p. 9. - "Ride the New Derby."
29 June 1913, p. Ed. 4. - "Adjoining . . ." [Castle Inn]
30 May 1915, p. Ed. 4. - "Is Now Open . . ."
21 April 1927, - [Ad]
25 May 1932, p. 23. - [Ad]

5 April 1936, p. 16, - "Opens April 9 . . ."
28 May 1936, p. 8. - "Decoration Day . . ."
8 April 1937, - "Opening . . ."
23 May 1937, p. 16C. - "New Band . . ."
29 May 1937, - "Opens Full Time . . ."
10 April 1938, p. 14C. - "New Dance Orchestra . . ."
22 April 1938, p. 14C. - "Open in Full . . ."
13 April 1939, p. 19. - "Jimmy Livingston . . ."
4 April 1940, [Opening]

14 May 1940, p. 14C. - "Opening May 25 . . ."
7 July 1940, p. 10B. - "5¢ Day . . ."
6 April 1941, p. 18B. - "Austin Wylie . . ."
18 May 1941, p. 16B. - "Gala Opening . . ."
24 June 1941, p. 12B. - "Free Fireworks . . ."
5 April 1942, p. 14B - "Opening . . ."
16 August 1942, "6¢ Day . . ."
27 June 1943, p. 14B. - [July 4th Ad]
14 April 1944, p. 13B. - "Opening . . ."

Newspaper Articles of the Postwar Years (1946 onward) on the Park: its closing (Sept. 1969), plans for its use, controversies over it, its destruction, fires at, changes to the acreage, and some memories.

in the *Cleveland News:*

23 Sept. 1946
4 Oct. 1946
12 April 1947
14 April 1947
25 April 1947

in the *Cleveland Plain Dealer:*

29 Aug. 1946
24 Sept. 1946
1 Oct. 1946
4 Oct. 1946
13 Nov. 1946
9 March 1947
25 April 1947
27 Aug. 1965
24 July 1969
1 Sept. 1969
3 Sept. 1969
20 Sept. 1969
29 Sept. 1969
2 Oct. 1969
19 Nov. 1969
22 Nov. 1969

23 Nov. 1969
15 Dec. 1969
11 Oct. 1970
26 Feb. 1972
28 March 1972
31 March 1972
5 April 1972
6 April 1972
7 April 1972
8 April 1972
11 April 1972
12 April 1972
13 April 1972
2 July 1972
12 Nov. 1972

in the *Cleveland Press* ·

22 Sept. 1946
24 Sept. 1946
4 Oct. 1946
13 Nov. 1946
27 Nov. 1946
12 April 1947
14 April 1947
23 May 1947
11 May 1965
15 June 1965
14 Feb. 1966
16 Feb. 1968
7 June 1968
11 Sept. 1968
29 April 1969
6 May 1969
4 Sept. 1969
18 Sept. 1969
20 Sept. 1969
15 Nov. 1969

17 Nov. 1969
20 Nov. 1969
22 Nov. 1969
11 Dec. 1969
15 Dec. 1969
7 May 1971
28 May 1971
28 Dec. 1971
25 Jan. 1972
28 Jan. 1972
25 Feb. 1972
31 March 1972
7 April 1972
10 April 1972
12 April 1972
29 April 1972
20 Sept. 1972
4 April 1973
2 Aug. 1975

in the *Scoop*
2 March 1972

ILLUSTRATIONS
FROM PROSPECTUS TO EXIT SIGN

307

CHAPTER V

CHAPTER VI

EPILOGUE

INDEX

FROM A.S.C.A.P. TO ZOOMER

Some notes for the reader using this index:

1. The contraction EBP refers to EUCLID BEACH PARK.
2. All MAP numbers cited are keyed to the numbers on the map on pp. 189 and 190.
3. All Illus. numbers are preceded by page numbers, e.g., Illus., p. 5 #6.
4. The order followed under each MAJOR HEADING is:
   1.) Subheadings (may also refer to Illus. or MAP numbers.)
   2.) **Illus., In boldface.**
   3.) MAP, IN CAPS.
   4.) *See* and/or *See Also In italics.*

Book Composition
Typography
Body Copy & Headlines — Souvenir
By: Great Lakes Typographers, Inc.
3869 Church Street
Willoughby, Ohio 44094

Lithoprinted by
Braun-Brumfield, Inc.
Ann Arbor, Michigan

   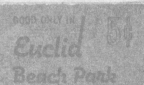